THE NEWSPAPER DESIGNER'S HANDBOOK

THE NEWSPAPER DESIGNER'S HANDBOOK

3rd edition

Written & designed by

TIM HARROWER

WCB Brown &
Benchmark
PUBLISHERS

Madison, Wisconsin • Dubuque, Iowa

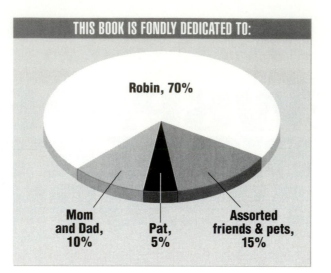

THIS BOOK IS FONDLY DEDICATED TO:

Robin, 70%

Mom and Dad, 10%

Pat, 5%

Assorted friends & pets, 15%

Book Team

Editor *Stan Stoga*
Developmental Editor *Kassi Radomski*
Production Editor *Debra DeBord*
Visuals/Design Developmental Consultant *Marilyn Phelps*
Visuals/Design Freelance Specialist *Mary L. Christianson*
Marketing Manager *Pamela S. Cooper*
Advertising Projects Coordinator *Susan J. Butler*

WCB Brown & Benchmark

A Division of Wm. C. Brown Communications, Inc.

Executive Vice President/General Manager *Thomas E. Doran*
Vice President/Editor in Chief *Edgar J. Laube*
Vice President/Marketing and Sales Systems *Eric Ziegler*
Director of Production *Vickie Putman Caughron*
Director of Custom and Electronic Publishing *Chris Rogers*

WCB Wm. C. Brown Communications, Inc.

President and Chief Executive Officer *G. Franklin Lewis*
Corporate Senior Vice President and Chief Financial Officer *Robert Chesterman*
Corporate Senior Vice President and President of Manufacturing *Roger Meyer*

The credits section for this book begins on page 218
and is considered an extension of the copyright page.

Cover illustration by Fred Ingram.

CONTENTS

INTRODUCTION

FOREWORD

A long, long time ago, people actually enjoyed reading newspapers. Imagine.

They'd flip a nickel to the newsboy, grab a paper from the stack, slap it open and gawk at headlines that shouted:

SOLONS MULL LEVY HIKE BID!

They'd gaze at those long, gray columns of type that looked like this:

— and they'd say: *"Wow!* What a lot of news!"

Today, people are different. We've got color TVs. Home computers. Portable CD players. Glitzy magazines. We collect data in a dizzying array of ways. We don't need long, gray columns of type anymore. We won't *read* long, gray columns of type anymore.

In fact, when we look at newspapers and see those long, gray columns of type, we say: *"Yuck!* What a waste of time!"

Today's readers want something different. Something snappy. Something inviting, easy to grasp, instantly informative.

And that's where you come in.

If you can design a newspaper that's inviting, informative and easy to read, you can — for a few minutes each day — successfully compete with all those TVs, CDs, computers and magazines. You can keep a noble old American institution — the newspaper — alive for another day.

Because let's face it: To many people, newspapers are dinosaurs. They're big, clumsy and slow. And though they've endured for eons, it may be only a matter of time before newspapers either:

◆ become extinct (this has happened to other famous forms of communication — remember smoke signals? The telegraph?). Or else they'll:

◆ evolve into a new species (imagine a combination video newspaper/TV shopping catalog that lets you tune into sports highlights, scan some comics, then view the hottest fashions on sale at your local TechnoMall).

FOREWORD

Those days are still a ways off. For now, we need to do our best with what we have: Black ink. White paper. Lots of lines, dots, letters and numbers. A good designer can put all those things together quickly and smoothly, so that today's news feels both familiar and . . . new.

But where do newspaper designers come from, anyway? Face it: You never hear children saying, "When I grow up, my dream is to *lay out the Opinion page.*" You never hear college students saying, "I've got a major in rocket science and a minor in *sports infographics.*"

No, most journalists stumble into design. Usually it's by accident. Without warning.

Maybe you're a reporter on a small weekly, and one day your editor says, "Congratulations! I'm promoting you to assistant editor. You'll start Monday. Oh, and . . . you know how to lay out pages, don't you?"

Or maybe you've just joined a student newspaper. You want to be a reporter, a movie critic, a sports columnist. So you write your first story. When you finish, the adviser says to you, "Uh, we're a little short-handed in production right now. You could really help us if you'd lay out that page your story's on. OK?"

Now, journalism textbooks usually discuss design in broad terms. They ponder vague concepts like *balance* and *harmony* and *rhythm.* They show award-winning pages from The New York Times or USA Today.

"Cool pages," you think. But meanwhile, you're in a hurry. And you're still confused: "How do I connect *this* picture to *this* headline?"

That's where this book comes in.

This book assumes you need to learn the rules of newspaper design as quickly as you can. It assumes you've been reading a newspaper for a while, but you've never really paid attention to things like headline sizes. Or liftout quotes, like the one at right. Or whether pages use five columns of text instead of six.

> "*I* am not the editor of a newspaper and shall always try to do right and be good, so that God will not make me one."
>
> **— MARK TWAIN**

This book will guide you through the fundamental building blocks of newspaper design: headlines, text, photos, cutlines. We'll show you how to shape them into a story — and how to shape stories into pages.

After that, we'll look at the small stuff (logos, teasers, charts and graphs, type trickery) that makes more complicated pages work. We'll even show you a few reader-grabbing gimmicks, like subheads, to break up gray columns of type:

YO! CHECK OUT THIS READER-GRABBING SUBHEAD

And bullets, to make short lists "pop" off the page:
- This is a bullet item.
- And so is this.
- Ditto here.

We'll even explore liftout quotes, which let you dress up a quote from somebody famous — say, Mark Twain — to catch your reader's eye.

Yes, some writers will do almost *anything* to get you to read their forewords. And if you made it all this way, ask yourself:

Did design have anything to do with it?

— Tim Harrower

SOME QUICK HISTORY

THE SIMPLE BEGINNINGS

Publick Occurrences, America's first newspaper, made its debut 300 years ago. But like most colonial newspapers, it looked more like a pamphlet or newsletter and was printed on paper smaller than the pages in this book.

Most colonial weeklies ran news items one after another in deep, wide columns of text. There were no headlines and very little art (though it was young Ben Franklin who printed America's first newspaper cartoon in 1754).

After the Revolutionary War, dailies first appeared and began introducing new design elements: thinner columns, primitive headlines (one-line labels such as *PROCLAMATION*) and — this will come as no surprise — an increasing number of ads, many of them parked along the bottom of the front page.

Colonial printing presses couldn't handle large sheets of paper, so when Publick Occurrences was printed in Boston on Sept. 25, 1690, it was only 7 inches wide, with two 3-inch columns of text. The 4-page paper had 3 pages of news (the last page was blank), including mention of a "newly appointed" day of Thanksgiving in Plimouth. (Plimouth? Publick? Where were all the copy editors in those days?)

THE 19TH CENTURY

Throughout the 19th century, all newspapers looked more or less the same. Text was hung like wallpaper, in long rows, with vertical rules between columns. Maps or engravings were sometimes used as art.

During the Civil War, papers began devoting more space to headline display, stacking vertical layers of *deckers* or *decks* in a dizzying variety of typefaces. For instance, The Chicago Tribune used 15 decks to trumpet its report on the great fire of 1871: *FIRE! Destruction of Chicago! 2,000 Acres of Buildings Destroyed....*

The first newspaper photograph was published in 1880. News photos didn't become common, however, until the early 1900s.

This 1865 edition of The Philadelphia Inquirer reports the assassination of President Lincoln with 15 headline decks. Like most newspapers of its era, it uses a very vertical text format: When a story hits the bottom of one column, it leaps to the top of the next to continue.

MORE QUICK HISTORY

THE EARLY 20TH CENTURY

By about 1900, newspapers began looking more like — well, like *newspapers*. Headlines grew bigger, bolder and wider. Those deep stacks of decks were gradually eliminated to save space. Page designs developed greater variety as news became departmentalized (*Crime, Foreign, Sports* and so on).

The '20s saw the rise of tabloids — those small, half-sheet papers packed with photos and sensational sledgehammer headlines.

As the years went by, papers kept increasing the traffic on each page, using ever more photos, stories and ads.

This 1898 edition of the New York Journal tries to stir up readers with sensational allegations about the destruction of the battleship Maine. Notice how loud the type is and how horizontal the page's design elements are: The headline, the illustration and even the text run the full width of the page in a very symmetrical layout.

THE NOT-TOO-DISTANT PAST

By today's standards, even the handsomest papers from 20 years ago look clumsy and old-fashioned. Others, like the page at right, look downright ugly.

Still, most of the current trends in page design were in place by the late '60s:

◆ more and bigger photos;

◆ quieter, more refined headline type (except for special feature stories and front-page banners);

◆ a move from 8- and 9-column pages to a standardized 6-column page;

◆ white gutters between columns instead of rules.

As printing presses continued to improve, full-color photos became common in the early '80s — thus ushering in a new era of newspaper design.

This 1966 sports page from The Oregon Journal is astoundingly bad — but to be fair, it's a typical example of mid-'60s design. The bizarre shapes of its photos and stories collide in a disorganized jumble. After printing pages like these for years, editors finally realized that taking page design seriously might not be such a bad idea.

CURRENT TRENDS

Compared to the newspapers of yesteryear, today's news pages look lively and sophisticated. That's partly due to technological advances. But today's editors realize that readers are inundated by slickly designed media, from movies to billboards to TV commercials. Sad to say, most consumers judge a product by the package it comes in. They simply won't respect a product — or a newspaper — that looks old-fashioned.

To look modern, newspapers now use:

◆ **Color.** Full-color photographs have become standard on section fronts across the country. Throughout the paper, color is applied both decoratively (in ads and illustrations) and functionally (in photos, in graphics, and in logos and headers that organize pages and guide readers).

◆ **Informational graphics.** Papers don't just report the news — they *illustrate* it with charts, maps, diagrams, quotes and fast-fact sidebars that catch readers' eyes and make information visual and easy to grasp.

◆ **Packaging.** Today's readers are busy. Picky. Impatient. So editors try to make every page as user-friendly as they can by designing briefs, roundups, scoreboards, promos and specially themed packages to be easy to find and quick to read.

◆ **Modular layout.** We'll explore this later. In a nutshell, it simply means all stories are neatly stacked in rectangular shapes.

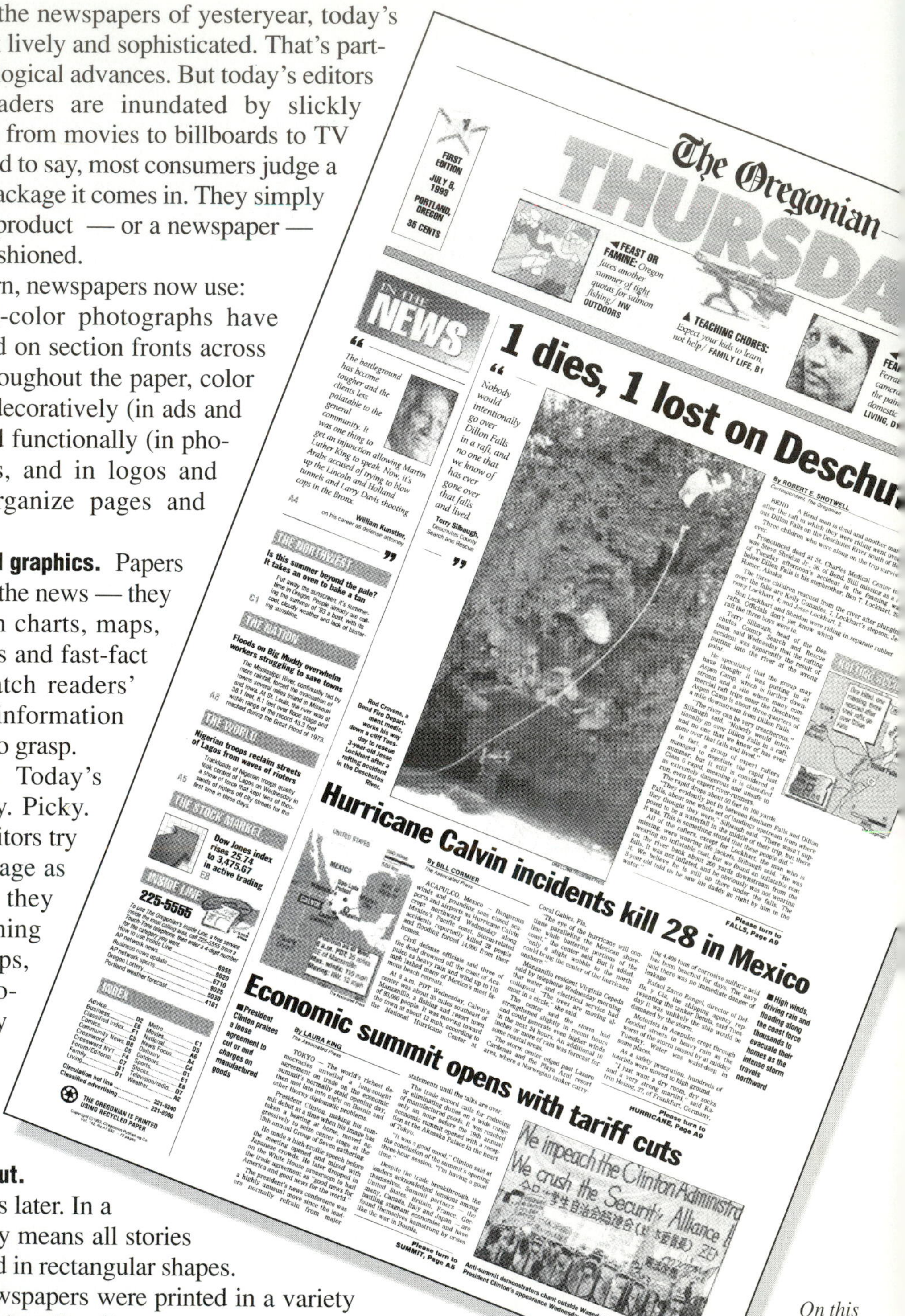

In the past, newspapers were printed in a variety of sizes. Today, virtually all newspapers are printed either as *broadsheets* (large, full-sized papers like USA Today or The Oregonian, shown above) or *tabloid* (half-sized papers like The National Enquirer — OK, maybe that's a bad example — or, say, The Christian Science Monitor).

In the pages ahead, we'll examine examples of modern American newspaper design. Most of these are broadsheet pages, but remember: whatever your paper's format, the same basic design principles apply.

On this front page you can see modern packaging at work in those news briefs, in the aggressive promos at the top of the page, and in the packaging of that lead news story.

CURRENT TRENDS

The Sun in Bremerton, Wash., devotes three-fourths of its front page to a special feature centerpiece on local gangs. Notice the stylish treatment of the story's lead art and headline. Alongside the flag, teasers promote stories inside the paper; two other news stories, without art, run along the right side of the page.

The London Free Press has designed a distinctive front-page package. Above the flag, a World Series promo combines text and graphics. A centerpiece story focuses on a controversial election issue. And the bottom third of the page provides a menu for the rest of the paper, with different-colored bars highlighting topics inside.

When war broke out in the Persian Gulf, most papers filled their front pages with text. But The Detroit News takes a different approach when major news breaks. Below that huge headline there's a map, diagrams of military hardware, a few key facts and an index. It's a bold, fast-paced billboard that instantly alerts and updates you.

PAGE ONE DESIGN

Today's Page One is a blend of traditional reporting and modern marketing that tries to answer the question: What *grabs* readers?

Is it loud headlines? Big photos? Juicy stories? Splashy colors? Or do readers prefer thoughtful, serious analyses of current events?

No one knows. Though newspaper publishers spend fortunes on readership surveys, they're still unsure what front-page formula is guaranteed to fly off the racks. As a result, most papers follow one of these Page One design philosophies:

◆ **The traditional:** No fancy bells or whistles — just the top news of the day. (For tabloids, that means 2-4 stories; for broadsheets, 4-7.) Editors combine photos, headlines, and text — usually lots of text — in a sober, straightforward style.

◆ **The magazine cover:** These pages emphasize *quality,* not quantity, as big art and dynamic headlines highlight a single topic. In tabloids, this package dominates the cover (and may even send you inside for the text); in broadsheets, a front-page centerpiece is given lavish play, flanked by a few subordinate stories.

◆ **The information center:** Here, the key words are *volume* and *variety.* By blending graphics, photos, promos and briefs, these fast-paced front pages serve as a window to what's inside the paper, a menu that serves up lots of short, appetizing tidbits to guide readers through the best of the day's entrees.

But the options don't end there. Some papers run editorials on Page One. Some add cartoons. Some print obituaries, entertainment calendars, contests — even ads. Almost anything goes, as long as readers accept it, enjoy it and *buy* it.

CURRENT TRENDS

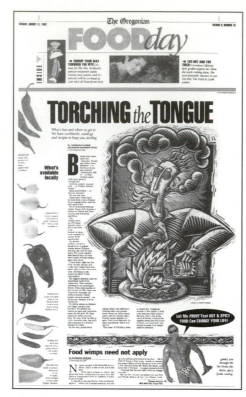

All three of these feature pages were produced by The Oregonian in Portland. Above, the cover of a spring fashion section uses a special headline and huge photo to seize readers' attention. (Note how the "Gypsy Soul" headline has been printed in white type — or reversed — over the photo.) Down the right side are teasers promoting other fashion stories inside the section.

This food page uses some outrageous design devices — note the hot-pepper cutouts running down the left side of the page, the silhouetted bodybuilder at the bottom speaking in a cartoon balloon ("Let me prove that hot & spicy food can CHANGE YOUR LIFE!"). In the headlines, text and artwork, this pages blends humor and design flair to communicate its message.

This Arts page is more refined and elegant than that food page next door. Even so, notice how it bends a number of design guidelines: One photo is round, another is tilted, while elephant ears poke up into the page header. Note, too, how every leg of text is a different width. Yet all these elements are tastefully sized and balanced; it's the designer's skill that holds this page together.

FEATURE PAGES & SECTIONS

As time goes by, feature sections become more and more popular — and their range gets broader and broader. Most modern feature sections offer a mix of:

◆ **Lifestyle coverage:** consumer tips, how-to's, trends in health, fitness, fashion — a compendium of personal and social issues affecting readers' lives.

◆ **Entertainment news:** reviews and previews of music, movies, theater, books and art (including comprehensive calendars and TV listings). Juicy celebrity gossip is always popular, too.

◆ **Food:** recipes, nutrition advice, new products for home and kitchen — all surrounded by coupon-laden advertising that shoppers clip and save.

◆ **Comics, columnists and crosswords:** from Dear Abby to Blondie, from Hagar to the horoscope, these local and syndicated features have faithful followings.

Feature sections often boast the most lively, ambitious page designs in the paper. It's here that designers haul out the loud type, play with color, experiment with unusual artwork and photo treatments.

Many feature sections dress up their front pages by giving one key story a huge "poster page" display. Other papers prefer more traffic, balancing the page with an assortment of stories, briefs, calendars and lists.

And while most papers devote a few inside pages to features, some bigger publications — those with plenty of writers and designers — produce daily themed magazines: *Money* on Mondays, *Health & Fitness* on Tuesdays, *Food* on Wednesdays, and so on.

CURRENT TRENDS

An award-winning sports page from The Asbury Park Press in New Jersey. Good sports pages offer readers plenty of variety — and notice how many different sports are represented on this page. Down the left side, photo briefs provide a visual rundown of the day's events. And the centerpiece package offers stat-by-stat comparisons of hoop stars Michael Jordan and Clyde Drexler.

Speaking of Clyde Drexler — here's a poster page that tells you everything you need to know about Portland's greatest player: his career points, rebounds, records, strengths and weaknesses, salary — and in the lower-left corner of the page, that's Clyde's actual shoe size (14). This was one of a series of poster pages The Oregonian printed in the middle of the 1991 basketball season.

Scholastic newsrooms produce outstanding sports packages, too. This tabloid soccer page is from The Epitaph in Cupertino, Calif. All the basics — the photo, text, soccer standings and calendar — are effectively displayed. But notice the graphic extras: the profiles along the bottom, the sidebars down the side (the outstanding athlete, the soccer trivia, the "Looking Back" box).

SPORTS PAGES & SECTIONS

Television seems to be the perfect medium for sports coverage. It's immediate. Visual. Colorful. Yet in many cities, more readers buy newspapers for sporting news than for any other reason. Why?

A good sports section combines dramatic photos, lively writing, snappy headlines and shrewd analysis into a package with a personality all its own. And while sports coverage centers around meat-and-potatoes reporting on games, matches and meets, a strong sports section includes features you won't find in any other medium:

◆ **Statistics:** scores, standings, players' records, team histories — true sports junkies can't get enough of this minutiae. It's often packaged on a special scoreboard page or run in tiny type (called *agate*).

◆ **Calendars and listings:** upcoming events, team schedules, ski reports, TV and radio listings — whether in small schools or big cities, fans depend on newspapers for the times and locations of sporting events.

◆ **Columnists:** opinionated writers whom sports fans can love or loathe — the more outspoken, the better.

◆ **Inside poop and gossip:** scores, injury reports, polls, predictions, betting lines, analyses and profiles that simply aren't available anywhere else.

Sports pages (like features) offer opportunities for designers to run photos more boldly, to write headlines more aggressively — and to create dynamic graphics packages that capture the thrill of victory in a visual way.

CURRENT TRENDS

This editorial page from The News in Boca Raton, Fla., contains the usual elements, but with a few modern twists: the sideways Opinion Page header; the editorial headline (which highlights THE ISSUE and what WE SUGGEST); the sidebar inset into the editorial (which explains how to write to the president); and, at bottom right, a smattering of opinions phoned in by readers.

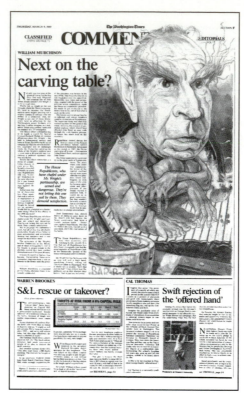

Opinion pages often run provocative cartoons to satirize public issues. On this Commentary page from The Washington Times, the lead story focuses on efforts to "carve up" then-House Speaker Jim Wright of Texas; the huge caricature shows Wright being roasted on a barbecue grill. The smaller stories on this page use more conventional art: a chart and a photo.

Another featurized treatment of a controversial topic — this time in tabloid form by the UCSD Guardian. This single-topic page examines the split decision in the 1992 Rodney King civil rights trial. A powerful headline anchors the page, flowing logically into the text and artwork below. Note how well-balanced the story elements are and how the bold type lends contrast to the page.

OPINION PAGES & EDITORIALS

Juxtaposing news and commentary is a dangerous thing. How are readers to know where cold facts end and hot opinions begin? That's why nearly every newspaper sets aside a special page or two for backbiting, mudslinging, pussy-footing and pontificating: It's called the editorial page, and it's one of the noblest traditions in American journalism.

The basic ingredients for editorial pages are nearly universal, consisting of:

◆ **An editorial cartoon,** a sarcastic illustration that lampoons public figures or political policy;

◆ **Editorials,** unsigned opinion pieces representing the newspaper's stance on topical issues;

◆ **Opinion columns** written by the paper's editors, by local writers or by nationally syndicated columnists;

◆ **Letters from readers,** and

◆ **The masthead,** which lists the paper's top brass (editors, publishers, etc.) along with the office address and phone number.

In addition — because editorial pages are often rigidly formatted — many papers run a separate opinion page (see example, top center). These pages provide commentary and opinion, too, as they examine current issues in depth. And like sports and feature sections, they set themselves apart from ordinary news pages by using stylized headlines, interpretive illustrations, and more elaborate design techniques.

CURRENT TRENDS

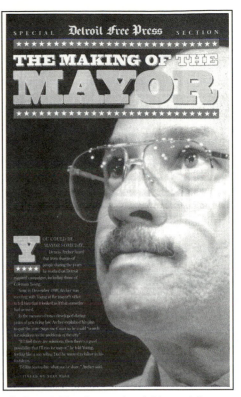

Most newspapers try, at least several times a year, to give their readers special reports on topical issues. These reports are printed either as a daily series or as a special section — such as the one shown here. This 12-page package, which ran in The Oregonian back in the Eighties, documented a local medical team's efforts to treat Ethiopian famine victims.

How can you entice kids to read the newspaper? Many papers produce special sections like this one, from The Chicago Tribune, in hopes of attracting young readers. Along with bright colors and zoomy images, these pages offer cartoons, puzzles, hobby tips, movie reviews, and opportunities for children to read their own words in print.

The Detroit Free Press printed this special election section two days after Detroit's new mayor was elected in 1993. The six-page section featured behind-the-scenes profiles of the candidates, photos from the campaign trail, exit polls, complete election totals and demographic analyses of voting trends. This bold, aggressive cover treatment has real stopping power.

SPECIAL PAGES & SECTIONS   Most newspapers settle into predictable routines from issue to issue, repeating the same standard formats — news, opinion, features, sports — day after day. (Fortunately, a little predictability is good: It keeps readers happy and editors sane.)

But opportunities often arise for producing special pages or sections with design formats all their own. These include:

◆ **Special enterprise packages** on hot topics or trends (*AIDS, The Homeless, How You Can Save Our Planet*).

◆ **Special reports** on news events, either printed in advance (*Baseball '95* or *Summer Olympics Preview*) or as a wrap-up (*The Tragedy of Flight 116* or *That Championship Season: The Phoenix Suns*).

◆ **Special-interest packages** — often printed regularly — that target a specific audience (pages for kids or teens; sections for women, senior citizens, hunters, farmers).

Editors now realize how specialized readers' tastes have become. Just look at the enormous variety of magazines and cable-TV channels consumers can choose from. That's why newspapers offer an increasingly wide range of pages and sections that cater to readers' diverse interests: Fitness. Computers. Religion. Skiing. After extensive readership surveys, one paper created a sewing page; another launched a weekly page of Civil War lore.

Every community is unique. What are *your* readers most interested in?

THE NEWSPAPER OF THE FUTURE

No, the "Digital Daily" doesn't exist — not yet, anyway. But imagine a computer that's thin, flat and portable, one that can show movies, play music, and yes — display instant news reports.

As you can see, this electronic newspaper is customized: It searches for news topics of interest to the user, then flashes the headlines below.

Simply touch the photo and it plays a video clip, complete with sound. Press the arrow button and the news story fills the screen, complete with text, graphics and videos — true multimedia journalism.

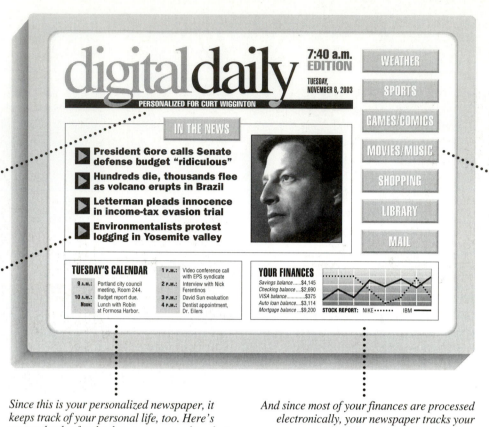

digital daily
PERSONALIZED FOR CURT WIGGINTON

7:40 a.m. EDITION
TUESDAY, NOVEMBER 8, 2003

WEATHER
SPORTS
GAMES/COMICS
MOVIES/MUSIC
SHOPPING
LIBRARY
MAIL

IN THE NEWS

▶ **President Gore calls Senate defense budget "ridiculous"**

▶ **Hundreds die, thousands flee as volcano erupts in Brazil**

▶ **Letterman pleads innocence in income-tax evasion trial**

▶ **Environmentalists protest logging in Yosemite valley**

TUESDAY'S CALENDAR

9 A.M.:	Portland city council meeting, Room 244.	1 P.M.:	Video conference call with EPS syndicate
10 A.M.:	Budget report due.	2 P.M.:	Interview with Nick Ferentinos
NOON:	Lunch with Robin at Formosa Harbor.	3 P.M.:	David Sun evaluation
		4 P.M.:	Dentist appointment, Dr. Eilers

YOUR FINANCES

Savings balance $4,145
Checking balance $2,690
VISA balance $375
Auto loan balance $3,114
Mortgage balance $9,200

STOCK REPORT: NIKE •••••• IBM ——

This is the 7:40 a.m. edition of your newspaper. But since the news is constantly revised and updated, you can access the paper anytime you like.

Down the right side of the screen is the index. Press these buttons to read the latest news, watch video clips of sports and movie highlights, enjoy the animated comics, do a little mail-order shopping, answer your electronic mail. . . . Get the picture? Best of all, anytime you want to explore a subject in greater depth, you can search the database in the newspaper's library.

Since this is your personalized newspaper, it keeps track of your personal life, too. Here's your calendar for the day, programmed to alert you as your next appointment approaches.

And since most of your finances are processed electronically, your newspaper tracks your current bank balances — in addition to monitoring the performance of your stocks.

Like what you see here? Or does it represent *the end of respectable journalism?*

Sure, it may seem far-fetched. But it isn't. If we're wise, we'll study prototypes like these and ask: What's to become of newspapers in 10 years? 20 years? Will paper still be plentiful, or will newspapers go electronic? Will *advertising* still be plentiful, or will newspapers go bankrupt?

As more and more newspapers bite the dust, publishers ponder their future. Some have begun exploring alternatives for 21st-century journalism:

◆ **Audiotext:** News by telephone — where you can dial up weather, sports, horoscopes or restaurant reviews — is already enormously popular in many cities.

◆ **Fax newspapers:** These, too, exist in many cities: 1- or 2-page minipapers that deliver headlines, sports scores and stock reports direct to your fax machine.

◆ **Computerized newspapers:** You'll soon read headlines on your portable computer. You'll also watch video clips, listen to sound bites, explore animated graphics. Keypads and touch-sensitive screens will let you ask questions, enter commands and search electronic databases. How will this interactive newspaper be delivered? Over fiber-optic cables. On CD disks. Or over the airwaves.

◆ **Personalized newspapers:** Instead of a mass-market publication, image a paper that caters to *your* personal interests. Want a paper that focuses on tennis, T-bills and Tasmania? Once you program your computer to prioritize your preferences, it'll edit the news for *you.*

Yes, newspaper technology is rapidly evolving. But questions remain: Who'll produce this new media? Who'll pay for all this expensive technology? What sort of device will display these computerized pages? And most importantly:

How will you wrap fish in it?

As we said in the Foreword — you *did* read the Foreword, didn't you? After all the work we put into it? Listen, it's not *nearly* as dull as it looks — you're probably eager to unravel the Mysteries of Page Design. But before you begin banging out prize-winning pages, you'll need to learn a few basics.

You'll need to know some vocabulary. You'll need to be familiar with the tools of the trade. But most of all, you'll need to understand the fundamental components of page design: headlines, text, photos and cutlines.

This book is designed so you can skip this chapter if you're in a hurry. Or you can just skim it and catch the highlights. So don't feel compelled to memorize everything immediately. But the better you understand these basics now, the more easily you'll be able to manipulate them later on.

To make this book handier to use, we've repeated the chapter contents in detail at the bottom of each chapter's introductory page. And each section within this book is cross-referenced, too, with those handy **MORE ON** guides in the upper-right corner of the page. As you study each topic, you can bounce back and forth through the book to expand upon what you're learning.

CHAPTER CONTENTS

WHAT IT'S CALLED

To succeed in the design world, you need to speak the lingo. In a typical newsroom, for instance, you'll find *slugs, bugs, bastards, dummies,* maybe even a *widow* in the *gutter.* (If our mothers knew we talked like this, they'd never let us become journalists).

Not all newsrooms use the same jargon, but there's plenty of agreement on most terms. Here are some common elements found on Page One:

Teasers
*These promote the best stories inside the paper (also called **promos** or **skyboxes**)*

Headline
The story's title or summary, in large type above or beside the text

Byline
The writer's name, often followed by key credentials

Display head
A jazzed-up headline that adds emphasis to special stories

Initial cap
*A large capital letter set into the opening paragraph of a special feature (also called a **drop cap**)*

Standing head
A label used for packaging special items (graphics, teasers, briefs, columns, etc.)

Index
A directory of contents

Logo
A small, boxed title (with art) used for labeling special stories or series

Flag
*The newspaper's name (also called the **nameplate**)*

Reverse type
White words set against a dark background

Infographic
A diagram, chart or map that conveys information pictorially

Deck
A smaller headline added below the main headline (shown here is a summary deck, which summarizes news stories)

Mug shot
A small photograph (usually just the face) of someone in the story

Refer
A brief reference to a related story elsewhere in the paper

Cutline
*Information about a photo or illustration (also called a **caption**)*

Jump line
A line telling the reader what page this story continues on

WHAT IT'S CALLED

As you can see, Page One is often loaded with devices designed to entice and entrap prospective readers. Inside the paper, however, graphic elements become more subtle, less decorative. They're there to inform and guide readers, not sell papers.

Here are some typical design elements used on inside pages:

MORE ON ▶

◆ **Terms:** *A complete glossary of design terms & jargon ... 212*

Folio
A line showing the page number, date, paper's name, etc.

Jump line
The page number this story continues from

Liftout quote
*A quotation from the story given graphic emphasis (also called a **pull quote** or **breakout**)*

Subhead
A boldface line of type used to organize the story and break up gray text

Gutter
The white space running vertically between elements on a page

Bastard measure
Type set in a different width than the standard column measure

Sig
*A special label set into stories giving typographic emphasis to the topic, title, writer's name, etc. (also called a **bug** or **logo**)*

Standing head
A label used for packaging special stories or features

Jump headline
A headline treatment reserved for stories jumping from another page (styles vary from paper to paper)

Photo credit
A line giving the photographer's name (often adding the paper or wire service he or she works for)

Text
Type for stories set in a standard size and typeface, stacked in columns (or legs)

Sidebar
A related story, often boxed, that accompanies the main story

Cutoff rule
A line used to separate elements on a page

Cutout
A photo in which the background has been cut away (also called a silhouette)

F12 + ■ THE SUNDAY OREGONIAN, JUNE 12, 1968

A BIG YEN FOR BASEBALL

Japan: Clubs hope when money talks, U.S. players listen

■Continued from Page F1

"$5 million can only buy a small condominium in the Tokyo area, so it doesn't seem like much money to us."

Masaaki Nagino,
Central League planner

A nondescript player in the U.S. major leagues, Randy Bass became a superstar with the Hanshin Tigers.

Associated Press

WARREN CROMARTIE
Ex-Expo now a Japanese veteran

BILL MADLOCK
Worth more than $1 million

BILL GULLICKSON
Packing 'em in in Tokyo

Not everyone likes Japan's best-loved team

By MICHIO YOSHIDA
The Associated Press

Is expansion in the works?

Drysdale's streak was highlight of 1968 — season of the pitcher

By LARRY BORTSTEIN
Knight-Ridder News Service

FOR THE RECORD

Don Drysdale (left) and Bob Gibson, shown during a joint appearance at a baseball camp, dominated National League pitching in 1968. Drysdale pitched 58 consecutive scoreless innings, a major league record.

Associated Press

TOOLS OF THE TRADE

In the old days, page designers spent a lot of time drawing boxes (to show where photos went). And drawing lines (to show where text went). And drawing *more* boxes (for graphics and sidebars and logos).

Nowadays, designers often do their drawing on computers. But those old tools of the trade are still handy: pencils (for drawing lines), rulers (for measuring lines), calculators (for estimating the sizes of those lines and boxes), and our old favorite, the proportion wheel (to calculate the precise dimensions of boxes as they grow larger or smaller).

Even if you're a computer whiz, you should know these tools and terms:

MORE ON ▶

◆ **The proportion wheel:** *A guide to how it works....* **103**

◆ **Terms:** *A complete glossary of design jargon* **212**

Pencil: *Yes, your basic pencil (with eraser) is used for drawing dummies. Designers who draw page dummies with pens are just showing off.*

Grease pencil: *These are used for making crop marks on photos. Afterward, these markings can easily be rubbed off with cloth.*

Knife: *In art departments and composing rooms, X-ACTO knives (a brand name) are used for trimming photos, cutting stories and moving items around during paste-up.*

Calculator: *Designers often need to use calculators for sizing photos and for computing line lengths in a hurry (unless you're a whiz with fractions). Test yourself: If you have an 18-inch story, and it's divided into 5 columns (or legs), and there's a map in the second leg that's 3 inches deep — how deep are each of the legs?*

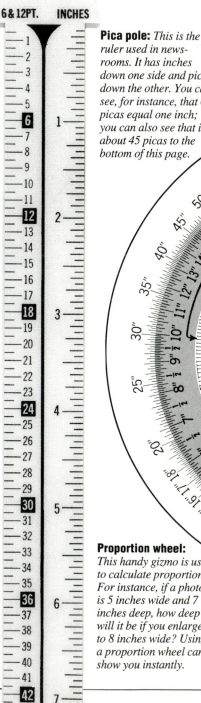

Pica pole: *This is the ruler used in newsrooms. It has inches down one side and picas down the other. You can see, for instance, that 6 picas equal one inch; you can also see that it's about 45 picas to the bottom of this page.*

Proportion wheel: *This handy gizmo is used to calculate proportions. For instance, if a photo is 5 inches wide and 7 inches deep, how deep will it be if you enlarge it to 8 inches wide? Using a proportion wheel can show you instantly.*

POINTS, PICAS, INCHES: HOW NEWSPAPERS MEASURE THINGS

If you're trying to measure something very short or thin, inches are clumsy and imprecise. So printers use *picas* and *points* for precise calibrations. There are 12 points in one pica, 6 picas in one inch — or, in all, 72 points in one inch.

This is a 1-point rule; 72 of these would be one inch thick.

This is a 12-point rule. It is 1 pica thick; 6 of these would be 1 inch thick.

Points, picas and inches are used in different places. Here's what's usually measured with what:

Points
◆ *Thickness of rules*
◆ *Type sizes (cutlines, headlines, text, etc.)*
◆ *All measurements smaller than a pica*

Picas
◆ *Lengths of rules*
◆ *Widths of text, photos, cutlines, gutters, etc.*

Inches
◆ *Story lengths*
◆ *Depths of photos and ads (though some papers use picas for all photos)*

TOOLS OF THE TRADE

The electronic newsroom has arrived. So if you're serious about newspaper design, you'd better get comfortable with computers. They're indispensable tools that improve performance and save time when it comes to:

◆ **Writing and editing stories.** Most newsrooms tossed out their typewriters 10 years ago. Today, reporters and editors use computers to type, edit, file stories, fit headlines and search databases.

◆ **Producing photos.** Digital photography lets you adjust the size, shape and quality of images electronically.

◆ **Pagination.** With desktop publishing programs you can create pages electronically (this book, for instance, was designed using QuarkXpress). In the future, all newspaper type, photos and art will be paginated.

◆ **Creating illustrations and graphics.** Drawing programs make it easy to create full-color artwork in any style. Several wire services produce computer graphics daily, transmitting them electronically to subscribers. This lets small papers package first-class graphics with each edition while expanding their libraries of maps and charts.

The most popular computer in newsroom art departments has been the Macintosh, produced by Apple Computer, Inc. (That's a Mac to the left of this text.)

MORE ON ▶

◆ **Scanning:** *How to import images into your computer electronically* **105**

◆ **Printing color:** *How computer drawing programs produce full-color art* **189**

COMPUTER ACCESSORIES

Floppy disks and CDs: *Information can be stored in a computer's internal memory drive, OR it can be transported from computer to computer via portable disks. Floppy disks (far left) came first; they can hold a megabyte or two. Compact disks (CDs) are far more powerful, storing 600 megabytes of data — perfect for photos, music and libraries.*

Scanner: *This device can capture photos or artwork electronically. It scans images like a photocopying machine, after which you can adjust their size, shape and exposure on your computer screen — avoiding the traditional darkroom process altogether. For more on scanning, turn to page 105.*

Printer: *Once you design your masterpiece on the computer, how do you print the thing out? Many desktop publishers use laser printers like this one: high-resolution devices that output near-typeset quality type and graphics.*

Modem: *A device that allows computers to communicate with each other and transmit data (text, images, page layouts) over telephone lines. Newer computers use their built-in modems to link users to electronic databases and information services.*

BASIC TYPOGRAPHY

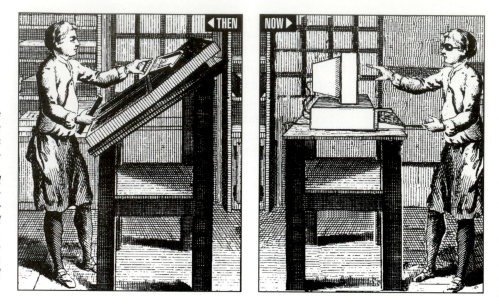

◄ THEN   NOW ►

For hundreds of years — since Gutenberg began printing bibles in the 15th century — type was set by hand. Printing shops had composing rooms where compositors (or typesetters) selected characters individually, then loaded them into galleys one row at a time: a slow and clumsy process.

Over time, printers began using machines to set type. A century ago, Linotype keyboards created type slugs from hot metal. In the 1960s, phototypesetters began using film to print typographic characters. And today, computers make typesetting so cheap and easy, almost anyone can create professional-looking type.

Before we start examining headlines and text, we need to devote a few pages to typography. After all, think how many hours you've spent reading books, magazines and newspapers over the years. And all that time you *thought* you were reading stories, paragraphs and words, you were actually processing long strings of *characters*, one after another. You're doing it now. Yet like most readers, you surf across these waves of words, oblivious to typographic details.

When you listen to music, you absorb it whole; you don't analyze every note (though some musicians do). When you read text, you don't scrutinize every character, either. But some designers do. They agonize over type sizes, spacing, character widths, line lengths. Because when you put it all together, it makes the difference between handsome type and type that looks like this.

All music starts with the 12 notes in the scale. All newspaper design starts with the 26 letters in the alphabet. If you want to understand the difference between Mozart and Metallica, you've got to ask, "How'd they do *that* with *those notes?*" If you want to understand the difference between good design and garbage, you've got to ask, "How'd they do *that* with *those letters?*"

Take the garbage below. Observe how it bombards you with a variety of sizes, shapes and styles, each with its own unique characteristics:

Upper-case boldface serif, 48 point

Lower-case sans serif, 29 point

Upper-case, boldface serif, reversed (white on black), 28 point

Lower-case serif outline, 46 point

Lower-case cursive, 60 point

Upper-case serif, expanded, 18 point

Upper-case sans serif, condensed, 60 point

Lower-case serif italic, 51 point

Lower-case serif with drop shadow, 36 point

BASIC TYPOGRAPHY

TYPE FONTS & FAMILIES

There are thousands of typefaces out there, with names like Helvetica and Hobo, Bookman and Blippo. Years ago — before printing became computerized — type foundries would cast each typeface in a variety of sizes. And each individual size of type was called a *font:*

MORE ON ▶

◆ **Display headlines:** *Tips on designing creative feature headlines* **182**

This is a font — a complete set of characters comprising one specific size, style and weight of typeface, including numbers and punctuation marks. As you can see, this Futura Condensed Bold font contains dozens of characters — and this font is just one member of the Futura family.

16-POINT FUTURA CONDENSED BOLD

ABCDEFGHIJKLMN OPQRSTUVWXYZ ·········· *Upper-case characters*

abcdefghijklmn opqrstuvwxyz ·········· *Lower-case characters*

1234567890 ·········· *Numbers*

&.,.:;""?!()•/#¢$%* ·········· *Punctuation marks*

All the individual Futura fonts are part of the great Futura *family.* And many type families (like Futura) include a variety of *weights* (lightface, regular, boldface) and *styles* (roman, italic, condensed).

Most type families are classified into two main groups: *serif* and *sans serif.*

Serif type *has tiny strokes, or serifs, at the tips of each letter. The typefaces at right are all members of the Times family — perhaps the most common serif typeface used today.*

This is 18-point Times.
This is 18-point Times Italic.
This is 18-point Times Bold.
This is 18-point Times Bold Italic.

Serif type families often include a wide variety of weights and styles. Times, however, is usually limited to two weights (regular and bold) and two styles (roman and italic).

Sans serif type *("sans" means "without" in French) has no serifs. The typefaces at right are all members of the Futura family, one of the most popular sans-serif typefaces used today.*

This is 18-point Futura.
This is 18-point Futura Condensed Light Oblique.
This is 18-point Futura Heavy Outline.
This is 18-point Futura Extra Bold.

The Futura family, on the other hand, is available in an extremely wide range of weights (from light to extra bold) and styles (including regular, oblique and condensed).

Some typefaces are too eccentric to be classified as either serif or sans serif. *Cursive type,* for example, mimics hand-lettered script. *Novelty type* strives for a more distinctive, decorative, and often outrageous personality.

Cursive type *looks like handwritten script. In some families the letters connect; in others they don't. This font is 18-point Diner Script.*

Dear John, I'm leaving forever, you slimy weasel.

HI-YO, SILVER! BOINGGG!!

Novelty type *adds variety and flavor. It works well in small doses (like headlines, ads and comic strips) but can call a lot of attention to itself.*

BASIC TYPOGRAPHY

HOW TO MEASURE TYPE SIZE

We measure type by *point size* — that is, the height of the font as calculated in points. (Points, you'll recall, are the smallest unit of printing measurement, with 72 points to the inch.) This sizing system originated in the 18th century, when type was cast in metal or wood. What's curious is this: Back in those olden days, a font's point size measured not the type characters but the printing block that *held* those characters:

MORE ON ▶

◆ **Raw-wrap headlines:** *Using them to keep headlines from butting* 62

◆ **Mortises and insets:** *Guidelines for overlapping photos* 135

Point size refers to the height of a font — or more specifically, the height of the slug that held the letters back in the days of metal type. Because those fonts were traditionally manufactured in only standard point sizes — 9, 10, 12, 14, 18, 24, 30, 36, 48, 60, 72 — those remain the most commonly used type sizes today.

100 pts.

Sizing type is a slippery thing because point sizes don't always correspond to reality. A 100-point typeface, for example, is never *exactly* 100 points tall. And what's more, the actual height of 100-point typefaces often varies from font to font.

And then there's *x-height,* the height of a typical lower-case letter. Fonts with tall x-heights look bigger than those with short x-heights — even when their point sizes are identical:

This line of 14-point Bookman looks bigger
than this line of 14-point Bernhard Modern.

As you can see, a number of variables come into play when you size a font. But by learning to identify the basic components of type — and how they affect readability — you'll be able to analyze type more intelligently:

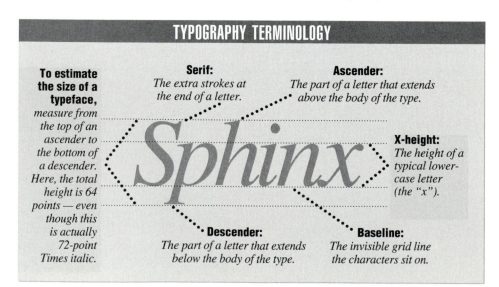

TYPOGRAPHY TERMINOLOGY

To estimate the size of a typeface, *measure from the top of an ascender to the bottom of a descender. Here, the total height is 64 points — even though this is actually 72-point Times italic.*

Serif: *The extra strokes at the end of a letter.*

Ascender: *The part of a letter that extends above the body of the type.*

X-height: *The height of a typical lower-case letter (the "x").*

Descender: *The part of a letter that extends below the body of the type.*

Baseline: *The invisible grid line the characters sit on.*

BASIC TYPOGRAPHY

Using type right out of the computer is like wearing a suit right off the rack — it won't look its best until you tailor it a bit. By tailoring type (adjusting shapes and spaces) you can increase its efficiency, improve its readability, and dramatically alter its personality.

Most page-layout software lets you modify type *vertically* and *horizontally:*

MODIFYING TYPE VERTICALLY

Point size: Changing the point size changes the height of a font. The bigger the size, the taller the type:

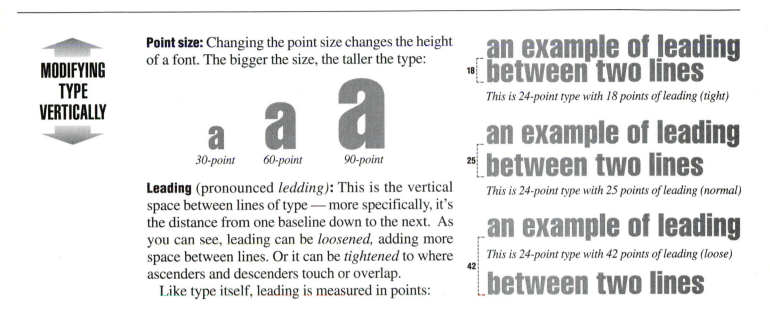

a *30-point*   a *60-point*   a *90-point*

Leading (pronounced *ledding*)**:** This is the vertical space between lines of type — more specifically, it's the distance from one baseline down to the next. As you can see, leading can be *loosened,* adding more space between lines. Or it can be *tightened* to where ascenders and descenders touch or overlap.

Like type itself, leading is measured in points:

18 an example of leading between two lines
This is 24-point type with 18 points of leading (tight)

25 an example of leading between two lines
This is 24-point type with 25 points of leading (normal)

42 an example of leading
This is 24-point type with 42 points of leading (loose)
between two lines

MODIFYING TYPE HORIZONTALLY

Tracking (or *kerning**)**:** Just as you can tighten or loosen the *vertical* spacing between lines, you can adjust the *horizontal* space between letters — though even the slightest changes in tracking can affect the type's readability:

tracking
This is 24-point type with normal tracking (no extra spacing between characters)

t r a c k i n g
This is 24-point type with loose tracking (+40 units between characters)

tracking
This is 24-point type with tight tracking (-10 units between characters)

Set width (or *scaling*)**:** Computers can stretch or squeeze typefaces as though they're made out of rubber — which can look lovely or lousy, depending. Set width is usually expressed as a percentage of the font's original width:

set width
This 24-point type has a normal set width (100%)

set width
This 24-point type is condensed, with a narrow set width (50%)

set width
This 24-point type is expanded, with a wide set width (200%)

* Technically, **tracking** is the overall spacing between *all* characters in a block of text, while **kerning** is the reduction of spacing between *pairs of letters.* For instance, if you kerned these two letters:

AW

— they'd look like this:

AW

THE FOUR BASIC ELEMENTS

Newspaper pages are like puzzles — puzzles that can fit together in a number of different ways.

Though pages may look complicated at first, you'll find that only four basic elements — four kinds of puzzle pieces — are essential. Because these four elements get used over and over again, they occupy 90% of all editorial turf. Once you master these four basic building blocks, you'll master page design. (Well, that's not entirely true — but it makes your job sound easier, doesn't it?)

The four elements are:
◆ **Headlines** — the oversized type that labels each story;
◆ **Text** — the story itself;
◆ **Photos** — the pictures that accompany stories; and
◆ **Cutlines** — the type that accompanies photographs.

This is how the page actually printed . . .

. . . and this is how we'll represent that page — and the four basic design elements — in this book:

Photo ··············

Cutline ············

Headline ···········

Text ··············

·············· Photo

·············· Cutline

·············· Headline

·············· Text

In the pages ahead, we'll examine each of these elements in quick detail. If you're interested only in page design, feel free to browse through this material and come back to it when you need it.

HEADLINES

When you study a page like the one at right — which probably happens every time you stand in the checkout line at the grocery store — there's one thing that leaps out, that grabs you, that sucks you in and forces you to dig down into your pocket, yank out some change and *buy* the thing:

The headlines.

Headlines can be mighty powerful. In fact, they're often the strongest weapon in your design arsenal. Stories can be beautifully written, photos can be vivid and colorful — but neither is noticeable from 10 feet away the way headlines are.

You may never write headlines as strange and tacky as these tabloid headlines are (although to give credit where it's due, notice how cleverly crafted they are). If you stick strictly to design, you may never even write heads at all (since most headlines are written by copy editors). But you still need to know what headlines are, where they go, and what styles, shapes and sizes are available.

Though this page has little to do with "serious" journalists like us, you've got to admit those Futura headlines are pretty effective.

WRITING GOOD HEADLINES

Because this is a book on design, not copy editing, we won't rehash all the rules of good headline-writing. But we'll hit the highlights, which are:

◆ **Keep them conversational.** Write the way people speak. Avoid pretentious jargon, odd verbs, omitted words (*Solons hint bid mulled*). As the stylebook for The St. Petersburg Times warns, "Headlines should not read like a telegram."

◆ **Write in present tense, active voice.** Like this: *President vetoes tax bill.* Not *President vetoed tax bill* or *Tax bill vetoed by president.*

◆ **Avoid bad splits.** Old-time copy-deskers were fanatical about this. And though things are looser these days, you should still try to avoid dangling verbs, adjectives or prepositions at the end of a line.

Instead of this: Try this:

Sox catch up with Yankees   **Sox catch Yankees in playoffs**

Above all else, headlines should be accurate and instantly understandable. If you can improve a headline by writing it a little short or by changing the size a bit — do it. Readability always comes first.

Remember, headlines serve four functions on a newspaper page:

1. They summarize story contents.

2. They prioritize stories, since bigger stories get bigger headlines.

3. They entice readers into the text.

4. They anchor story designs to help organize the page.

HEADLINES

TYPES OF HEADLINES

This headline is from The New York Sun of April 13, 1861. Papers often wrote a dozen decks like this before finally reaching the start of the story. Why no wide horizontal headlines in those days? Because the old type-revolving presses used metal type locked into blocks to print each page. Type set too wide tended to come loose and fly off the cylinder as the presses spun around.

THE LATEST NEWS.

BY TELEGRAPH TO THE N. Y. SUN.

Civil War Begun!

THE MADNESS OF TREASON.

FORT SUMTER ATTACKED !

FURIOUS BOMBARDMENT.

GALLANT DEFENCE OF THE FORT.

" Our Flag is Still There "

Arrival of the Relief Fleet !

PRELIMINARY OFFICIAL CORRESPOND. ENCE.

A century ago, most newspaper headlines:
- ◆ Mixed typefaces at random.
- ◆ Combined all caps and lower case.
- ◆ Were centered horizontally.
- ◆ Stacked layers of narrow decks atop one another, with rules between each deck.

Today's headlines, by comparison:
- ◆ Are generally written downstyle (that is, using normal rules of capitalization).
- ◆ Run flush left.
- ◆ Are usually wide rather than narrow.
- ◆ Use decks optionally, as in this example:

Hula hoops have Americans all a-twirl

That '60s trend is back, and it's hotter than ever

That's called a *banner* headline, and it's the standard way to write a news headline. But it's not the only way. Below are some alternatives — headline styles that go in and out of fashion as time goes by. (These headlines all use Helvetica.)

Kickers

Kickers lead into headlines by using a word or phrase to label topics or catch your eye. They're usually much smaller than the main head, set in a contrasting style or weight.

A TREND RETURNS
Hula hoops are on a roll

Hoop-la
Hula hoops are sweeping the nation this summer

Hammers

Hammers use a big, bold phrase to catch your eye, then add a lengthier deck below. They're effective and appealing, but are usually reserved for special stories or features.

Slammers

Who dreams up these nutty names? This two-part head uses a boldface word or phrase to lead into a contrasting main headline. Some papers limit these to special features or jump headlines.

Hula hoops: A hot new hit

HULA HOOPS: They were hot in the '60s, but they're hotter today

Tripods

This head comes in three parts: a bold word or phrase (often all caps) and two lines of deck squaring off alongside. Like most gimmicky heads, it usually works better for features than for hard news.

Raw wraps

Most headlines cover all the text below; this treatment lets text wrap alongside. It's a risky idea — but later on, we'll see instances where this headline style comes in handy.

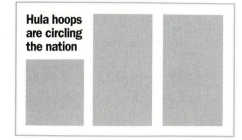

Hula hoops are circling the nation

Hula hoops are circling the nation this summer

Sidesaddle heads

This style lets you park the head beside, rather than above, the story. It's best for squeezing a story — preferably, one that's boxed — into a shallow horizontal space. Can be flush left, flush right or centered.

HEADLINES

HOW TO SIZE HEADLINES ON A PAGE

If we had to generalize about headline sizes, we could say that *small* headlines range from 12- to 24-point; *midsize* headlines range from 24- to 48-point; *large* headlines range upwards from 48-point.

Beyond that, it's difficult to generalize about headline sizes. Some papers like them big and bold; others prefer them small and elegant. Headlines in tabloids are often smaller than headlines in broadsheets — though not always.

Still, this much is true: Since bigger stories get bigger headlines, headlines will generally get smaller as you move down the page. Here are some examples:

MORE ON

◆ **Butting headlines:**
When it's permissible and how it works... **69**

◆ **Standing heads:**
How they differ from headlines **123**

◆ **Display headlines:**
Treatments that add variety and graphic pizzazz to feature headlines **182**

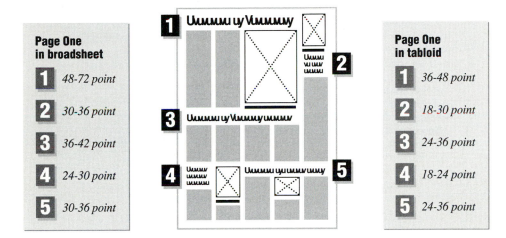

Page One in broadsheet

1. *48-72 point*
2. *30-36 point*
3. *36-42 point*
4. *24-30 point*
5. *30-36 point*

Page One in tabloid

1. *36-48 point*
2. *18-30 point*
3. *24-36 point*
4. *18-24 point*
5. *24-36 point*

NUMBER OF LINES IN A HEADLINE

Traditionally, newspapers have used a coding formula for headlines that lists: 1) the *column width,* 2) the *point size* and 3) the *number of lines.* Using that formula, a 3-30-1 headline would be a 3-column, 30-point headline that runs on one line, like this:

Rock 'n' roll causes acne, doctor says

(Not shown actual size)

Headlines for news stories usually run on top of the text. That means a wide story needs a wide headline; a narrow story needs a narrow one. So in a narrow layout, that headline above could be rewritten as a 1-30-3 (1 column, 30-point, 3 lines deep):

Rock 'n' roll causes acne, doctor says

Since 5-10 words are optimum for most headlines, narrow stories may need 3-4 lines of headline to make sense; wide headlines can work in a line or two.

The chart below will give you an idea of how many lines usually work best:

HOW MANY LINES DOES A HEADLINE NEED?					
If headline is this wide (in columns):	1	2	3	4	5	6
Then make it this deep (in lines):	3-4	2-3	1-2	1	1	1

Text is the most essential building block of newspaper design. It's the gray matter that communicates the bulk of your information.

But text doesn't have to be gray and dull. You can manipulate a wide range of typographic components to give text versatility and personality.

Take this record review, for instance:

Typeface & size
These record titles use 9-point Futura Condensed bold (note the variety of type styles.)

This text uses 9-point Palatino —a common typeface and size for newspaper text.

Leading
The text uses 10 points of leading. Since it's 9-point type, that means there's one point of space between descenders and ascenders.

Tracking & set width
We've tightened the tracking just a bit (-2), so the characters nearly touch. And the set width is slightly condensed (95%).

Paragraph indents
The first line of each new paragraph is indented 9 points.

Hanging indents
In a way, these are the opposite of paragraph indents. The first line is flush left; all subsequent lines are indented to "hang" along the edge of those black bullets (or dingbats).

Extra leading
We've added 8 points of extra leading between the end of one review and the beginning of the next. There's also 3 points of extra leading between the boldface title info and the text that follows.

BITE YOU LIKE A DOG
Toe Jam
(Nosebleed Records) ★★★

Looking for some tunes that'll make your eardrums bleed and melt 50 points off your I.Q.?

Grab yourself some Toe Jam.

On "Bite You Like A Dog," these veteran Seattle death-metal-mongers unleash testosterone-drenched blasts of molten sonic fury, from the opening salvo of "Lost My Lunch" to the gut-wrenching closer, "Can't Love You No More ('Cuz I'm Dead)." Lead vocalist Axl Spandex has never sounded more satanic than on the eerie "Sdrawkcab Ti Yalp."

Of course, the big question for every Toe Jam fan will be: Does this record match their ageless 1992 classic, "Suckadelic Lunchbucket"?

Sadly, no. But really, what could?
— *Forrest Ranger*

THE VILLAGE IDIOTS UNPLUGGED
The Village Idiots
(Doofus Records) ★

What awesome potential this band has! You'd have to be living in a cave on some remote planet not to remember how the music biz was abuzz last year when these rock legends joined forces, refugees from such stellar supergroups as:

● Nick O. Teen and The Couch Potatoes;
● Men With Belts;
● Potbelly; and, of course,
● Ben Dover and the Silvery Moonbeams.

What a letdown, then, to hear this dreck. One listening to "The Village Idiots Unplugged" and it's your *stereo* you'll want unplugged.
— *Ruby Slippers*

HOG KILLIN' TIME
Patsy Alabama
(Big Hair Records) ★★★★

Some still call her "The Nashville Madonna." But Patsy Alabama now swears her days as "The Cuddle-Bunny of Country Music" are over.

IN YOUR EAR

REVIEWS, PREVIEWS & MUSICAL MUSINGS

And with her new record — and her new band, The Rocky Mountain Oysters — she proves it.

Patsy's songwriting is a wonder: sweet, sassy, and so doggone *powerful*. In the waltzy weeper "I Love When You Handle My Love Handles," she croons:

Some nights are rainbows
Some are cartoons
And some call you softly to dance
    below the moon
© 1994, Millie Moose Music, Inc.

Aw, shucks. That gal will dang near bust your heart. Buy some hankies. Then buy this record.
— *Denton Fender*

ROCKS IN YOUR SOCKS
Ducks Deluxe
(NSU-Polygraph) ★★

If the idea of a 22-piece accordion orchestra appeals to you — playing such polka-fied disco classics as "Shake Yer Booty" fronted by a vocalist named Dinah Sore, whose fingernails-on-the-blackboard screechings make Yoko Ono sound like Barbra Streisand — then friend, this is your lucky day.

For the rest of you, avoid this sonic spewage like the plague.
— *C. Spotrun*

NEWS & NOTES: The April 14 benefit for **Window-Peekers Anonymous** has been canceled. . . . Rapper **Aaron Tyres** will sign autographs at noon Sunday at The Taco Pit. . . . **The Grim Reapers** are looking for a drummer. Interested? Call 555-6509.

Got a music news nugget? A trivia question? A cure for the common cold? Write to In Your Ear, P.O. Box 1222.

Sans serif type
Papers often use sans-serif faces to distinguish graphics, logos and side bars from the main text. This Futura font is centered, all caps, and reversed (white type on a black background).

Italic type *is used to emphasize words — as in "powerful" here. It's also used for editor's notes (below), foreign words, or literary excerpts — as in the song lyrics here.*

Agate type
Fine print set in 5- or 6-point. Also used for sports scores and stocks.

Flush right type *runs flush to the right edge of the column.*

Flush left type *runs flush to the left edge of the column. Many papers also run cutlines and news briefs flush left (ragged right).*

Justified type
The text has straight margins on both the right and left edges.

Boldface type
Boldface is often used to highlight key words or names. It's hard to read in large doses, however.

Editor's note
This uses Palatino text type — but note how the extra leading, italics and ragged-right style set it apart from the text.

TEXT

Newspapers measure stories in inches. A short filler item might be just 2 inches long; a major investigative piece might be 200. But since one inch of type set in a *wide* leg is bigger than one inch of type in a *narrow* leg, editors avoid confusion by assuming all text will be one standard width (that's usually around 12 picas).

You can design an attractive newspaper without ever varying the width of your text. Sometimes, though, you may decide to stretch or shrink the width of a column; those non-standard column widths are called *bastard* measures.

Generally speaking, text becomes hard to follow if it's set in legs narrower than 10 picas. It's tough to read, too, if it's set wider than 20 picas.

The ideal depth for text is between 2 and 10 inches per leg. Shorter than that, legs look shallow and weak; longer than that, they become dull, gray stacks. (We'll fine-tune these guidelines in the pages ahead.)

MORE ON ▶

◆ **Story designs**
using only text....... **40**
◆ **Text shapes:** *How to choose the best configurations when dummying stories...* **45**
◆ **Page designs**
using only text........ **68**

SHAPING TEXT INTO COLUMNS

Text is flexible. When you design a story, you can bend and pour the text into different vertical and horizontal configurations, as these examples show:

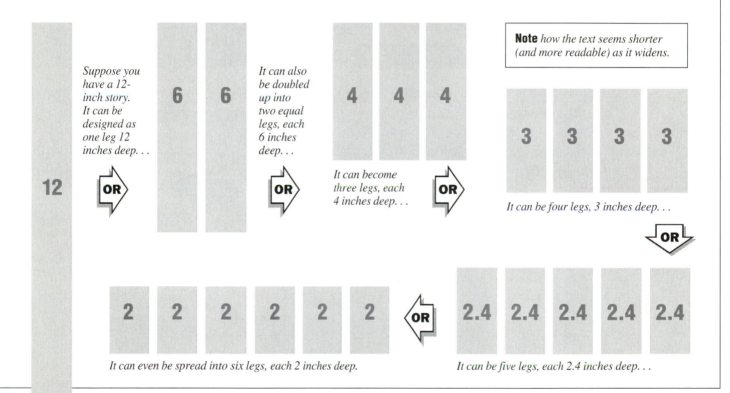

12

Suppose you have a 12-inch story. It can be designed as one leg 12 inches deep. . .

OR

6 **6**

It can also be doubled up into two equal legs, each 6 inches deep. . .

OR

4 **4** **4**

It can become three legs, each 4 inches deep. . .

OR

Note *how the text seems shorter (and more readable) as it widens.*

3 **3** **3** **3**

It can be four legs, 3 inches deep. . .

OR

2 **2** **2** **2** **2** **2**

It can even be spread into six legs, each 2 inches deep.

OR

2.4 **2.4** **2.4** **2.4** **2.4**

It can be five legs, each 2.4 inches deep. . .

A lot of math is involved in page design, especially when you calculate story lengths and shapes. To succeed, you need a sense of geometry and proportion — an understanding of how changing one element in a story's design affects every other element.

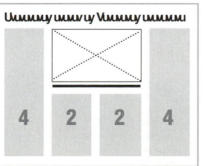

Here's that same 12-inch story — but now it wraps around a photograph. Can you see how, if the photo became deeper, each column of text would need to get deeper, too?

PHOTOS

There's nothing like a photograph to give a page motion and emotion. As you can see in these classic images from pages of the past, photojournalism lies at the very heart of newspaper design:

Clockwise from top:
Babe Ruth says farewell to baseball; Harry Truman waves a famous election headline; a captured Viet Cong officer is shot in Saigon; the space shuttle Challenger explodes after launch; Buzz Aldrin walks on the moon; Jack Ruby shoots accused Kennedy assassin Lee Harvey Oswald.

Every picture tells a story — and every story deserves a picture. Today's readers are so spoiled by TV and magazines that they now expect photos — color photos, yet — to accompany every story they read.

Now, you may not have the space for that many photos. You may not have enough photographers to *shoot* that many photos. And printing color may be downright impossible.

But try anyway. Add photos every chance you get. Without them, you simply can't create an appealing newspaper.

MORE ON ▶

◆ **Horizontals:**
Tips on sizing and designing 46

◆ **Verticals:**
Tips on sizing and designing 49

◆ **Plus:** *A complete chapter on photos* .. 91

THE THREE BASIC PHOTO SHAPES

It sounds obvious, but news photos come in three basic shapes. Each of those shapes has its strengths and weaknesses. And each is best suited to certain design configurations.

The three shapes are *rectangular:* horizontal, vertical and square.

Horizontal
This is the most common shape for news photos. We view the world horizontally through our own eyes, and when you pick up a camera, this is the shape you instantly see — though some subjects (like basketball players and space shuttle launches) may demand a vertical composition.

Vertical
Vertical shapes are often considered more dynamic than either squares or horizontals. But verticals can be trickier to design than squares or horizontals. Because they're so deep, they often seem related to any stories parked alongside — even if they're not.

Square
Squares are sometimes considered the dullest of the three shapes. In fact, some page designers and photographers avoid squares altogether. Remember, however, that the content of a photo is more important than its shape. Accept each photo on its own terms, and design it onto the page so it's as strong as possible — whatever its shape.

CUTLINES

You're browsing through the newspaper. Suddenly, you come face-to-face with a photo that looks like this:

You look at the pig. You look at the men. You look at the bulldozer. You look back at the pig. You wonder: *What's going on here?* Is it funny? Cruel? Weird? Is this pig *doomed?*

Fortunately, there's a cutline below the photo. It says this:

Highway workers use a loader to lift Mama, a 600-pound sow, onto a truck Monday on Interstate 84 near Lloyd Center. The pig fell from the back of the truck on its way to the slaughterhouse. It took the men two hours to oust the ornery oinker.

Ahhhh. Now it makes sense.

Sure, every picture tells a story. But it's the cutline's job to tell the story behind every picture: *who's* involved, *what's* happening, *when* and *where* the event took place. A well-written cutline makes the photo instantly understandable and tells readers *why* the photo — and the story — are important.

CUTLINE TYPE STYLES

Cutlines are quite different from text. And to make sure that difference is clear to readers, most newspapers run cutlines in a different typeface than text. Some use boldface, so cutlines will "pop" as readers scan the page. Some use italic, for a more elegant look. Some use sans serifs, to contrast with serif text. (This book uses a serif italic font — Times — for its cutlines.)

SERIF BOLDFACE, JUSTIFIED

President Bill Clinton greets Boris Yeltsin at the White House Thursday as the two leaders begin a new round of high-level summit talks.

SERIF ITALIC, RAGGED RIGHT

President Bill Clinton greets Boris Yeltsin at the White House Thursday as the two leaders begin a new round of high-level summit talks.

SANS SERIF, JUSTIFIED, WITH BOLDFACE LEAD-IN

SUMMIT BEGINS — President Bill Clinton greets Boris Yeltsin at the White House Thursday as the two leaders begin a new round of high-level summit talks.

CUTLINES

How long should cutlines be? Long enough to describe — briefly — all significant details in the photo. Some photos are fairly obvious and don't require much explanation. Others (old historical photos, works of art, photos that run without stories) may need lengthy descriptions.

And what about photos of clubs or teams? Should every face — all 19 of them — be identified? Most newspapers set guidelines for such occasions, so it's hard to generalize. But remember that readers expect cutlines to offer quick hits of information. So don't overdo it.

Where do you dummy cutlines? On news pages, they generally run *below* each photo. But for variety, especially on feature pages, cutlines can also run *beside* and *between* photos, as shown below:

MORE ON ▶

◆ **Mug shots:** *They've got their own style of cutlines* **42**

◆ **Photo spreads:** *Cutline treatments and placement* **111**

BELOW

The Bugle-Beacon/PAT MINNIEAR

*Cutlines below photos usually align along both edges of the photo. They should **never** extend beyond either edge. Some papers set extra-wide cutlines in two legs, since wide type — such as the type in this cutline — can be difficult to read. Another rule of thumb: in wide cutlines, be sure the last line extends at least halfway across the column. (This line barely makes it.)*

BESIDE

*This cutline is set **flush right** along the edge of the photo. (Notice how ragged left type is somewhat annoying to read.) Try to dummy cutlines like this along the outside of the page. That way, the cutline won't butt against any text type, confusing your readers and uglifying your page.*

*This ragged right cutline is **flush left** against the photo and flush to the bottom. And it's too thin. Cutlines should always be at least 6 picas wide. If they're narrow, they shouldn't be very deep.*

BETWEEN

Ideally, every photo should get its own cutline. But photos can also share one common cutline, as these two do. Just be sure you make it clear which photo (at left or at right) you're discussing. And be sure the cutline squares off at either the top or bottom. Don't just let it float. (Note how this cutline is justified on both sides.)

A SAMPLE DUMM

Editing Exercise

This is a typical page dummy for a 6-column broadsheet newspaper. Most broadsheets use a 6-column format like this; most tabloids use a 5-column format that's not as deep.

How dummies work:

◆ *The numbers along the left margin show you inches measured down from the top of the page. The entire page, as you can see, is 21½ inches deep.*

◆ *The numbers along the right margin show inches measured up from the bottom of the page. These are useful for dummying ads.*

◆ *The vertical lines represent columns. A 6-column photo, for instance, would be as wide as the entire page.*

◆ *Each horizontal line represents an inch of depth. A leg of text that's 1 inch deep would take up just one of those segments.*

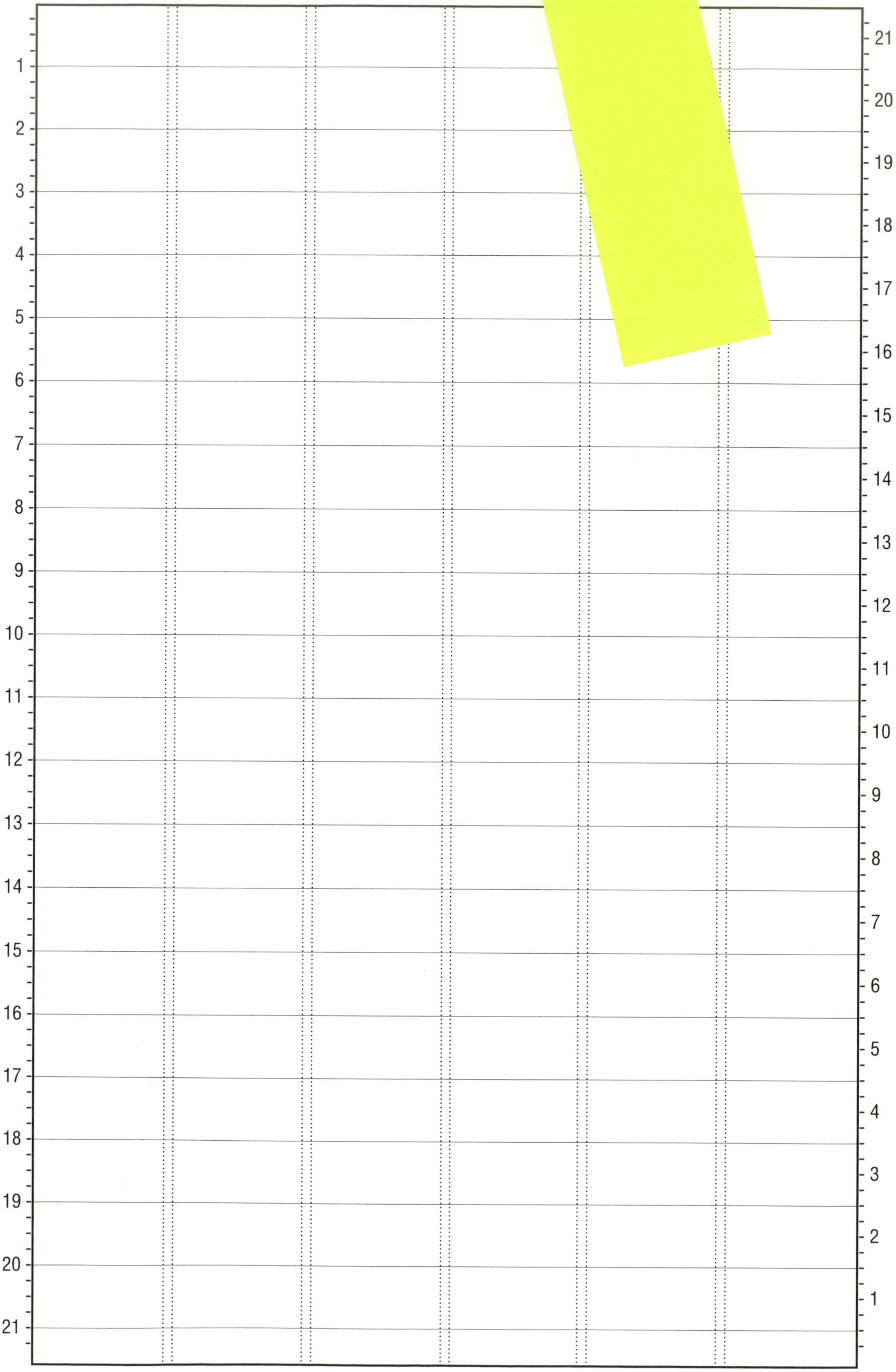

Need a dummy?

You'll need lots of blank page dummies like this to do the exercises at the end of each chapter. Feel free to duplicate this dummy as often as you like if no others are available for you to practice on.

But better yet: *Create a page dummy like this that's customized for your newspaper.*

DRAWING A DUMMY

How can you show your colleagues, in advance, where stories will go on a page? Or what size headlines should be? Or where the photos run?

Mental telepathy? No. You draw a dummy.

Now, you might be tempted (especially if you build pages on a computer) to bypass dummy-drawing and, instead, squat in front of a computer and noodle aimlessly for hours until you *discover the solution.* Wrong. Big waste of time. You'll work more efficiently if you draw a detailed page diagram in advance — a dummy — before you try to assemble the real thing.

Dummies are generally about half the size of actual pages but proportioned accurately (i.e., if your design calls for a thin vertical photo, it shouldn't look square on the dummy.) For greater precision on complex pages, designers often draw life-sized dummies. But for most pages, a small-sized dummy like the one below is sufficient.

And quite necessary.

MORE ON ▶

◆ **Modular design:**
Want to see how this page would look if the story elements were scrambled? Turn to page 76

This is how most pages begin. An editor or designer draws a series of lines and boxes to indicate where photos, cutlines, headlines and text will go. This page is pretty simple: not too many stories or extras.

And here's how that dummy translated into print. Note how every story jumps (continues on another page). That makes the page easier to build, since text can be cut according to the diagram on the dummy.

DRAWING A DUMMY

Drawing a dummy isn't an exact science. Stories don't always fit the way you want. And even when you're dead certain you've measured everything perfectly, you'll inevitably find yourself fudging here and there once you start pasting things up.*

So relax. When it's time to fine-tune a page, you can always trim a photo. Plug in a liftout quote. Write a bigger headline. Shuffle ads around. Add extra air between paragraphs. Cut an inch or two from the story. Or (worst of all) start over.

MORE ON ▶

◆ **Making stories fit:** *Options to try when stories turn out too short or too long ...* **80**

> *In the old days — like, say, oh, 10 years ago — photos, headlines, cutlines and text were printed individually on separate strips of paper, then pasted into place on a grid sheet. That camera-ready page was called a *paste-up* (though all those strips of paper were stuck on with wax, not paste). Some of you old-timers may still build pages this way; the rest of you probably use computer programs like PageMaker or QuarkXpress.

AN EXAMPLE OF HOW DUMMYING WORKS

Let's take a finished layout and build a dummy from it — a reverse of the usual procedure. That way, you can see how the different parts of a dummy work together to create a finished page.

The Oregonian / KRAIG SCATTARELLA

Highway workers use a loader to lift Mama, a 600-pound sow, onto a truck Monday on Interstate 84 near Lloyd Center. The pig fell from the truck on the way to slaughter.

Freeway closed for two hours as ornery oinker hogs traffic

Westbound traffic on Interstate 84 near the Lloyd Center exit was backed up for nearly two miles early Monday when a 600-pound hog on the way to slaughter fell from the back of a truck.

For nearly two hours, the sow refused to budge.

Fred Mickelson told police that he was taking six sows and a boar from his farm in Lyle, Wash., to a slaughterhouse in Carlton when Mama escaped.

"I heard the tailgate fall off, and I looked back and saw her standing in the road," Mickelson said with a sigh. "I thought: 'Oh, no. We've got some real trouble now.'"

Mickelson said Mama was "pretty lively" when she hit the ground, lumbering between cars and causing havoc on a foggy day. There were no automobile accidents, however.

After about an hour of chasing the pig with the help of police, Mickelson began mulling over his options, which included having a veterinarian tranquilize the hog.

About 10 a.m., a crew of highway workers arrived and decided to use a front-end loader to pick up the sow and load her back into the truck.

DRAWING A DUMMY

**STEP BY STEP:
HOW TO DRAW
A DUMMY**

1 Measure all the elements in the example on page 34, and this is what you'll find:

◆ **Text:** The text is in two legs. Each leg is 12 picas and 2 points wide — often written *12p2* (which is a pretty standard column width for newspaper text). Each leg is 2 inches deep. The whole story, then, is 4 inches long.

◆ **Headline:** Measure from the top of an ascender to the bottom of a descender, and you'll find it's a 24-point headline. There are two lines, with a slight space *between* lines. So the whole headline is about 48 points (4 picas) deep.

◆ **Photo:** We usually measure photo widths in picas or columns. (This one is two columns wide — or 25p4.) And though some papers measure depths in inches, it's better to use picas. (This photo is 18 picas — 3 inches — deep.)

◆ **Cutline:** Note the spacing above and below this cutline. From the bottom of the photo to the top of the headline is roughly half an inch — 3 picas.

MORE ON ▶

◆ **Basic terms:** *Definitions of terms like picas and points* **16**

◆ **Headlines:** *How they're measured and how to code them* ... **25**

---

2 Suppose we want to design this story into the top left corner of the page. Grab a page dummy. Find the two left-hand columns. Move up to the top, and we'll begin drawing in the elements.

At the top of the page, draw a box to represent the photo. Make it two columns wide; count down 3 inches for the depth. Run a big "X" into the corners. (The "X" is a traditional way to indicate this is a photo, not an ad or a box for another story.)

HOG
2X18

Always remember to write the size of the photo. In this case, it's 2 columns wide, 18 picas deep — or 2 X 18, for short.

---

3 Next comes the cutline. There are different ways to indicate cutlines on dummies, but here's how we'll do it:

Calculate how many lines of cutline there'll be (in this case, two). Allowing a little air under the photo, draw a line where the bottom of the cutline will be. Here, it's about a half-inch below the photo.

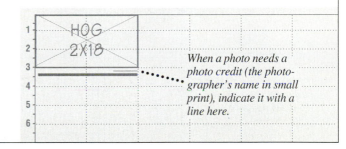

When a photo needs a photo credit (the photographer's name in small print), indicate it with a line here.

---

4 Now dummy a 2-24-2 headline. Most designers just draw a horizontal line and jot down the headline code — and that's quick and easy.

But you might want to imitate the *feel* of the headline by drawing either a row of X's or a squiggly horizontal wave to represent each line of headline. Then write the headline code at the beginning of the line.

Allow a few picas of space between the cutline and the headline. Like this:

HOG
2X18
2-24-2

This effect is easy to do: just waggle a pencil up and down, back and forth along the edge of a ruler.

---

5 Finally, indicate where the text goes. There are many ways to do this: straight lines, wavy lines, arrows — some papers just leave blank space.

For now, let's use a directional line. Write the name (or *slug*) of the story where the text begins; under it, draw a line down the center of the leg. When you reach the bottom of the leg, jog the line up (the way your eye moves) to the top of the next leg. This will trace the path of the text, like so:

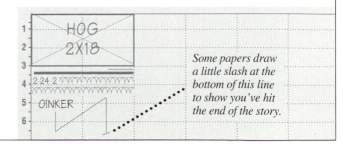

Some papers draw a little slash at the bottom of this line to show you've hit the end of the story.

DRAWING A DUMMY

WHAT EVERY GOOD DUMMY SHOULD SHOW

Every newspaper has its own system for drawing dummies. Some, for instance, size photos in picas; others use inches, or a combination of picas and inches. Some papers use different colored pens for each different design element (boxes, photos, text). Some use wavy lines to indicate text, while others use arrows — or nothing at all.

Whatever the system, *make your dummies as complete and legible as you can.* Be sure that every dummy contains:

Page or section headers, if any

Column logos, sigs or bugs, clearly labeled

Any rules, boxes or borders, clearly marked

Sizes and slugs for all art (photos, maps, charts, etc.), with cropping instructions, if necessary

Cutlines and credit lines for all photos

Story name (or slug) and column width, if it's in a bastard measure; slug can be circled for emphasis

Arrows or lines to show position and movement of text

Any special instructions to the composing room (layout advice, late stories, trimming directions, etc.)

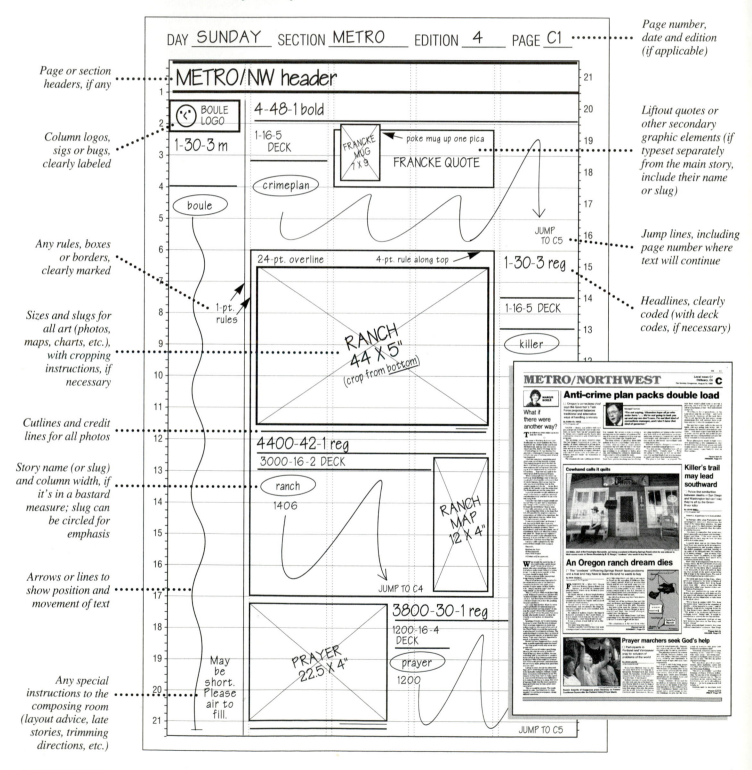

Page number, date and edition (if applicable)

Liftout quotes or other secondary graphic elements (if typeset separately from the main story, include their name or slug)

Jump lines, including page number where text will continue

Headlines, clearly coded (with deck codes, if necessary)

Why ask why?

ANSWERS ▶ 196

1 Examine the headline above. What is the:

Typeface _____

Weight _____

Point size *(within 3 points)* _____

Why ask why?

2 What three things have we now done to that line above:

1. _____

2. _____

3. _____

3 Examine the type at right. Identify five important type characteristics. ▶

> Here is another
> typographic brain-teaser

1. _____   4. _____

2. _____   5. _____

3. _____

4 What four things have we done to that boxed type in question three? ▶

> HERE IS ANOTHER
> TYPOGRAPHIC BRAIN-TEASER

1. _____   3. _____

2. _____   4. _____

5 What are the pica dimensions of that box in question three? _____

6 How thick is the border of that box in question three? _____

7 What are the four differences between the column on the left and the column on the right?

Best picture: "Schindler's List"
Best actor: Tom Hanks in
"Philadelphia"
Best actress: Holly Hunter in
"The Piano"

● **Best picture:** "Schindler's List"
● **Best actor:** Tom Hanks in
"Philadelphia"
● **Best actress:** Holly Hunter in
"The Piano"

7 Below is a three-column news story. Draw a dummy for this layout. (If necessary, use a copy of the dummy sample sheet on page 30.) Be sure to include headline coding.

Crazed pig closes freeway again

For the second time, an ornery oinker causes chaos on the highway

Mama is one freedom-loving hog.

Twice in the same day, Mama broke free from her captors and bolted for daylight. Twice in the same day, she created massive traffic jams.

And twice she was dragged, kicking and squealing, back into captivity.

Westbound traffic on Interstate 84 near Lloyd Center was backed up for two miles Monday when Mama, a 600-pound hog on the way to slaughter, fell from the back of a truck.

For nearly two hours, the sow refused to budge.

Fred Mickelson told police that he was taking six sows and a boar from his farm in Lyle, Wash., to a slaughterhouse in Carlton when Mama escaped.

"I heard the tailgate fall off, and I looked back and saw her standing in the road," Mickelson said with a sigh. "I thought: 'Oh, no. We've got some real trouble now.'"

Mickelson said Mama was "pretty lively" when she hit the ground, lumbering between cars and causing havoc on a foggy day. There were no automobile accidents, however.

After about an hour of chasing the pig with the help of police, Mickelson began mulling over his options, which included having a veterinarian tranquilize the hog.

About 10 a.m., a crew of highway workers arrived and decided to use a front-end loader to pick up the sow and load her back into the truck.

The Oregonian / KRAIG SCATTARELLA

Highway workers use a loader to lift Mama, a 600-pound sow, onto a truck Monday on Interstate 84 near Lloyd Center. The pig fell off the truck on the way to slaughter.

8 The display headline below uses fairly common typefaces. If you have access to a typesetting or page-layout computer program, duplicate this headline as closely as possible; if not, describe as completely as you can the various typographic components involved:

larry MOE & Curly

ANSWERS ▶ 196

Headlines, text, photos, cutlines. Those are the basic pieces in the great Newspaper Design Puzzle. Over the years, page designers have tried assembling their puzzles in every conceivable way. Some solutions worked; others didn't.

In the pages ahead, we'll show you what works, what doesn't, and what comes close. You may think there are thousands of design combinations for every story and every page, but there are really just a few basic formats you can count on. And those formats are well worth knowing.

In this chapter, we'll show you the different shapes a story can take, whether it's:

◆ a story without art;
◆ a story with a mug shot;
◆ a story with a large photograph;
◆ a story with two photographs.

Later on, we'll show you how to combine stories to make a page. But first things first.

There's a lot of information in the pages ahead. Don't try to absorb it all at once. Many of these examples were designed to be swipeable formats; the next time you're laying out pages, look through the section that applies, explore your options, and choose a format that fits the bill. You'll soon understand why some layouts succeed and others fail.

STORIES WITHOUT ART

In a typical newspaper — whether it's The New York Times or a small rural weekly — 70% of the stories run without any art, 25% use just one piece of art (a photo, chart or map), and only 5% use two or more pieces of art.

See for yourself:

MORE ON ▶

◆ **Designing pages without art:** *Tips and techniques for creating attractive pages when photos aren't available ....* **68**

Here's a typical section front from the Portland Press Herald in Maine. There's a huge fire photo in the center of the page (but the actual story is on the following page). One other story uses one photo — and the other three stories, along with the news briefs, use only headlines and text. When you turn the page. . .

. . . on the second page of that section there's another fire photo (this time with text). That top story adds a map and a small sidebar. All the other elements on the page use only text: the news story in the top left corner; the four jump stories (continued from the previous page); the calendar along the bottom.

So relax. Most of the stories you'll design will consist of just headlines and text. And since there are only a few ways to design stories without art, it's hard to goof them up.

Basically, when you combine headlines and text, they tend to run along the page either *vertically* or *horizontally:*

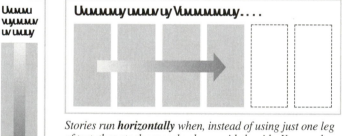

*Stories run **vertically** when the headline is on top, the text drops straight down below it — and that's that until the text ends.*

*Stories run **horizontally** when, instead of using just one leg of text, they stack several columns side by side. You can keep adding new legs — and extending the headline — until you run out of room at the right edge of the page.*

SHAPING STORIES INTO RECTANGLES

One of the key design guidelines is this: **Whether square, horizontal or vertical, stories should be shaped into rectangles.**

STORIES WITHOUT ART

VERTICAL STORY DESIGN OPTIONS

A hundred years ago, stories were all dummied vertically. Printers would simply lay in strips of text below the headline, and when they reached the bottom of the page, they'd either end the story or jump the text up into the next column.

Nowadays, that's considered dumb dummying. In fact, you should try to avoid dummying legs more than 12 inches deep, since long legs look dull, gray and intimidating. In short: the longer the story, the more it needs to go horizontal.

In news stories (right), the headline usually sits atop the text. (In features, as you'll soon see, that rule is frequently broken.)

Vertical stories are clean and attractive. They're the easiest shape to follow — just start at the headline and read straight down. Vertical design does have drawbacks, however:
◆ *Long vertical legs like these can be very tiring to read.*
◆ *Headlines are harder to write when they're this narrow.*
◆ *Pages full of these long, skinny legs look awfully dull.*

HORIZONTAL STORY DESIGN OPTIONS

Horizontal shapes are pleasing to the eye. And they create the illusion that stories are shorter than they really are.

Again, avoid dummying legs deeper than 12 inches. But avoid short, squat legs, too. For most stories, legs should generally be at least 2 inches deep — never shorter than 1 inch.

Horizontal layouts flow left to right, the way readers naturally read. You'll create the most attractive designs by keeping legs between 2 and 10 inches deep. Note how the headline covers the story, and how it touches the start of the text.

TWO UNUSUAL OPTIONS TO PONDER

Probably 99% of all stories look like those above: basically vertical or horizontal, with the headline running above the text, covering the entire story like an umbrella.

Life is full of exceptions, however, and here are two more: the raw wrap and the sidesaddle head (below). They both break the rule about headlines running above all the text. And they're both potentially troublesome. (See how those right-hand legs of text could collide into any text above them?)

But in the right situations, they're handy. For now, view them with suspicion — but stay tuned.

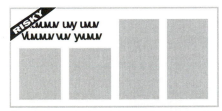

Raw wrap: *The headline is indented into the left-hand legs while the text wraps up alongside and aligns with the top of the headline.*

Sidesaddle headline: *The headline runs in the left-hand column — flush left, flush right or centered. The text runs alongside.*

MUG SHOTS

Yes, you can design stories without art. But that can look awfully gray. And for readers, it can seem downright dull.

Most stories are about people: people winning, losing, getting arrested, getting elected. Readers want to know what those people *look* like. So show them.

Remember, mug shots attract readers. And attracting readers is your job.

◆ **Size:** Mugs usually run the full width of a column, 3-4 inches deep (though you can indent half-column mugs into the text).

◆ **Cropping:** Mug shots should fill the frame tightly — but not *too* tightly. Leave a little air above the hair; avoid slicing into ears, foreheads or chins.

◆ **Cutline:** Every mug needs a cutline. Mug cutlines often use a two-line format: The first is the person's name; the second is a description, title, etc.

HILLARY CLINTON
Supports new health care proposals.

VERTICAL STORY DESIGN OPTIONS

In vertical designs, mug shots go at the very top of the story. In descending order, then, arrange story elements like this: *photo, cutline, headline, text.* Any other sequence may get you into trouble.

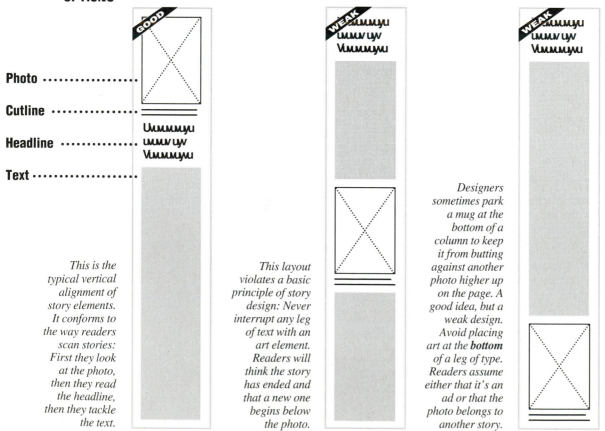

Photo ··············

Cutline ··············

Headline ··············

Text ··············

This is the typical vertical alignment of story elements. It conforms to the way readers scan stories: First they look at the photo, then they read the headline, then they tackle the text.

This layout violates a basic principle of story design: Never interrupt any leg of text with an art element. Readers will think the story has ended and that a new one begins below the photo.

Designers sometimes park a mug at the bottom of a column to keep it from butting against another photo higher up on the page. A good idea, but a weak design. Avoid placing art at the **bottom** of a leg of type. Readers assume either that it's an ad or that the photo belongs to another story.

MUG SHOTS

HORIZONTAL STORY DESIGN OPTIONS

Because mug shots are usually one column wide, it's easy to attach them to a horizontal story: Simply square them off beside the headline and text.

And this is where a little math comes in. Assume the mug is 3 inches deep. Assume the cutline is roughly a half-inch deep. That adds up to a total depth of 3½ inches.

For short stories like this, headlines are small: roughly a half-inch to an inch deep. That makes every leg of text in this design approximately 3 inches deep.

Here's a typical layout for a 6-inch story:

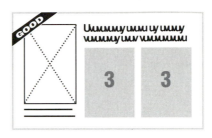

To keep the story rectangular, the headline aligns with the top of the photo; the bottom of each leg squares off with the bottom of the cutline. To make sense, the headline needs to be two lines deep.

If each leg of text in this design is roughly 3 inches deep, that means you can keep adding on legs to accommodate a 9-, 12-, or even a 15-inch story.

Note how, as the headline gets wider, it goes from two lines (above) to one (left). But since bigger stories use bigger headlines, the depths of the legs will stay roughly the same.

You can position mug shots at either end of the story, too. Since the mugee generally stares straight ahead, one side's just as good as the other:

Note how the headline covers only the text — not the photo. Sometimes, though, extending the headline above the mug may help all the elements fit better.

Longer stories need more depth, so they'll wrap beneath the mug. **Note:** Since the text has just grown one column wider, note how the headline needs to extend one more column, too:

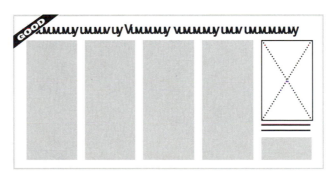

The mug can now go in any leg except the first — and many designers would choose one of the middle legs. Always allow at least 1 pica of air between the cutline and the text. And always dummy at least 1 inch of text under any photo.

In longer stories, a mug can run in any leg (except the first leg — nothing should come between the headline and the start of the text). Or you can park several mugs side by side:

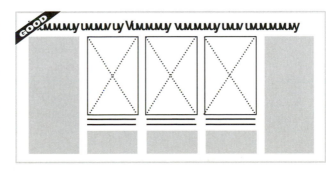

Note how these three mugs are evenly aligned. Two reasons for that: 1) It's ordered, balanced and pleasing to the eye; 2) It gives each mug equal weight instead of emphasizing one person disproportionately.

MUG SHOTS

SOME EXTRA STORY DESIGN OPTIONS

Don't think that layouts *must* be either vertical or horizontal. We've simply made those distinctions to help you develop a feel for story shapes. You'll soon see that, as stories get more complex, they expand both vertically *and* horizontally — and that's where you'll begin improvising and bending the rules.

For example:

Here's a layout that isn't purely vertical, since it uses not one but two legs side by side. And it's not purely horizontal, since it's more deep than wide. But it's a good design solution when you need to fit a short story into a square-shaped hole. And it could easily be deepened to accommodate a longer story.

Note the rules we've observed in dummying this story:
◆ *The headline covers all the text.*
◆ *All elements align neatly with each other.*
◆ *There's at least an inch of text below the photo.*
◆ *The entire story is shaped like a rectangle.*

We've now examined all the basic configurations for stories with mugs. The preceding examples also work well for nearly any story where you add a small graphic (a one-column map, chart, list, etc.) instead of a mug shot.

Now examine these new variations below. Notice the top two designs; they show you what happens when the headline fails to cover all the text.

Remember the raw wrap? Here it is again, this time with a mug atop the second leg. This design works well in a 2-column layout like this: it would keep headlines from butting if another story began to the right of this one.

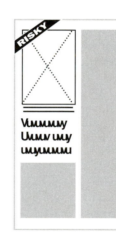

This is a variation of the raw wrap, but few papers use it. It's basically a vertical design cut in half, with the bottom half parked alongside the top. The question is: What happens if there's a story above this one?

Half-column mugs let you add a photo without wasting too much space. These wraparounds work best in wide legs; text should be at least 6 picas wide where it wraps around a mug or it's too thin to read comfortably.

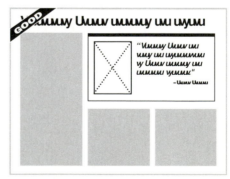

This popular format combines a mug with a liftout quote. It's more attractive and more informative than just a mug shot by itself.

TEXT SHAPES

To repeat once more: You should always shape stories into rectangles. That means all four edges of the story should align — or "grid off" — with each other, as in this example:

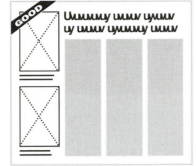

This story is designed into a square-shaped rectangle. The legs are all even lengths, and all outside edges of the story align with each other. It's a clean, well-ordered story design.

This example, by the way, shows you another solution for adding two mugs to a story: putting one atop the other. It's a well-balanced treatment that gives both mugs equal weight.

Beginning designers often find themselves wrenching text into bizarre shapes as they try to make stories fit. Or they'll choose risky, offbeat designs — like raw wraps — when simpler designs would be better.

One way to keep your layouts under control is to watch the shape of your text block. Some text shapes, as you'll see below, are better than others:

TEXT SHAPES: THE GOOD, THE BAD & THE UGLY

Ranked from best to worst, these are the most common text shapes you'll encounter. Arrows follow the flow of the reader's eye through the text.

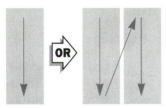

1 *This is the safest shape of all: a rectangle. Whether in one leg or many, it's clean and clear: no odd wraps, leaps or bends.*

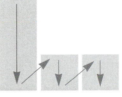

2 *L-shaped text results when text wraps under a photo. It's still a neat and readable shape.*

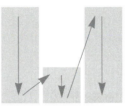

3 *U-shapes break up boring stacks of text, but beware of giant leaps to the top of that right leg.*

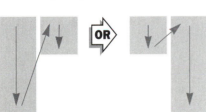

4 *These shapes (called doglegs) are often inevitable when you design around ads. Try to avoid them otherwise, since art placed below text is often mistaken for an ad.*

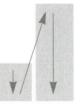

5 *This backward "L" is a risky shape. Readers may think the text starts in that second leg; besides, that second leg will butt into any leg above it. Be careful.*

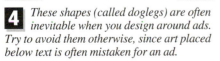
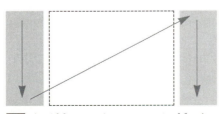

6 *Avoid fragmenting your text and forcing readers to jump blindly across art parked in the middle of one leg or sandwiched between two legs. It's risky. It's confusing. Beware.*

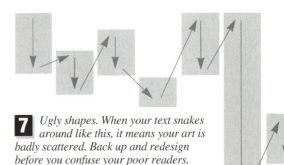

7 *Ugly shapes. When your text snakes around like this, it means your art is badly scattered. Back up and redesign before you confuse your poor readers.*

ONE HORIZONTAL PHOTO

The principles of story design are logical and consistent. In fact, you can probably dummy photos onto pages without ever actually *seeing* the photos. Just stack all the pieces in a clean, pleasing way, and there you are.

That's possible. But it's not recommended. Every photo is unique; every image needs special consideration before you size it and shove it in a convenient slot. Here, for instance, is a typical photo, along with typical considerations you should make before doing any designing:

MORE ON ▶

◆ **Photos:** *A complete chapter on cropping, photo spreads and more* **91**

A FEW FACTS ABOUT THIS PHOTO

1 *In 1985, photographer Lois Bernstein of The Virginian-Pilot came upon three bloodied youngsters huddled by the side of the road. The girl, 16, and her twin 12-year-old brothers had just left the wreckage of their car after smashing into a tree.*

The photo caused a stir when it ran in the paper the next day. "Three of my children were still in hospital beds," said the children's father. "I was hurt. I was upset." The family's friends accused the paper of using a tragedy to sell papers.

Yet the photo is honest and powerful. It later won numerous awards. Would you have run this photo if you had been in the newsroom that day?

5 *Many photos are directional — i.e., the action in the photo moves strongly left or right, requiring you to design the story so the photo faces the text. Here, the children are facing slightly right. But that's not directional enough to matter; text could be dummied on either side of the photo.*

6 *Many design gurus insist that you crop photos into a rectangular shape known as the "golden mean." This shape — basically 3 X 5, roughly the shape of the photo shown here — was discovered by the ancient Greeks and is often thought to be the most harmonious proportion known to man. That's pretty cosmic. Unfortunately, not too many ancient Greeks design newspapers these days, so don't worry about golden rectangles. Just use the shape that best suits the image.*

2 *How big should this photo be played? An image this dramatic has maximum impact if it runs 3 or 4 columns wide — i.e., quite a bit bigger than shown here. Run larger than that, the photo's grisly content would offend some readers; run smaller, the photo's drama and emotion would be lost.*

3 *For some stories, you need several photos to show readers what happened. Here, for instance, the photographer may also have shot the wrecked car, the tree it collided with, the police at work, and so on. But would additional photos have robbed this shot of its impact? Would they have been necessary — or just padding?*

4 *Notice the cropping on this photo. Along the right edge, you can see a hint of a car's bumper; along the bottom, the shoulder of the road. When this photo first ran in the paper, Bernstein cropped it as you see it here. But she now prefers a crop that focuses more tightly on the arms and faces of the children. Which do you prefer?*

Unlike mug shots — which come in one standard shape and size and are generally interchangeable — full-sized photos require thoughtful analysis. So before you begin designing a story, you must consider each photo's:

◆ **Size.** How big must the photo run? (If it's too small, faces and places become undecipherable; if it's too big, you hog space.) Does the photo gain impact if it's larger? Is there room on the page for jumbo art?

◆ **Direction.** Does the action in the photo flow strongly in one direction (someone running, pointing, throwing a ball)? If so, it's best to design the story so the photo *faces* the text. Images that seem to move into the wrong story — or off the page — may misdirect your readers.

◆ **Content.** Is one photo enough to tell the story? Is the package more informative with two or more? Or is the photo meaningless, routine, expendable — something that could make room for another story?

ONE HORIZONTAL PHOTO

VERTICAL STORY DESIGN OPTIONS

As we've previously seen with stories using mug shots, this vertical layout conforms to the way most readers scan stories. They're attracted by the photo; they read down, through the cutline, into the headline; then, if they're still interested, they read the text.

The main factors to consider are: 1) keeping all elements in the proper order; 2) avoiding long, gray legs of text; and 3) avoiding confusion if you park another story beside the photo (we'll explore this in the next chapter).

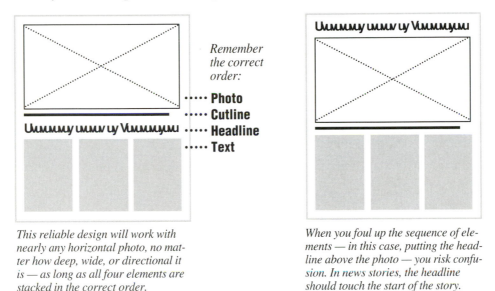

Remember the correct order:

···· **Photo**
···· **Cutline**
···· **Headline**
···· **Text**

This reliable design will work with nearly any horizontal photo, no matter how deep, wide, or directional it is — as long as all four elements are stacked in the correct order.

When you foul up the sequence of elements — in this case, putting the headline above the photo — you risk confusion. In news stories, the headline should touch the start of the story.

HORIZONTAL STORY DESIGN OPTIONS

As we saw on page 45, the safest shape for text blocks is a rectangle (as opposed to L-shapes, U-shapes, doglegs, etc.) So that makes the examples on this page — both vertical and horizontal — safe, simple solutions.

Whenever you try to square off text beside a photo, you'll probably need to wrestle with photo shapes and story lengths to make the math work out. But remember: Every story is (be careful, but it's true) *cuttable.*

If the photo faces right:
*This is the better solution, since the action of the photo will flow into the text. To anchor this design, both the photo and the text block need ample width; the photo should be **at least** two columns wide.*

If the photo faces left:
Simply flop the elements so the text is parked on the left. Remember that all elements must square off at both the top and the bottom; this design won't work if the text comes up too short.

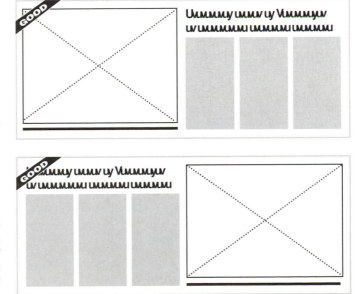

*In these examples, note how the headline runs **beside** the photo, covering only the text. That's the cleanest way to dummy a headline in this format. But here's another variation: running the headline all the way across both the text **and** the photo (it's often called an "armpit"):*

The advantages:
◆ *It connects the photo to the text more tightly. On busy pages, that can help organize stories.*
◆ *One long, loud banner headline can give the story more punch.*

ONE HORIZONTAL PHOTO

SOME EXTRA STORY DESIGN OPTIONS

To a designer's eye, the previous examples are appealing because they're so neatly aligned, so cleanly balanced. Yet these two designs directly below are more common, and perhaps more effective.

The reason? Notice how effectively the headline and text surround the photo to create a self-contained package. There's no way a reader can mistake which story the photo belongs to.

MORE ON ▶

◆ **Raw-wrap headlines:**
Using them to keep headlines from butting.................. **72**

◆ **Feature designs:**
A chapter on special headlines and photo treatments **167**

Here, an L-shaped text block wraps below the photo. If you wanted to play the photo bigger, you could run it 3 columns wide. For longer stories, you could deepen each leg of type — or wrap another leg of type along the right side of the photo and extend the headline further.

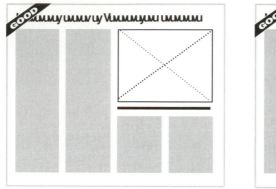

Here, the text wraps around three sides of the photo. Some editors prefer this layout to the one at left because 1) it's symmetrical, and 2) it breaks up those long, gray legs of text more effectively.

Other design options are risky or downright clumsy. Here are several examples to consider — or to avoid altogether:

This, you'll recall, is a raw wrap — where instead of covering the entire story, the headline is parked in a left-hand leg or two. It's not necessarily a bad solution. But it's best reserved for times when you dummy two stories side by side and you need to keep headlines from butting. With a raw wrap, the photo lets you get away with that.

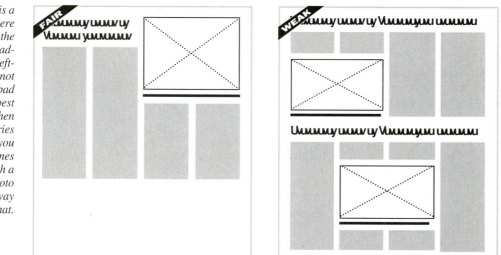

Avoid running photos below text. There's too great a danger readers will think the photo's an ad, or that it belongs to a story below. Wrap text below or beside art — not above it.

Wrap text around art, did we say? Dropping art into the middle of a story disrupts the logical flow of the text; readers will fumble to figure out which leg goes where. Avoid interrupting a leg of text with a photo.

SWIPEABLE FEATURE FORMATS

These designs are intended for special feature stories. Some of them will need fancy headlines, long decks or text wraps to work effectively.

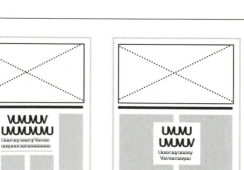

Very symmetrical. A graceful U-shape centers the headline and deck.

More symmetry. Here, the text encircles the headline (which could also be boxed).

This sidesaddle headline uses a long deck. The text squares off alongside.

Another sidesaddle head in a narrow stack. This one squares off beside the photo.

ONE VERTICAL PHOTO

If you understand the design options for horizontal photos, you'll have no problem with verticals. If anything, verticals offer fewer design options than horizontals. They're more dramatic, shape-wise, but it's often difficult to get them to mesh smoothly with their accompanying text.

MORE ON ▶

◆ **Photos:** *A chapter on cropping, sizing, photo pages, etc. ...* **91**

A FEW FACTS ABOUT THIS PHOTO

1 *This photo of rocker Billy Idol was shot by Joel Davis during a concert in Portland. Getting high-quality action photos of pop superstars is usually a difficult, demanding task. The lighting is poor. Photographers are often forced to stand far away, using telephoto lenses and grainy high-speed film. And photos are sometimes allowed only during a few selected songs at the start of the show. It's no wonder, then, that concert photos often fall flat.*

2 *Designers should avoid dictating in advance what photographers should shoot. But here, you know before the concert even starts that you'll want a shot of Billy (not the band). Since he's a singer, you'll probably want a dramatic close-up of him while he's singing. And since he doesn't play piano or guitar, you can assume the photo will be vertical. This shot, then, is exactly what the designer — and the readers — might expect.*

3 *Would you run this photo in your newspaper? There's something decadent, almost obscene about Billy's facial expression and hand position — but you could argue that it's a classic rock-rebel pose, perfectly capturing the spirit of his music. (You could also argue that we see more lewd behavior on MTV all day long.)*

4 *Shortly after this photo was taken, Billy invited fans to rush the stage, prompting a riot in which several people were injured. As a result, the review became a late-breaking news story without any photos at all — thus, this dramatic image never ran in the paper. But if it had, how big should it have been?*

5 *One dramatic photo like this can easily carry a story by itself. For some performers, however, additional photos enhance the story's appeal by showing other musicians, wild sets, crazily attired crowd members or onstage action (dancing, guitar-bashing, etc.). Bigger stars deserve bigger spreads.*

◆ **A word about square photos:** On previous pages, we explored design options using horizontal photos. In the pages ahead, we'll explore options for vertical photos. So what about squares?

Squares, you'll recall, have a reputation for being dull. Some designers avoid them (though that's overdoing it). But because square photos can adapt to all the design options we're showing you, we won't give them special treatment. Just modify the principles you've learned and you can dummy squares easily.

ONE VERTICAL PHOTO

VERTICAL STORY DESIGN OPTIONS

Remember the correct order:

Photo ···············
Cutline ··············
Headline ············
Text ·················

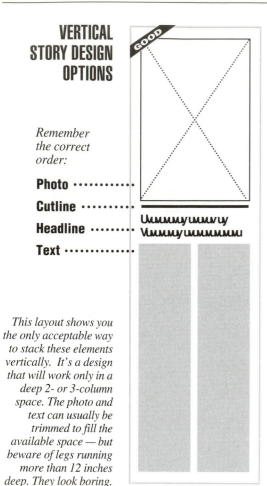

This layout shows you the only acceptable way to stack these elements vertically. It's a design that will work only in a deep 2- or 3-column space. The photo and text can usually be trimmed to fill the available space — but beware of legs running more than 12 inches deep. They look boring.

Since vertical photos usually run either 2 or 3 columns wide, that makes them pretty deep — anywhere from 5 to 15 inches deep. Stick a headline and a story below that, and you've got a sleek, dynamic design (if you have enough room for a layout that deep). The only drawback is that it's so far from the top of the photo to the bottom of the story: Will readers get tired — or lost?

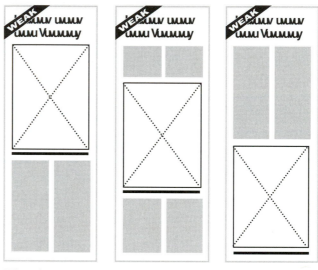

When elements are stacked incorrectly, problems result. Here, we see three basic guidelines ignored. From left to right: 1) The headline should always touch the start of the story. 2) Avoid interrupting any leg of text with an art element. 3) Avoid running art below text.

HORIZONTAL STORY DESIGN OPTIONS

Stacking photos and stories side by side requires careful measurement but creates a graceful design. Note how, in the examples below, the headline covers only the text. (Running a wide headline atop both the photo and the text is a secondary option — see page 47.)

Note, too, how both examples use 2-column photos. A 3-column vertical photo would be extremely deep (8-15 inches). And that could make those legs of text dangerously deep and gray.

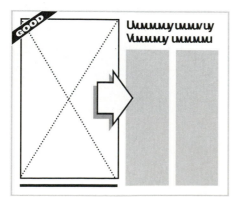

For directional photos: *Position the photo on the proper side — whichever side forces the action in the photo to move toward the text . . .*

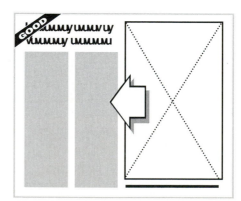

. . . but remember that non-directional photos work well on either side. Your decision should be based on how the overall page fits together.

ONE VERTICAL PHOTO

**OTHER
STORY DESIGN
OPTIONS**

In this L-shaped wrap, all the elements work well together. But consider how deep those left-hand legs could become, especially with a 3-column photo. To break up the gray, designers often dummy a liftout quote into that second column.

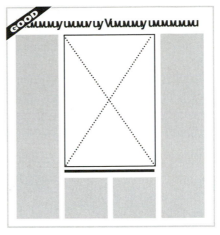

This U-shaped wrap keeps those two long legs of text from merging into one gray slab. But beware: 1) Those two legs under the photo will look flimsy if they're not deep enough; and 2) It's a long trip from the bottom of the third leg to the top of the fourth.

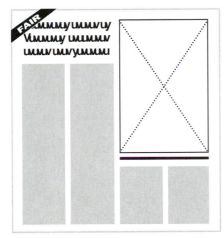

Raw wraps (like this one) keep headlines from butting when stories are dummied side by side. But this layout is less graceful than those above. The headline is often huge to keep from being overpowered by the photo and text. Still, it's acceptable.

As a rule, news headlines should run above all text — and only text. But there are times, especially on Page One, when you need a big photo-big headline combo. Running a 1-column headline over that leg of text gives you a cleaner design, but a lot less oomph.

**SWIPEABLE
FEATURE
FORMATS**

These designs are intended for special feature stories. Some of them will need fancy headlines, long decks or text wraps to work effectively.

A symmetrical, centered U-shape. Box this design if other stories run above.

Here, the headline runs above the photo. Again, may need to be boxed.

An airy design, one that can look awkward if all the proportions aren't right.

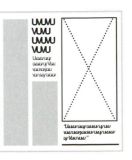

A somewhat risky L-shape, with a headline sandwiched between the text and photo.

THE DOMINANT PHOTO

Generally speaking, editors and page designers try hard to be fair. And that's admirable. But as you'll soon discover, some news is more important than others. Some stories are more interesting than others. And some photographs, for one reason or another, are simply *better* than others.

Readers expect newspapers to make decisions for them: to decide which stories are the biggest, which photos are the best. Readers want editors to edit — not just shovel everything onto the page in evenly sized heaps.

Equality, in short, can be boring. Take a look:

Here's what happens when you give every photo equal weight. For one thing, you lose all sense of priority. Who figures prominently in this story? Whose face is most interesting? But secondly, see how the design suffers? This page is static, boxy — like a page from a scrapbook. There's no sense of movement because the design isn't guiding your eyes. This effect results anytime you park two or more similarly sized photos near each other.

Here's a page that emphasizes the best images, mixing shapes and sizes. Feel the difference? This page has motion. Variety. Impact. We see that some photos (and some characters) clearly have more impact than others.

This principle applies whether there are two or ten photos on the page: **Always make one photo dominant — that is, substantially bigger than any competing photo.**

THE DOMINANT PHOTO

CHOOSING A DOMINANT PHOTO

A strong photograph will anchor a story — or a page. Two evenly sized photos side by side, however, will work against each other. They'll compete. They'll clash. Or worse, they'll just sit there in two big, boring lumps.

There are times when photos may work better if they're equally sized (a before-and-after comparison, a series of mugs, some frames of time-elapsed events). But usually, you must make one photo dominant.

When you evaluate photos to decide which gets bigger play, ask yourself:

◆ **Do we *really* need two photos?** Are they that different from each other? Does the story require this extra graphic information? If so, keep asking:

◆ **Does one have better content?** Does it capture a key moment of drama? Does it show motion and/or emotion? Does it enhance and explain the story?

◆ **Does one have higher readability?** Does it need to be BIG to show faces, details or events? Or will it pack some punch in a smaller space?

◆ **Does one have better quality?** Better focus? Exposure? Composition?

◆ **Does one have a better shape?** Would I prefer a vertical? A horizontal? A square? Will one shape create a stronger overall design for the story?

Below are four photos from a news feature we'll call "Hog Farm Holiday." In the pages ahead, we'll pair the photos in different ways to create different story designs. But first, ask yourself: Which should be the lead (dominant) photo?

MORE ON ▶

◆ **Dominant photos:** *Using art to anchor a page design* 75

◆ **Photos:** *A complete chapter on cropping, sizing, creating photo spreads, etc.* 91

Left: *It's not every day you see a girl riding a pig. That's a memorable image, one that's bound to arouse the curiosity of readers. It's probably the stronger of the two verticals, since it also shows more of the barnyard than any other photo.*

Below: *The baby pigs are cute, and this photo provides our only look at animals minus the humans. This photo doesn't read as well as the others when it's run small, however.*

Above: *This image of a man nuzzling a pig is an attention-getter with immediate impact. It's certainly stronger than the other horizontal (far right, bottom), though it shows us less of the barnyard than the other shots do.*

Right: *This photo of the farmer is his only appearance in these four shots. And though this photo isn't as engaging as the other vertical, it would be a good choice for a secondary photo if the farmer plays an important role in the story.*

BIG VERTICAL, SMALL HORIZONTAL

Suppose you choose to use these two photos to accompany your story. The girl riding the pig will be your dominant (or lead) photo; the guy nuzzling the pig is secondary. Since neither is strongly directional, you have some flexibility in placement.

In the examples below, we'll show you the most common story designs for news pages (as well as swipeable feature layouts). We can't show you every possible solution, so feel free to explore other options.

STORY DESIGN OPTIONS

*Here's what you get when you stack the photos **vertically:***

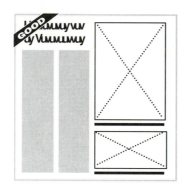

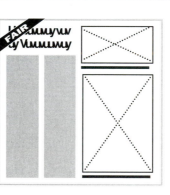

*Putting the lead photo atop the secondary photo (**left**) is a good, clean solution — if the text is deep enough. Putting the smaller photo on top (**right**) is OK when it's a before-and-after sequence: the setup, then the punchline. But it's usually best to lead with your strongest image.*

*Here, the photos share a cutline, and the shapes become less blocky, less tightly packed than the example above. Note that the cutline goes to the **outside** of the story. For longer stories, the text wraps below the photos, and the headline extends. . .*

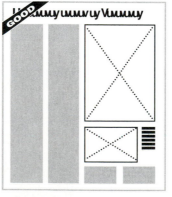

. . .across the two new right-hand legs of text. The danger here is that those two left-hand legs of text are getting awfully deep. A liftout quote in the second leg would help. . .

. . .but better yet, moving the photos into the middle two legs creates a U-shaped text block that's not as gray-looking. The question remains: Is it too high a jump to that last leg?

BIG VERTICAL, SMALL HORIZONTAL

STORY DESIGN OPTIONS

Here's what you get when you stack the photos horizontally:

The biggest problem with those preceding examples is space — having enough depth on the page to stack the photos on top of each other, and having enough text to square off alongside.

The examples below extend horizontally and are a bit more flexible:

MORE ON ▶

◆ **Feature page design:** *A chapter on special headlines and photo treatments* **169**

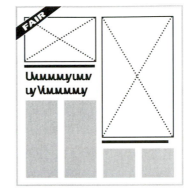

*This layout works only with text short enough to square off along the bottom edge of the dominant photo. Another option: If that horizontal photo were less wide, you could dummy a joint cutline **between** the two photos.*

Stack the photos side by side this way and what do you get? A raw wrap. Not bad — the package holds together pretty well. Still, look for better options before using this one.

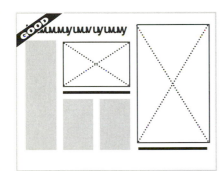

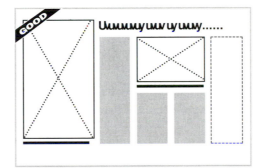

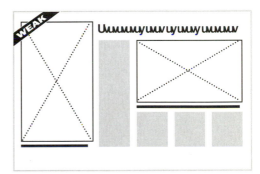

This is probably the most common design for a big vertical, small horizontal (as long as the lead photo isn't directional to the right). The text is L-shaped; everything is dummied to the left of the lead photo. . .

. . . or, for longer stories (or if the lead photo is strongly directional to the right), the whole design can be flopped. The text is still L-shaped. If needed, you can add an additional leg of text and extend the headline one more column, as well.

Remember: You must keep the sizes of the photos properly balanced. Here, the secondary photo is played too big and competes with the lead photo. Note, too, that this sort of L-shaped text — one tall leg, several squat ones — isn't always graceful.

SWIPEABLE FEATURE FORMATS

These designs are intended for special feature stories. Some of them will need fancy headlines, long decks or text wraps to work effectively.

A 1-column photo is OK if the leg is set wide like this. If the story's boxed or at the bottom of the page, the photo can go below the text.

We've warned you not to let art separate legs of text. But if the story is boxed and the design is symmetrical, this might still work.

Centering the small photo above the lead creates room on the left side for a joint cutline, room on the right for a headline/deck combo.

This wraparound text treatment lets you run the small photo a column-and-a-half wide. Don't let those legs of text get too skinny, however.

BIG HORIZONTAL, SMALL VERTICAL

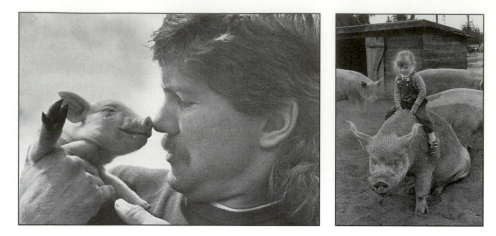

With a different pair of photos — the pig-smooching close-up as lead art, the pig-riding shot as secondary art — you create an appealing package focusing more on the people than the barnyard. And since neither photo is strongly directional, you'll have plenty of freedom in positioning the art.

As on previous pages, the designs below represent some common solutions for pairing these two photos. Studying them will give you a sense of how some design principles work — and why others *don't*.

STORY DESIGN OPTIONS

If you have enough width, you can stack the photos side by side. Note that the photos are exactly 3 and 2 columns wide, squaring off with the columns of text below. This looks OK, but it's a bit blocky, and the cutlines butt.

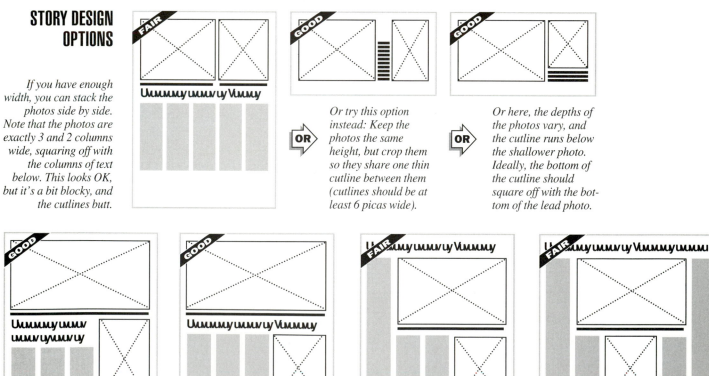

Or try this option instead: Keep the photos the same height, but crop them so they share one thin cutline between them (cutlines should be at least 6 picas wide).

Or here, the depths of the photos vary, and the cutline runs below the shallower photo. Ideally, the bottom of the cutline should square off with the bottom of the lead photo.

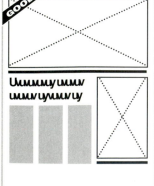

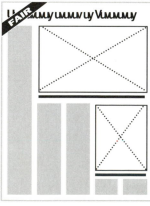

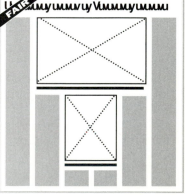

A clean, common layout. All the elements square off neatly. And note that the smaller photo could go on either side of the page.

For longer stories, text can wrap below the smaller photo, with a wider headline. That photo could move to the middle, if you prefer.

Look at the shape of the text: a stairstep with a mile-high first leg. For long stories, this layout works in the 5-column format here...

... and in a 6-column format, you could try this version, which is symmetrical, almost elegant. But the outside legs are awfully steep, and the text shape is odd.

BIG HORIZONTAL, SMALL VERTICAL

ANOTHER OPTION: RAW-WRAP HEADLINES

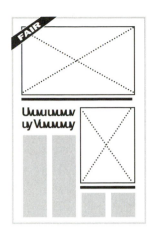

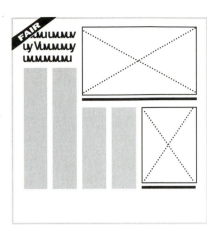

Compare these two designs with the two middle patterns at the bottom of page 56. Which do you prefer? The only difference is that these use raw-wrap headlines. If you want to use a display headline — or if you need to avoid a long horizontal head — then these are preferable. Otherwise, beware the awkward text wrap.

MORE ON ▶

◆ **Raw-wrap headlines:**
Using them to keep headlines from butting **72**

◆ **Mortises & insets:**
Guidelines for overlapping photos **181**

ONE-COLUMN PHOTOS: BIG ENOUGH?

As a rule, mug shots are the only photos that consistently work in a one-column size. And horizontals almost *never* "read" (i.e., show details clearly) when they're that small. But on occasion — when space is tight, or you just want to squeeze in a bit more art — you can run a vertical photo one column wide instead of two. Just make sure the photo *reads:*

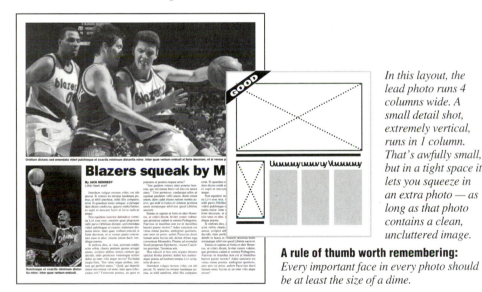

Ortilium dictare; sed emendata videri pulchraque et exactis minimum distantia miror. Inter quae verbum emicuit at forte deconum, et si versus p

Blazers squeak by M

By JACK KENNEDY
Little Hawk staff

Pulchraque et exactis minimum distantia miror. Inter quae verbum emicuit.

In this layout, the lead photo runs 4 columns wide. A small detail shot, extremely vertical, runs in 1 column. That's awfully small, but in a tight space it lets you squeeze in an extra photo — as long as that photo contains a clean, uncluttered image.

A rule of thumb worth remembering:
Every important face in every photo should be at least the size of a dime.

SWIPEABLE FEATURE FORMATS

These designs are intended for special feature stories. Some of them will need fancy headlines, long decks or text wraps to work effectively.

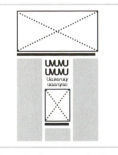

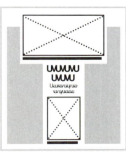

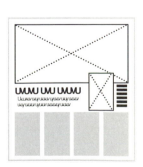

A vertical, symmetrical design. A narrow head and deck are centered in 3 wide bastard legs. This layout...

...gets flashier (and riskier) if you wrap text around the top photo and create a blind jump over the center leg.

A sidesaddle headline (with deck) creates a neat, logical design. But box this layout or keep other stories away.

A new twist: mortising the small photo on top of the dominant photo. The head then fills in alongside.

TWO VERTICALS

Always try to vary the sizes *and* shapes of the photos you use. Though there's nothing wrong with dummying two verticals together, you'll see in the layouts below that your options are limited — and less than ideal.

STORY DESIGN OPTIONS

Stacking vertical photos vertically is a problem. Whether the dominant photo's on top or not, you end up with an extremely deep design that hogs space, makes the text legs too deep and creates too much dead space below the cutline. As we saw earlier, 3-column vertical photos are tricky to deal with.

Stacking the photos side by side is an appealing solution: clean, tight, attractive. Two slight problems: 1) It's tough to size the photos and the headline so that they square off cleanly; 2) Note that the headline is an odd new variation. Though not exactly a raw wrap, it doesn't extend across the full text width.

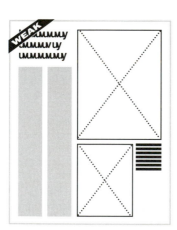

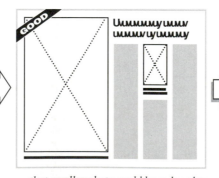

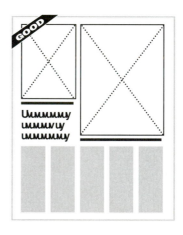

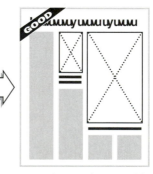

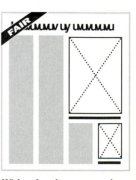

A common and solid solution, provided the text squares off evenly. You could also flop this layout and dummy the lead photo to the right of the smaller photo. Or...

...that smaller photo could be reduced to 1-column size — but only if it reads well that small. At that size, you could park it in either of the two right-hand legs...

...or the two photos could trade places. Note that here we've run the lead photo 2 columns wide instead of 3.

With a 1-column secondary photo, you can stack both photos vertically — though the text legs are a bit long.

TWO VERTICALS

WHAT HAPPENS WHEN STORIES COLLIDE

Designing stories into rectangular shapes (also called *modular design,* since pages consist of movable, interrelated modules) is an attractive way to create well-ordered pages — as long as you follow the rules.

But even when you follow the rules, confusion occasionally results from a bad juxtaposition of elements. Especially when you dummy text alongside a large vertical photograph. See for yourself:

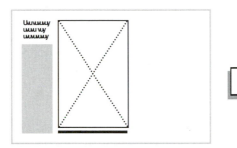

1 *Here's a simple and common story design: a big vertical photo with the text running vertically down the left side. So far, there's no problem, no confusion.*

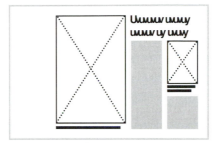

2 *Here's another common design: This time, it's a story dummied to the right of a big vertical photo. And again, it's a clean, correct layout. No problems yet.*

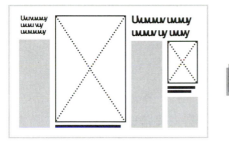

3 *But if you saw this page in a newspaper, how would you decide which story goes with the big vertical photo? The layout works either way. You'd have to scan both stories, then try to decide.*

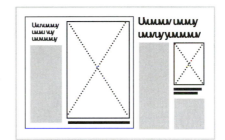
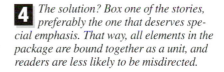

4 *The solution? Box one of the stories, preferably the one that deserves special emphasis. That way, all elements in the package are bound together as a unit, and readers are less likely to be misdirected.*

Later on, we'll look more closely at guidelines for boxing stories. But for now, be aware that your story designs may seem quite simple and obvious to you — but quite ambiguous and confusing to your readers.

SWIPEABLE FEATURE FORMATS

These designs are intended for special feature stories. Some of them will need fancy headlines, long decks or text wraps to work effectively.

A wide headline, a photo at the bottom, a small amount of text: It's risky, but will work if boxed or run at the bottom of the page.

This odd design puts three vertical stacks side by side: 1) lead art and joint cutline; 2) sidesaddle head, deck and small photo; 3) text.

Another 1-column secondary photo. But here, the photo is centered between the two columns, and the text wraps around it.

This design insets the small photo over the corner of the lead photo and fills in the other elements from there. Beware — this one's risky.

TWO HORIZONTALS

Pairing two horizontal photos is more common — and a bit less limiting — than pairing two verticals. Remember, however, that it's important to vary the shapes of the photos you use. So avoid running two horizontals together if a better combination is available.

Which of these two photos should be dominant? Most would choose the guy nuzzling the piglet, since it's more appealing and better composed. Keep in mind, however, that the second photo — the row of piglets — won't read if it's too small (as you see it printed here, it's about a column-and-a-half wide). That means it *must* run at least two columns wide.

STORY DESIGN OPTIONS

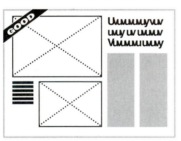

Stacking the photos vertically works well. Note the shared cutline; there's a danger of wasted white space in the bottom corner if the bottom photo is too narrow or the cutline is too short.

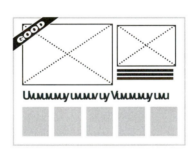

Stacking the photos horizontally also works well. A shared cutline like this will generally butt tightly against both photos. It's OK if it comes up a bit short, but aligning tightly is better.

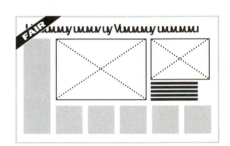

Stacking the photos horizontally works well in this configuration, too — though you need the full width of a 6-column page for this layout. Note how we've indented the cutline a half-column to add some white space.

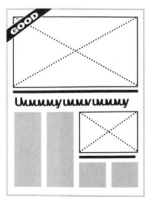

Another common solution. The smaller photo is dummied into the upper-right corner of an L-shaped text block...

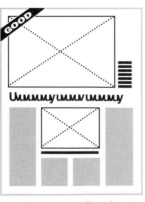

...or here, the smaller photo is centered. Note the cutline treatment for the lead photo, an option offering more flexibility.

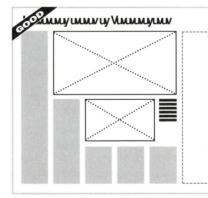

Again, note the added flexibility of sharing a cutline: in this case, the smaller photo can be 2-3 columns wide. You also have the option of adding another leg of text along the far right.

This raw-wrap headline treatment is acceptable, but not preferable. Use it if you're avoiding a horizontal headline.

TWO HORIZONTALS

SOME ODD OPTIONS — AND WHY THEY DON'T WORK

Throughout this chapter, we've offered common solutions to common design situations. If we wanted to, we could easily fill several pages with rejects — designs which, for one reason or another, are too ugly to print.

Instead, we'll take a moment here to analyze a few close calls. These layouts are well-intentioned, but still wrong enough to be avoided.

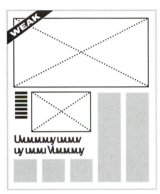

This layout demonstrates the basic problem with text shaped like a backward "L": Too many readers won't know where the story starts. Even if the headline ran horizontally between the two photos, your eye would ignore those short legs on the left and assume the story starts in that fourth column.

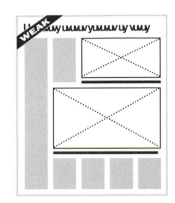

Here's a configuration that looks magazine-y, somehow. But in newspapers, you're smart to avoid confusing layouts like this. Where does the reader go at the end of that first leg: under the big photo, or all the way back up to the top? This is the risk you take whenever art interrupts the flow of the text.

There are two things wrong with this design: 1) The headline is too small, thin and insignificant (a very unnecessary raw wrap). 2) Too many readers will think the story starts to the right of that second photo. Remember: Readers often assume that the tallest leg is the one that starts the story.

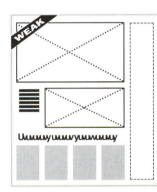

Here's a design with a subtle flaw— it gives us a package in two totally independent chunks: a photo chunk at the top and a story chunk below. Since it's so far down to the story, the elements don't work together. In fact, those photos could mistakenly be paired with any story running in an adjacent column.

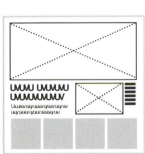

With the right photos in the right place on the right page, this design might look pretty hip. But as a rule, resist the temptation to run photos under text or to run the dominant photo under the secondary photo. It might work on features — especially if they're boxed — but be careful with hard news.

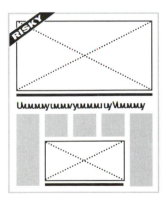

Here's another layout you'd see in a magazine. It might even work, boxed, on a feature page. But for most news stories, avoid dummying photos at the bottom of a story. Readers assume that's an ad position. Or that any photo parked below one story belongs to the next story. Why risk confusing readers if you don't have to?

SWIPEABLE FEATURE FORMATS

These designs are intended for special feature stories.

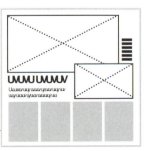

Here are three variations of the same idea: Put the small photo below the lead, then square off the headline beside one of the photos. All three will work, depending on the headline wording and photo cropping.

ADDING MUG SHOTS

Most of the photos you'll dummy with news stories will be *live* (meaning they're timely and unstaged). Mug shots, on the other hand, are *canned* (that is, shot at some neutral time and place, then put in the can — stored — until you need them).

And though it's a good idea to add mug shots to stories whenever possible, try not to confuse the reader by mixing live and canned photos. Add mugs — but dummy them slightly apart from news photos, as a signal to readers.

Also, consider adding liftout quotes to mugs whenever possible. Combining someone's face with his words connects him to the story, provides extra commentary, and creates a graphic hook to attract more readers.

MORE ON ▶

◆ **Mug shots:** *Tips for dummying them with stories* **42**

◆ **Liftout quotes:** *How to design and dummy them effectively* **126**

*Legs of text usually run alongside dominant vertical photos. And mug shots can be added atop any leg except the first. Here, a liftout quote was included with the mug (assuming the quote is either **by** or **about** the person pictured).*

Here, the quote runs below, rather than beside, the mug shot. Either way is acceptable. You could even park a second mug shot — with its own quote — alongside this one.

With a big horizontal photo, the text will usually run underneath. The most logical spot for a mug shot (with or without an added lift quote) is in one of the middle legs, to help break up the repetitive grayness of the text.

If appropriate, two or three mugs can run alongside each other at the top of those middle legs of text. Those mugs, all evenly sized, work together as a unit. And the headline helps distance them from the live photo at the top of the story.

With a dominant vertical and a secondary horizontal, a mug can be dummied into the far corner of the text. Note how this layout helps distance the mug from the two live photos. And even with this growing number of elements, the whole story holds together as a unit.

With a dominant horizontal and a secondary vertical, you can always add a mug in the middle leg. Again, in this design the two live photos are dummied tightly together, while the mug is kept separate by either the headline or text.

EXERCISES

*Designing a story is like performing brain surgery: You can't learn to do it by reading a book. You've got to **practice**. And doing these exercises lets you practice what you've learned so far. If you want to use a dummy sheet, you can trace or copy the sample dummy on page 32.*

ANSWERS ▶ 198

1 What are your two best options for dummying a 5-inch story without any art? How would you code the headline for each option if it were dummied at the top of Page One? At the bottom of an inside page?

2 You've got a 9-inch story with one mug shot. (Assume your newspaper runs its mug shots 3 inches deep). What are your three best options for dummying this story?
Will this story work in a 3-column format?

3 Here's a layout that uses two mug shots. There are several things wrong with it. How many problems can you identify?

4 Today is a busy news day. Your top story is a 12-inch piece about a fire that destroyed this man's home. This photo accompanies that story:

Hint:
As printed here, this photo is 29 picas wide and 17½ picas deep. Assuming you work at a paper where columns are roughly 12 picas wide, here's how deep this photo would be if it were sized for:

❏ *1 column: 7 picas*
❏ *2 columns: 15 picas*
❏ *3 columns: 23 picas*
❏ *4 columns: 31 picas*
❏ *5 columns: 39 picas*
❏ *6 columns: 47 picas*

For more on sizing photos by using a proportion wheel, see page 103.

There are a number of ways you could dummy this story for a 6-column broadsheet newspaper. But what design solution would you recommend?

EXERCISES

5 Here are the two best photos from last night's Bruce Springsteen concert. Your editor wants you to run them both. Which one should be the dominant photo?

The review that accompanies these photos is 20 inches long. There's space on the Arts page for a deep layout that's 5 columns wide. What's your strongest design if you use the horizontal photo as dominant art? If you use the vertical?

To make this exercise easier, don't worry about sizing these photos exactly. Instead, dummy them using their rough shapes and assume you can crop them slightly to fit the layout that works best.

6 What's wrong with each of these news story designs?

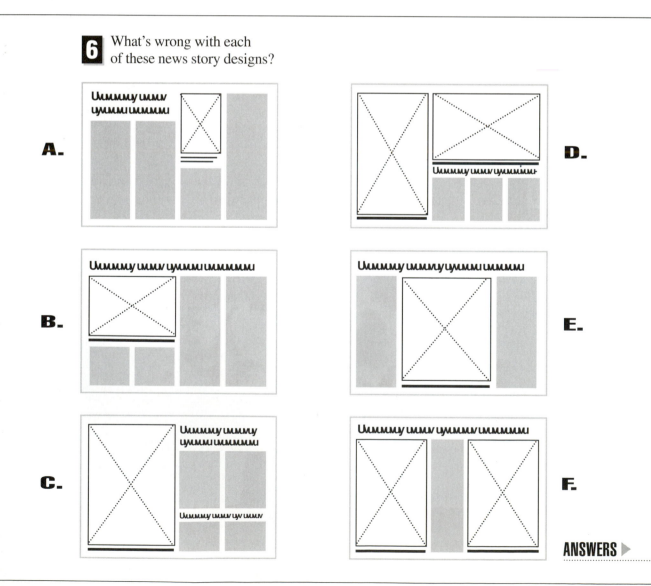

A.

B.

C.

D.

E.

F.

ANSWERS ▶ 198

Design trends come and go. What's cool today will look hopelessly lame in a decade or two (if newspapers still *exist* in a decade or two). Tastes change. Journalistic philosophies change, too.

The same goes for theories of page design. Some design experts insist that the upper-left corner is a page's prime position; thus, you should put your top story there. Others claim that the upper-*right* corner is the best-read spot on the page, and that you should put your top story *there*. Still others advise putting *strong* elements in *weak* positions (like the bottom corners) to ensure that readers will stay interested wherever their eyes wander.

Confusing, eh? Then forget what the experts say and remember this: Readers will look where you *want* them to. If you know what you're doing, you can create a page that's logical, legible and fun to read — and you can guide the readers' eyes wherever you choose.

This chapter explores current principles of page design. Now that we've looked at stories as independent units — modules — we'll begin examining ways you can stack those modules together to create attractive, well-balanced pages.

Once you understand how these principles work, you can adapt them to any pages you design — whatever the style or topic.

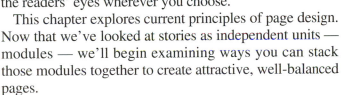

GRIDS

Before you design a page, you've got to know: What *grid* does this page use? What's the underlying pattern that organizes this page into columns? A page grid provides the structure — the architecture —that divides elements into rows, keeping photos and stories evenly aligned:

2-column grid: *Newsletters often use this grid, but note how limited the options are for photo and text widths.*

3 columns: *Also popular in newsletters. Tabloids use it too, but it doesn't offer much variety or flexibility.*

4 columns: *A common grid for tabloids. More flexible than a 3-column grid, and the text is comfortably wide.*

5 columns: *Probably the most popular tabloid grid. It's also commonly used on broadsheet section fronts.*

6 columns: *The standard grid for broadsheets, since most ads are sold in these universal column widths.*

BROADSHEET GRIDS

Newspapers, you'll recall, come in two basic sizes: broadsheet and tabloid. Broadsheets are twice the size of tabloids. And the big broadsheet page provides room for longer text, bigger photos, more expansive headlines.

Most broadsheets use a 6-column grid — especially on inside pages, where ads are sold in standard widths that require columns about 12 picas wide.

On section fronts, however, broadsheet news pages use a variety of grids:

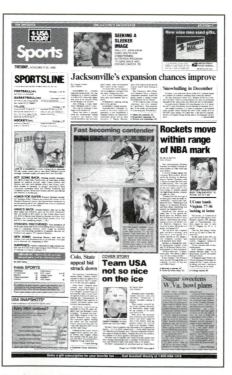

6 columns: *At The Portland Press Herald, all elements (except those downpage promos) align along a 6-column grid. Note how column rules separate those butting stories along the bottom.*

7 columns: *USA Today uses a rigidly formatted 7-column grid that accepts only minor changes from day to day. Note how those two left-hand legs become one wide column of briefs.*

11 columns: *This unusual grid helps to create margins (or "rails") along both sides of those news stories in the middle. Editors can add quotes, graphics, cutlines, etc. into those rails.*

GRIDS

TABLOID GRIDS

Though large-circulation dailies are usually broadsheets, many other papers — including weeklies, student newspapers and special-interest journals — prefer the advantages of the tabloid format:

◆ Their smaller size makes tabs easier to produce and cheaper to print.

◆ They're popular with readers — handier, less bulky, faster to scan.

◆ Editors and advertisers find that their stories and ads can dominate a page more effectively than in a broadsheet.

Tabloids are roughly half the size of broadsheets. If you took broadsheet paper, turned it sideways and folded it, you'd create two tabloid pages:

MORE ON ▶

◆ **Special grids :** *How rails can help you display graphic extras* 166

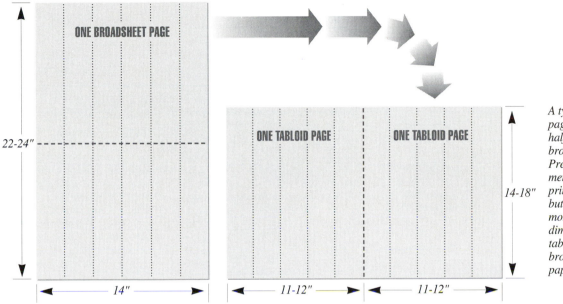

ONE BROADSHEET PAGE

22-24"

14"

ONE TABLOID PAGE   **ONE TABLOID PAGE**

14-18"

11-12"   11-12"

A typical tabloid page is roughly half the size of a broadsheet page. Precise measurements vary from printer to printer, but these are the most common dimensions for tabloid and broadsheet paper sizes.

Though the 5-column format is most common in tabloids, some prefer 4 columns — while others are experimenting with 6-, 7-, even 9-column grids:

The Epitaph, a high-school tabloid in Cupertino, Calif., uses a 4-column grid but loads the page with sophisticated design devices (labels, icons, summaries and sidebars). The wide legs anchor the design and keep the page from becoming chaotic.

The Little Hawk, a high-school tabloid in Iowa City, uses an innovative 7-column grid. Note how the narrow outer rails provide a logical and attractive home for graphic extras: lists, statistics, quotes, cutlines and so on.

PAGES WITHOUT ART

NOTE ▶

Some of you work with tabloids. Some of you work with broadsheets. As a compromise, the examples in this chapter — like the one below — will use 5 columns (like most tabloids) but will show the shape and depth of broadsheet pages.

Until now, we've looked at different ways of designing *stories*. Now, we're ready to design *pages*. And a well-designed page is really nothing more than an attractive stack of stories. Sounds simple, right?

So we'll start simply. With just text — no photos. That way, you'll be able to see that, with or without art, you build a page by fitting rectangles together as neatly as you can.

In the old days, editors designed pages by stacking stories side by side in deep vertical rows. Today, the trend is more horizontal, and it's possible to build pages in long, horizontal rows like the example below. Simple as it is, a page like this works fairly effectively:

MORE ON ▶

◆ **Headlines and headline sizes:** *A quick guide for both broadsheet and tabloid*.................. 25

◆ **Designing pages with art:** *Guidelines for adding photos to gray pages like this one* 74

◆ **Inside pages:** *Creating modular designs, working with ads* 82

This page design is simple, but it still observes some basic design principles:

Story placement:
The strongest story goes at the top of the page. By "strong," we're referring to news value, impact or appeal. As you move down the page, stories become less significant.

Headline sizing:
Page position dictates headline size. The lead story will have the biggest headline; headlines then get smaller as you move down the page.

Story shapes:
As we've learned, stories should be shaped like rectangles. And here, you can see how keeping stories rectangular keeps pages neat and well organized. Whether stories are stacked vertically or horizontally, whether they use art or not, that principle always applies on open pages like this. (Later, when we look at pages with ads, you'll see it's not always this easy to keep stories rectangular.)

The design of this page is clean, but its impact on readers is probably weak. Why? It's too gray. Too monotonous. There's nothing to catch our eye. The only contrast comes from the headlines.

In a perfect newspaper, every story might have some sort of art: a photo, a chart, a map or — at the very least — a liftout quote. In reality, though, actually *producing* all those extras would take a colossal amount of work and might actually look chaotic.

A better rule of thumb is this: *Make every page at least one-third art.* In other words, when you add up all the photos, graphics, teasers and display type on a page, they should occupy at least a third of the total real estate. Some pages should use even more art than that (sports, features, photo spreads).

There are times, however, when photos just don't exist. When there are no quotes to lift. When there's no time — or no artist — to add a chart or graph. Your page may be gray, but it doesn't have to be dull. Instead of simply stacking stories in rows (as in the example above), you can add variety by:

◆ **Butting headlines.**
◆ **Boxing stories.**
◆ **Using bastard measures.**
◆ **Using raw wraps and alternative headline treatments.**

In the pages ahead, we'll see how these techniques work on pages without art.

PAGES WITHOUT ART

BUTTING HEADLINES

TOM MIX DIES IN CRASH

Troy Tops Illini 13-7; Texans Beat Bruins 7-0

115,000 to Join Pontifical Mass for Peace Today

Cleric Leaders Aiding Papal Envoy in Coliseum

By Kenneth Macker
While nations war in *Reader Overture*

Western Film Hero Killed in Arizona

KIMBROUGHS DRIVE GAINS EARLY SCORE

Jackie Robinson, Uclan Star, Hurt, Removed From Game; Fumbles Mar Coliseum Fray

By Al Santoro
The powerful Texas Aggies defeated the Bruins of U.C.L.A., 7 to 0 in their intersectional game in Memorial Coliseum yesterday afternoon.

TROY ATTACK IN 3D PERIOD DOWNS ZUPPKE

Robertson Scores Twice for Victors in See-Saw Battle Before 40,000 at Champaign

By Davis J. Walsh
CHAMPAIGN, Ill., Oct. 12.—Southern California's Trojan juggernaut really got rolling this afternoon for the first time this season, the men of Troy eking out an avoid hard-

Hitler Warned By Greece; Nazis Seize Bucharest

U-Boats Stage Battle With British Navy

BERLIN, Oct. 12.—(INS)—An unusual sea battle off southern Eng-

Von Wiegand Says:

Europe Conflict Moving to Egypt

Axis Plans Check of British in Mediterranean

Troops March in Triumph to Balkan Capital

ATHENS, Greece, Oct. 12.—(P)—High Greek authorities, pushing defense measures as German military power spread in near-by Ru-

Nobody likes ugly heads. But it took newspapers years to figure out how to slap headlines onto every story without jamming them into a chaotic jumble. Until the 1960s, most newspapers ran vertical rules in the gutters between stories. When their headlines stacked alongside each other, they looked like tombstones (hence the term *tombstoning,* another name for butting heads).

For years, the First Commandment of Page Design has been: *Don't butt heads.* That's good advice. Butt-headed design can cause confusion like this:

Princess Diana meets Frisbee title-holder pope at Dover Beach to challenge record

By Robin Fox/ **The Times**   By John Hamlin/ **The Times**

Occasionally, though, you'll need to park two stories alongside each other. When you do, their heads may butt. But here's how to minimize the problem:

◆ **Mix styles, fonts or sizes.** The idea here is: If headlines must butt, make them very dissimilar. If one's boldface, make the other light or italic. If one's a large, 1-line horizontal, make the other a small, 3-line vertical.

◆ **Write short.** Let a little air separate the two headlines. That usually means writing the headline on the left a few counts short, just to be safe.

With stories stacked like this — in wide horizontal layers — you're not forced to butt any headlines. But should we add some vertical motion to break up the monotony?

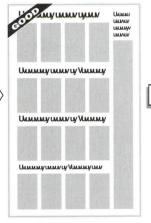

Here, the top two headlines butt a bit. But the one on the left is bigger (by at least 12 points) and it's written short. The page now has a vertical element to relieve the tedium.

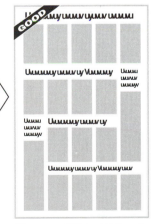

Here, two different pairs of headlines butt. But some would say the page now has more motion, more interesting shapes. By bending the rules, we've added variety.

PAGES WITHOUT ART

BOXING STORIES

Another way to break up monotonous gray page patterns is by boxing stories. As we saw on page 59, putting a box around a story (with a photo) is one way to avoid confusing readers with ambiguous designs:

MORE ON ▶

◆ **Bad juxtapositions:** *How they happen, and how to avoid them* **86**

◆ **Rules and boxes:** *Where (and where not) to use them ...* **133**

 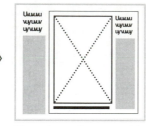

Which story does this photo belong to? Hard to tell. You'd have to scan the text and the cutline to figure it out.

If you draw a box around the story and its photo, you join them into one package — and avoid confusing readers.

Boxing a story also gives it visual emphasis. It's a way of saying to the reader, "This story is *different* from the others; it's *special.*"

Don't box a story just because you're bored with a page and want to snazz it up. Or because you need extra air between two butting heads.

Instead, save boxes for stories that deserve special treatment:
◆ A light feature on a page full of hard news.
◆ Small sidebars attached to bigger stories.
◆ Standing columns (news briefs, opinion, etc.) that appear regularly.
◆ Stories with risky or complicated designs whose elements might otherwise collide with *other* stories and confuse readers.

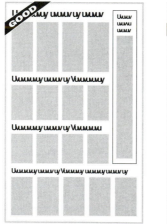  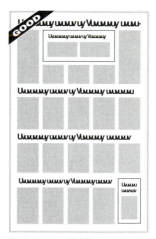

*Boxing this deep vertical story breaks up the monotony of the page and says to the reader, "This story is different." Give this treatment, then, **only** to special stories or columns.*

Here, we've created the effect of two lead stories on one page: one across the top and one that's boxed. See how these story shapes move your eye around the page?

At the top, we've boxed the lead story's sidebar — and it's obvious that the two stories work together as a unit. At the bottom, we've given a graphic nudge to a small feature.

When you put text inside a box, column widths become bastard measures. To figure out how wide those legs should be:
1) **Measure** the width of the box (in picas);
2) **Decide** how many legs of text you want inside the box;
3) **Subtract** 1 pica for each gutter inside the box (including the two gutters on the outside edges); and
4) **Divide** by the number of legs.

PAGES WITHOUT ART

BASTARD COLUMN MEASURES

OK, stop snickering. Bastard measures are *serious* typographic devices. And they're handy, too — especially when you need extra flexibility in sizing photos. (More on this later.)

As we've seen, most papers use a fixed number of columns on each page. Bastard measures let you deviate from the standard text width:

MORE ON ▶

◆ **Bastard measures:**
How they add extra flexibility in sizing photos 81

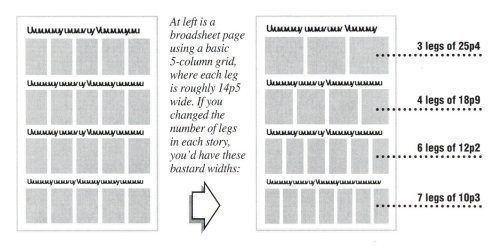

At left is a broadsheet page using a basic 5-column grid, where each leg is roughly 14p5 wide. If you changed the number of legs in each story, you'd have these bastard widths:

3 legs of 25p4

4 legs of 18p9

6 legs of 12p2

7 legs of 10p3

Bastard measures add graphic emphasis to a story by freeing it from the rigid page grid. (In the above left example, see how the columns and gutters align in a strict vertical pattern?) Changing column widths is a subtle but effective way to show that a story is special or different:

GOOD

GOOD

WEAK

A good combination: a box with a bastard measure. This adds emphasis to the lead story and helps set it apart. The page is orderly; the relative news value of each story is clear.

A wider measure can enhance a columnist or other special piece (right column and bottom). Note, too, how the cutoff rule helps separate that right column from the other stories.

Too many bastard measures can get confusing. Why create two competing lead stories? Why run that bottom story in wide legs? In short: Don't ignore your basic page grid.

Bastard measures alter the grid patterns on a page — which can be either good (relieving monotony) or bad (creating chaos). Some papers don't allow any bastard measures; others allow them only when a story is boxed. Like other design devices, bastard legs can cause problems if used carelessly.

A warning about something that should be obvious by now: *Don't change column widths within a story.* Widths may change from story to story, from page to page — but once you start a story in a certain measure, each leg of that story on that page should stay the same width. No cheating.

PAGES WITHOUT ART

USING RAW WRAPS

Raw wraps let you park two stories side by side without butting their headlines. But use raw wraps with caution. They work only at the top of a page, beneath a rule, or beneath a boxed story; otherwise, as you can see, they'll collide with other columns of text and confuse your readers:

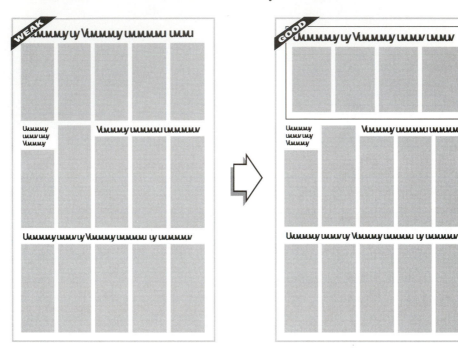

Here's that typical photo-less page again. You can see how that raw-wrapped headline adds variety to the story shapes. But see how the second leg of that raw-wrapped story collides with the text above it? That's the danger of raw-wrapping stories in the middle of the page.

*A better combination. Here, the lead story is boxed in a bastard measure. That gives it extra emphasis and staggers the column alignment, making it unlikely that readers will be misdirected. You **could** box the raw-wrapped story instead, but remember: Save boxes for stories whose content is special. Don't use boxes to salvage weak designs.*

OPTIONAL HEADLINE TREATMENTS

No one ever said all headlines had to look the same. Adding variety to your headlines can add oomph to your page designs. But don't overdo it. Save special headline treatments for special stories. If you use too many offbeat headlines on a page, their styles may clash and create distraction.

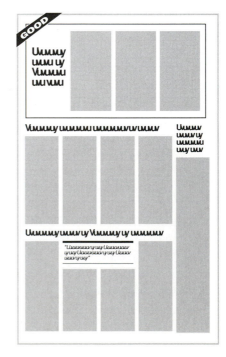

At the top of the page: a raw-wrap headline inside a boxed story (in bastard measure). Some papers raw-wrap headlines at the top of the page simply to avoid an excess of long, 1-line banner heads. Below, a hammer head (with deck) gives extra impact to a special analysis or feature story.

At the top of the page: a sidesaddle headline. Like raw wraps, these must be used carefully to avoid collisions between legs of different stories. Note, too, that if the story's legs are too deep, the headline will float in too much white space. At the bottom of the page, a liftout quote lures readers as it breaks up the gray text.

PAGES WITHOUT ART

A BETTER SOLUTION: PACKAGING

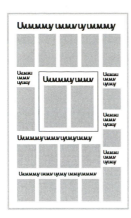

If your pages consistently look like the one at left — a gray hodgepodge crowded with short stories — you may need another photographer. Or you may need to start packaging short, related items into special formats.

The advantages:

◆ Instead of scattering news briefs or calendar listings throughout the paper, you anchor them in one spot. That's a smarter, cleaner solution.

◆ You create more impact for your main stories by keeping those smaller ones out of their way.

◆ You appeal to reader habit (since most of us prefer finding material in the same spot every issue).

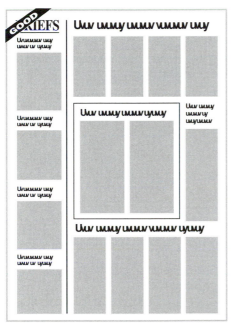

"Roundup" packages of briefs usually run down the left-hand side of the page. By stacking briefs vertically, it's easier to add or cut material to fit precisely. Note how this column runs in a wider measure, separated from the rest of the page by a cutoff rule. A box would also work well to isolate these briefs.

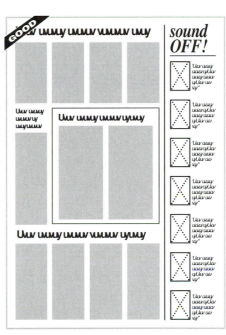

By flopping the page design at far left, we can see how the page looks when you run a special column down the right-hand side. Here, a "man-in-the-street" interview uses mugs and quotes to anchor and enliven an otherwise gray page.

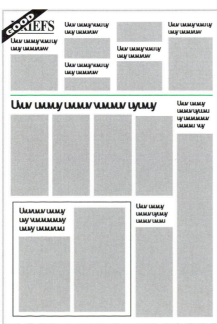

Some papers run news roundups horizontally across the top of the page, though the text often wraps awkwardly from one leg to another. Note the raw wrap at the bottom of the page. This is how it looks when you box a raw-wrapped story (in bastard measure) below another story. Is that solution acceptable?

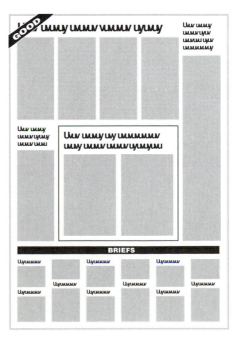

Here's how a roundup column looks when it's stripped across the bottom of the page. Again, the biggest drawback is the awkwardness of wrapping short paragraphs from one leg to the next. In this example, a black bar labels the column and separates it from the rest of the page.

PAGES WITH ART

As a page designer, your job isn't just drawing lines, stacking stories and keeping everything from colliding. It's *selling* stories to readers. People won't swallow food that looks unappetizing; they won't ingest information that looks unappetizing, either. And that's why you gotta have art.

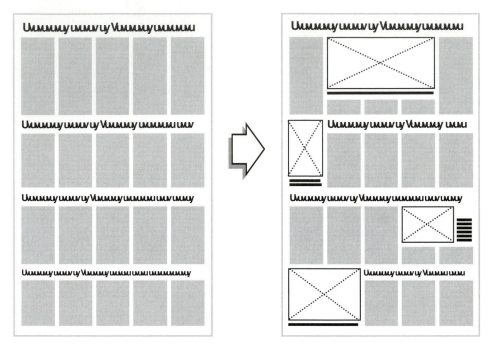

Here's that gray page again. Sure, it's clean, well-ordered, crammed with information. But it's dull. Lifeless. Nothing grabs your attention or arrests your eye. The stories may be wonderful, but they may never get read.

Here's that same page, with art. There's less room for text now, so stories must either be shortened or jump to another page. But it's worth it. Remember, most readers browse around until something compels them to stop. By adding photos, maps or charts, you catch their interest — then deliver the information.

Art is essential. And informational art — not just decoration — is the very heart of newspaper design. Adding art to your pages:
- Supplements *textual* information with *visual* information.
- Adds motion, emotion and personality that's missing in text alone.
- Attracts readers who might otherwise ignore gray type.
- Increases the design options for each page.

GUIDELINES FOR PAGES WITH ART

When you add art to page designs, you enhance their appeal. You also increase the risk of clutter and confusion. So go slowly at first. Once you feel comfortable adding art to stories, keep adding it. It's better to make a page too dynamic than too dull. Or as one veteran designer put it: "I like to take a page right to the edge of confusion, then back off a bit."

There's a dizzying number of rules and requirements to remember when you design full pages. The most important guidelines are:
- **Keep all story shapes rectangular.** You've heard this a dozen times. But it's the key to good modular design.
- **Vary your shapes and sizes** (of stories as well as art). Avoid falling into a rut where everything's square. Or vertical. Or horizontal. Or where all the stories are 10 inches long. Give readers a variety of text and photo shapes.
- **Emphasize what's important.** Play up the big stories, the big photos. Place them where they count. Let *play* and *placement* reflect each story's significance as you guide the reader through the page.

On the next page, we'll look more closely at three crucial guidelines:
- **Give each page a dominant photo.**
- **Balance and scatter your art.**
- **Beware of butting headlines.**

PAGES WITH ART

GIVE EACH PAGE A DOMINANT PHOTO

Most beginning page designers run art too small. As a result, pages look weak. Meek.

So be bold. Run your best art big. And when you use two or more photos on a page, remember that one of them should dominate.

Even if there's only *one* photo on a page, it should run big enough to provide impact and interest — to visually anchor the page.

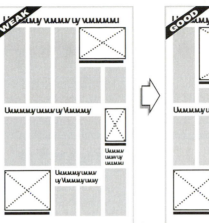
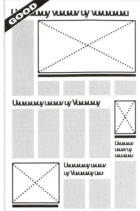

Here's a page where no photo dominates. As a result, it looks gray. Meek. Unexciting.

Here, that top photo is two columns wider — and now it dominates a dynamic page.

BALANCE & SCATTER YOUR ART

Use photos to anchor your pages, but remember to balance and separate your art, too. When photos start stacking up and colliding, you get a page that's:

◆ **confusing,** as unrelated art distracts us and intrudes into stories where it doesn't belong. *Or:*

◆ **lopsided,** as photos clump together in one part of the page and text collects in another.

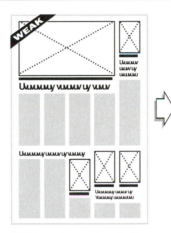
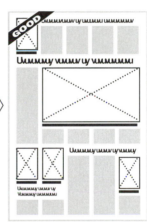

This layout seems to pair the lead photo and top mug, as well as the three mugs below. It's confusing and top-heavy.

With smarter photo placement, there's no collision or confusion. And the page is better-balanced when the art's apart.

BEWARE OF BUTTING HEADLINES

We've seen how you can bump heads (carefully) when you *need* to. But on most well-designed pages, head butts are unnecessary. Clumsy. And confusing to readers.

Instead, think ahead. Rather than butting headlines, use art to separate stories. In many cases, that's where raw-wrapped headlines offer a smart alternative to a crowded page.

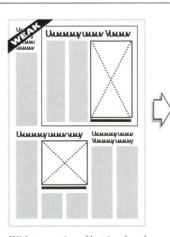
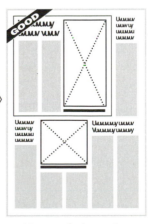

With two pairs of butting headlines, this layout is clumsy and confusing. But if you use the photos to separate stories...

...it's a much cleaner layout. Notice how the raw wrap (bottom left) provides an easy way to run two stories side by side.

MODULAR PAGE DESIGN

We've mentioned the term *modular design* before. And as you begin designing full pages, the idea of treating stories as modules — as movable, interchangeable units — gains new meaning.

Take a moment to study the sports page below. Notice how every story is a rectangle — and how all those rectangles fit together into a well-balanced, well-organized page:

C section   The Orange County Register   Tuesday, July 26, 1988

Sports

America's Cup is on for September

Judge rules US must face New Zealand

MARK WHICKER

Giants nearly let Dodgers off the hook

Catcher Mike Scioscia stops the Giants' Donell Nixon from scoring with a body block, but the Dodgers couldn't stop San Francisco, losing, 3-1.
The Associated Press

Mitchell's homer sinks Dodgers

Giants break through against Fernando, 3-1

Safety's wish is granted

Rams give Cromwell release after 11 years

By Don Seeholzer
The Register

McCaskill, Angels come out on top, 2-1

He throws three-hitter to beat Stewart, A's

By Peter Schmuck
The Register

INSIDE

Irvine boxing: Paul Gonzales scores a unanimous decision over Javier Diaz in a flyweight bout/2

Starting call? Quarterback Jim Plunkett, at age 40, is optimistic about his fate with the Raiders/3

Jets sign Cadigan: Ex-USC lineman Dave Cadigan agrees to a four-year, $2 million deal with New York/3

The AL East: New York overtakes Detroit for first place; Boston, behind Roger Clemens, wins 12th in a row/4

Double duty: Several jockeys will commute between Del Mar and Los Alamitos race courses to ride at both tracks/6

DC Tennis Classic: Jimmy Connors beats Andres Gomez in straight sets, his first singles title since 1984/7

Sports Today/2   The NFL/3
Baseball/4-5   Sports Etc./7
The SportsLine (714) 953-7723

Third baseman Jack Howell fails to stop Jose Canseco's line drive in the Angels' 2-1 victory over Oakland.
Chris Covatta/The Register

MODULAR PAGE DESIGN

Could that page have been assembled differently — or better? Let's rearrange
the modules to see how other options might have turned out:

The problem: two thin vertical stories side by side, their heads nearly butting. That's a weak juxtaposition, though the rest of the page is OK.

Move the dominant photo all the way to the top and you get two gray text blocks dulling things up in the middle of the page. Otherwise, it's OK.

To break up that gray (example at left), move that bottom story up, then dummy the America's Cup story along the bottom. A good balance.

Could that small photo run at the top of the page? Well, not like this. The two photos collide, and now there's no art at all downpage.

Here, we lead with the smaller photo. Does this design feel odd? Usually, big photos play better when they're near the top of the page.

*A mirror image of the original. Nothing wrong with it, but columnists traditionally run down the **left** side of the page. Does that matter?*

FRONT PAGE DESIGN

Every paper has its own news philosophy. And that news philosophy is most visibly reflected on Page One: in the number of stories, the play of photos, the styles of headlines, the variety of graphics.

Designing the front page is no tougher than designing any other page. But the standards are higher — and deadlines are often tighter.

Here are a few current examples of broadsheet Page One design. Study them closely. Have they observed the design principles we've discussed?

MORE ON ▶

◆ **Page One design:**
Current trends and philosophies............ 7

The Seattle Times uses elegant typography to create a formal, handsome look. Unlike many newspapers, the Times uses very little boldface headline type. As a result, the page is quiet, almost sedate. Notice how the center story runs an italic overline above the photo, then a standard headline below it — a solution many papers use on Page One when a story's headline appears below the fold.

The Colorado Springs Gazette Telegraph runs its front-page stories ragged right and boxed. Notice how every box is labeled ("CRIME," "SPORTS," HEALTH," etc.) to help readers quickly identify topics of interest. Is that device effective — or does this design style become too boxy and busy?

There's a lot of traffic on this page from Ball State University's daily paper. But study how the main package — a coach's resignation — has been assembled. Though it combines headline elements, quotes, mug shots and sidebars, it remains organized and focused. Does the symmetry help hold the pieces together?

An unusual approach to Page One: Notice how little traditional text this page contains. Instead, it combines a Q&A, a calendar, and a sideways flag (with promos) down the left-hand edge. Still, the page is anchored by traditional story elements: a package using a dominant photo and a hammer headline. Does it all work?

FLOW CHART: SECTION FRONT DESIGN

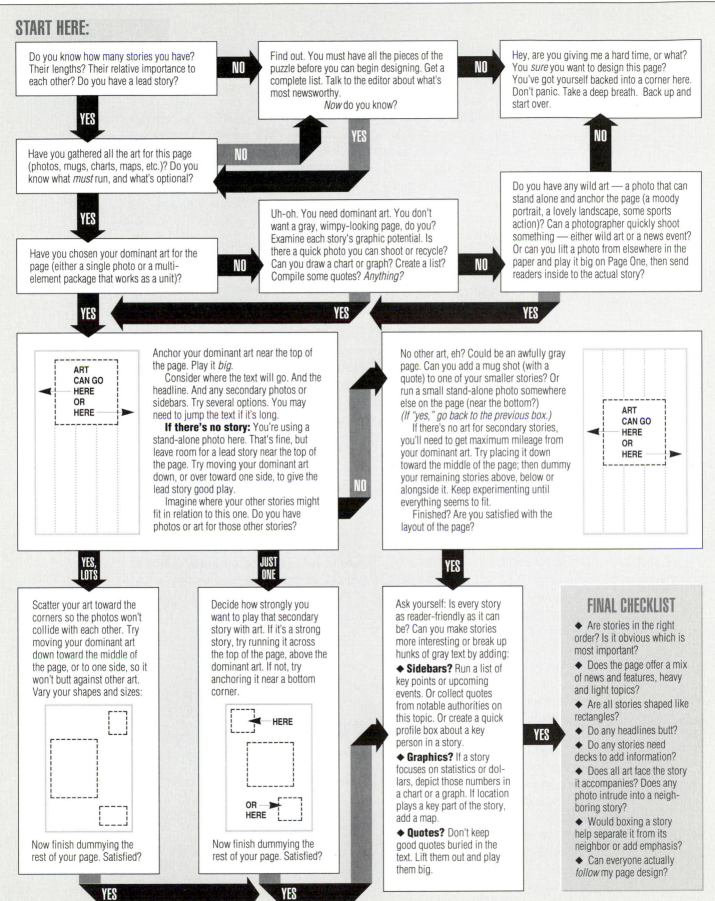

START HERE:

Do you know *how many* stories you have? Their lengths? Their relative importance to each other? Do you have a lead story?

NO → Find out. You must have all the pieces of the puzzle before you can begin designing. Get a complete list. Talk to the editor about what's most newsworthy.
Now do you know?

NO → Hey, are you giving me a hard time, or what? You *sure* you want to design this page? You've got yourself backed into a corner here. Don't panic. Take a deep breath. Back up and start over.

YES ↓

Have you gathered all the art for this page (photos, mugs, charts, maps, etc.)? Do you know what *must* run, and what's optional?

NO →

YES (from Find out box)

YES ↓

Have you chosen your dominant art for the page (either a single photo or a multi-element package that works as a unit)?

NO → Uh-oh. You need dominant art. You don't want a gray, wimpy-looking page, do you? Examine each story's graphic potential. Is there a quick photo you can shoot or recycle? Can you draw a chart or graph? Create a list? Compile some quotes? *Anything?*

NO → Do you have any wild art — a photo that can stand alone and anchor the page (a moody portrait, a lovely landscape, some sports action)? Can a photographer quickly shoot something — either wild art or a news event? Or can you lift a photo from elsewhere in the paper and play it big on Page One, then send readers inside to the actual story?

NO ↑ (to Hey box)

YES ↓   **YES**   **YES**

ART CAN GO HERE OR HERE

Anchor your dominant art near the top of the page. Play it *big*.
Consider where the text will go. And the headline. And any secondary photos or sidebars. Try several options. You may need to jump the text if it's long.
If there's no story: You're using a stand-alone photo here. That's fine, but leave room for a lead story near the top of the page. Try moving your dominant art down, or over toward one side, to give the lead story good play.
Imagine where your other stories might fit in relation to this one. Do you have photos or art for those other stories?

No other art, eh? Could be an awfully gray page. Can you add a mug shot (with a quote) to one of your smaller stories? Or run a small stand-alone photo somewhere else on the page (near the bottom)? (*If "yes," go back to the previous box.*)
If there's no art for secondary stories, you'll need to get maximum mileage from your dominant art. Try placing it down toward the middle of the page; then dummy your remaining stories above, below or alongside it. Keep experimenting until everything seems to fit.
Finished? Are you satisfied with the layout of the page?

ART CAN GO HERE OR HERE

NO ↓ (between the two bottom sections)

YES, LOTS ↓   **JUST ONE** ↓   **YES** ↓

Scatter your art toward the corners so the photos won't collide with each other. Try moving your dominant art down toward the middle of the page, or to one side, so it won't butt against other art. Vary your shapes and sizes:

Now finish dummying the rest of your page. Satisfied?

Decide how strongly you want to play that secondary story with art. If it's a strong story, try running it across the top of the page, above the dominant art. If not, try anchoring it near a bottom corner.

HERE

OR HERE

Now finish dummying the rest of your page. Satisfied?

Ask yourself: Is every story as reader-friendly as it can be? Can you make stories more interesting or break up hunks of gray text by adding:

◆ **Sidebars?** Run a list of key points or upcoming events. Or collect quotes from notable authorities on this topic. Or create a quick profile box about a key person in a story.

◆ **Graphics?** If a story focuses on statistics or dollars, depict those numbers in a chart or a graph. If location plays a key part of the story, add a map.

◆ **Quotes?** Don't keep good quotes buried in the text. Lift them out and play them big.

YES →

FINAL CHECKLIST

◆ Are stories in the right order? Is it obvious which is most important?

◆ Does the page offer a mix of news and features, heavy and light topics?

◆ Are all stories shaped like rectangles?

◆ Do any headlines butt?

◆ Do any stories need decks to add information?

◆ Does all art face the story it accompanies? Does any photo intrude into a neighboring story?

◆ Would boxing a story help separate it from its neighbor or add emphasis?

◆ Can everyone actually *follow* my page design?

YES →   **YES** →

Eventually, all newspaper pages will be *paginated* — assembled electronically. Computers will estimate the *exact* length of each story, calculate the *exact* sizes of photos, and manipulate everything *exactly* into place.

Until that day, though, things may get a bit sloppy.

No matter how hard you try, no matter how carefully you plan, no matter how goof-proof your page designs seem, stories will still come up short. Or long.

Once a page is assembled, minor tweaking is easy. Major repairs, however, can be tricky and time-consuming. You may need to back up and re-dummy a story or two. But first, find out what went wrong. Ask yourself:

◆ **Was there a planning problem?** Did someone change a story's length? Did someone swap or re-crop photos? Were ads sized wrong? Omitted? Killed? Or:

◆ **Was there a production problem?** Were text and photos correctly placed? Headlines correctly sized? Are all elements — bylines, cutlines, refers, logos, liftout quotes — where they're supposed to be?

If a story's close to fitting — say, within a few inches — try some of these options, either while you're designing the page or after it's typeset:

MORE ON ▶

◆ **Sizing photos:** *How to use a proportion wheel* **103**

◆ **Liftout quotes:** *Some basic styles and guidelines* **126**

◆ **Decks:** *Styles and guidelines for sizing and dummying* **128**

IF A STORY TURNS OUT TOO LONG

◆ **Trim the text.** As a rule of thumb, stories are usually cuttable by 10%. For instance, a 10-inch story can usually lose an inch without serious damage; a 30-inch story can lose a few inches. (And your readers may thank you.)

◆ **Trim a photo.** Shave a few picas off the top or bottom, if the image allows it. Or, if necessary, re-size the photo so you can crop more tightly.

◆ **Trim an adjacent story.** If you find that a story is trimmed to the max, try tightening the one above or below it.

◆ **Drop a line from the headline.** But be careful — short headlines that make no sense can doom an entire story. (See chart, page 25).

◆ **Move an ad.** Either into another column or onto another page.

IF A STORY TURNS OUT TOO SHORT

◆ **Add more text.** If material was trimmed from a story, add it back. Or if you have time, break out a small sidebar that highlights key information.

◆ **Enlarge a photo.** Crop the depth more loosely. Or size it a column larger.

◆ **Add a mug shot.** But be sure it's someone *relevant.*

◆ **Add a liftout quote.** Use meaningful material that draws in readers. And follow our advice at right.

◆ **Add another line of headline.** Or better yet, expand the decks on those long and medium-sized stories.

◆ **Add some air between paragraphs.** This old composing-room trick lets you add a 1-4 points of extra leading between the final paragraphs of a story. But be careful: If you overdo it, those paragraphs begin to float apart.

◆ **Add a filler story.** Keep a selection of optional 1- or 2-inch stories handy to drop in as needed.

◆ **Add a house ad.** Create small promos for your paper. Have them ready in a variety of widths and depths.

◆ **Move an ad.** Try another column or page for it.

In addition to these quick fixes, there are two more techniques — using bastard measures and jumping stories — that are a bit more complicated:

"
If you add a liftout quote, try to make it provocative and enticing. And designing in some white space below (like we're doing here) can help you fill deeper holes.
"

MAKING STORIES FIT

NON-STANDARD (BASTARD) MEASURES

Most of the time, photos fit fine into standard column widths. But on some pages, they're just too small in one column measure — and just too big in another.

At times like these, bastard measures can be the answer — especially on feature pages, where photos often dominate.

Take this column of text you're reading right now, for instance. Most text in this book is set 29 picas wide. But to maintain the best possible proportions for those four examples at right, we've narrowed this leg of text, running it in a bastard width — 9 picas — alongside the illustrations.

1 *Suppose you're dummying a 6-inch story with a mug. You need to fill this space that's 3 columns wide, 5 inches deep. What's your best option?*

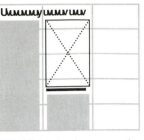

2 *With a 1-column mug, the story fits in 2 legs, leaving a column empty. (A 2-line headline would force text into that third leg, but wouldn't fill it.)*

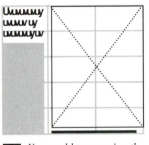

3 *You could try running the mug 2 columns wide, but it wastes way too much space. Only 3½ inches of text will fit into that left-hand column.*

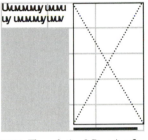

4 *The solution? Running 2 bastard legs in place of the usual 3. The text is 4 inches deep, but it's half-again as wide as a 1-column leg — so it fits.*

MORE ON ▶

◆ **Jump headlines:** *Guidelines for making jump stories effective... 136*

JUMPING STORIES

There will be times — many, many times — when you'll need to fit a 30-inch story into a 10-inch hole. When that happens, you can either:

❑ Cut 20 inches from the story (lots of luck), or
❑ Start the story on one page and finish it on another.

When stories runneth over like that, they're called *jumps*. Jumps are controversial. Many editors hate them. Many readers hate them, too. But designers love them, because they give you the freedom to stretch and slice stories in otherwise unimaginable ways.

(That age-old journalistic question — "Do readers actually follow stories that jump?" — has yet to be answered definitively. My own hunch? If a story's engrossing enough, readers will follow it *anywhere*. Otherwise, they'll use the jump as an excuse to bail out.)

When you jump a story:

◆ **Make it worth the reader's while.** It's pointless — and annoying — to jump just a few short paragraphs at the end of a story. Jump *at least* 6 inches of text, unless the story is simply uncuttable and there's no other option.

◆ **Start the story solidly** — with *at least* 4 inches of text — before you jump it. Otherwise, the story may look too insignificant to bother reading.

◆ **Jump stories to the same place** whenever possible. Readers will accept jumps more easily once they're trained to always turn to the back page, the top of Page 2, the bottom of Page 3, etc.

◆ **Jump stories once** — and once only. You'll lose or confuse too many readers if you jump a few inches to Page 2, then snake a little more along Page 3 and

Please turn to **JUMPS,** *Page 136* ▶

INSIDE PAGES

**ADS:
THREAT OR
MENACE?**

News stories exist to inform readers. Ads exist to make money for publishers. Can you guess which is more important?

Right. *Ads.*

The big difference between a front page and an inside page is that, on inside pages, you coexist with a loud, pushy heap of boxes — ads — stacked upward from the page bottom. Now, some stacks look better than others. But whatever format they use, ad stacks are dummied onto pages before the news is — and thus dictate the shape of the news hole you're left with.

Today, these three formats are most often used for dummying ads:

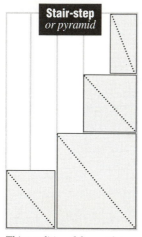

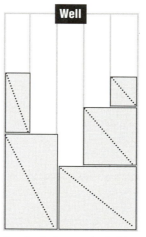

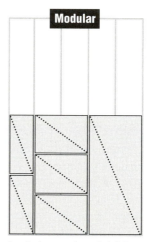

This traditional format lets every ad touch news copy, which is important to many advertisers. But for editors, it creates ugly-looking news holes. It also creates a pyramid effect on facing pages.

As ads stack up on both sides of the page, a well forms in the middle — hence the name. Like stair-stepped ads, wells can get ugly; designers have been known to call them "Ad Stacks From Hell."

Looks better, doesn't it? By stacking ads in modular blocks, pages looks more orderly and attractive, and readership actually improves. This solution may become more common in the future.

As you can see, those two old-fashioned ad configurations — stair-step and well — offer tough challenges for page designers. What's the best way to squeeze stories into those oddly shaped spaces? Here's some advice:

**GUIDELINES
FOR AD
LAYDOWN**

Many pages are doomed to ugliness before you even start designing. That's because the ad staff and the newsroom aren't communicating. As a result, ad laydowns become unmanageable, forcing you to waste precious time trying to overcome unnecessary obstacles.

To avoid headaches, work with the ad staff to:

◆ **Use modular ad formats.** Snaking stories around steeply stair-stepped ads punishes both readers and advertisers. Square off ads whenever possible.

◆ **Use house ads** to smooth out any small, awkward holes.

◆ **Establish guidelines for key pages.** Negotiate dependable news holes where you need them most. Reach an agreement that Page 2 will always be open, for instance, or that Page 3's left-hand column is off-limits to ads.

◆ **Establish limits.** If ads are stacked too high — say, an inch from the top of the page — dummying even the simplest headline and story is impossible. Ideally, ads should either stack clear to the top or start at least 2 inches down.

◆ **Get permission to move ads.** Ad positions aren't etched in stone. Reserve the right to move ads if necessary. Just don't abuse the privilege.

INSIDE PAGES

GUIDELINES FOR DESIGNING INSIDE PAGES

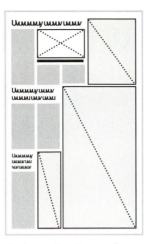

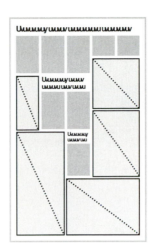

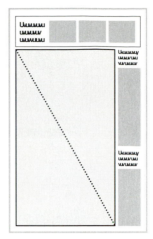

As these ads stair-step down the page, stories square off alongside. You may need to cut some text to create these modular shapes, but the page will be more readable than one full of doglegs.

The more crowded the page, the less necessary (and more difficult) it is to add photos. Note how this page plays up one dominant story — and how slight doglegs around ads are not a problem.

With a banner headline, that top story would have looked shallow and awkward. But by using a sidesaddle head, the elements fit together neatly. The box and the bastard measures are both optional.

◆ **Give every page a dominant element.** On crowded pages with tiny news holes, this may be impossible. And on other tight pages, even squeezing in a small photo may be difficult. But try to anchor each page with a strong image or a solid story. Don't just crowbar cluttered clumps of copy together.

◆ **Work with the ad stacks.** Yes, it's best to dummy stories into rectangles — but on pages crowded with ads, that may not work. Doglegging text is common on inside pages, and it's often your only option.

Before you begin dummying, explore how best to subdivide each page. Work with the ads to block out clean, modular story segments. Start at the bottom, if necessary; sometimes you can smooth things out by stretching one wide story atop an uneven stack of small ads. Or try working backwards from an awkward corner. But wherever possible, square off stories along the edges of ads.

◆ **Use alternative headline treatments.** When ads crowd up at the top of a page, you may barely have enough depth for a headline and an inch of text. That's where sidesaddle headlines come in handy (see the example at the top of the page, far right).

Another option: use raw-wrap headlines to dummy two stories side by side at the top of a crowded page.

◆ **Avoid dummying photos or boxed stories near ads.** Ads are boxes. Photos are boxes. And readers can't always tell one box from another. So unless you want photos and sidebars mistaken for ads, always keep a little text between the two (see example at right).

◆ **Save good stories for pages with good news holes.** Instead of trying to dummy your best stories and photos around your worst ad stacks, can you pour in flexible material like calendar listings? Briefs? Obituaries? Many papers successfully relegate low-priority material to pages where ads are ugliest.

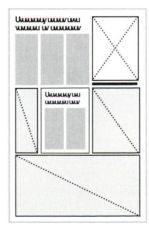

Two problems here: That top photo sits on an ad — and could easily be mistaken for an ad itself. In the middle of the page, that boxed story is sandwiched between ads — and, like the photo, seems to turn into another ad.

DOUBLE TRUCKS

This two-page "Tall Ships" spread was produced in 1984 on the front and back pages of the Upfront feature section in the Rochester (N.Y.) Times-Union. Designed by art director Ray Stanczak, this double-truck design lifted many of its ideas from a "tall ships" page previously done by The Boston Globe. It took several artists several days to research and execute this layout, which previewed the arrival of a fleet of sailing ships by showing readers fun facts, a diagram, a map of the route, etc. This "Tall Ships" page became a favorite of many Times-Union staffers . . .

. . .and years later, a Times-Union feature editor, Felix Winternitz, moved to The Cincinnati Enquirer. Though he hadn't worked on the original "Tall Ships" page, Winternitz said, "I always loved it, and I thought, 'Someday I'm gonna find a way to use this.' " And in 1989 he helped create this "Tall Stacks" page.

The design and illustrations for "Tall Stacks" took three months. Like the "Tall Ships" spread, it used the front and back pages of the feature section. Unlike "Tall Ships," it printed in black and white ("Tall Ships" originally ran in color) to achieve a more antique effect.

As Winternitz said: "Ideas are made to be stolen."

DOUBLE TRUCKS

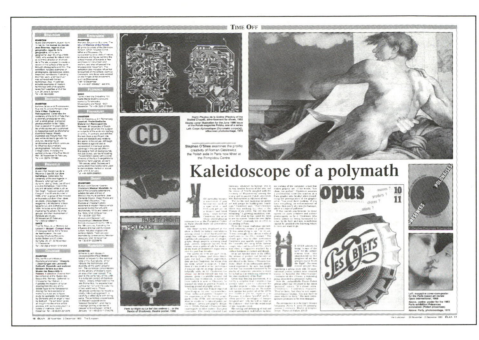

This double-truck spread from The European combines a weekly arts calendar (at left) with a lavishly illustrated feature story to form a handsome, magazine-style package. Note how the design flows right across the central gutter. (Note, two, how that lead headline forms an awkward armpit.)

When two facing pages print across the gutter on one sheet of newsprint — say, the two pages in the center of a section — it's called a *double truck*. Double trucks are rare in broadsheets, but popular in tabloids. They'll work best if you:

◆ **Clear off all ads.** Make it one big, modular, editorial block. Any ads will either intrude, get buried, or be mistaken for editorial matter.

◆ **Treat both pages as one horizontal unit.** If you're used to dealing with vertical formats, this is a good chance to rethink your approach. Ignore the gutter between pages; spread your elements from left to right in a balanced, orderly way. Keep the flow of text clean. Anchor the design with a bold headline and strong dominant photo. But above all, package only related topics together.

◆ **Save them for special occasions.** Readers expect these packages to be special; don't let them down. Save double trucks for news features, infographics, photo layouts or major events. Add color and graphic effects. Think big. Have fun.

DESIGNING TWO FACING PAGES

You can also apply special treatment to two facing pages anywhere in the paper (these are sometimes called "double trucks out of position").

As with true double trucks, it's important to view facing pages as one wide unit and balance your elements accordingly. If you're careful, you can even run some elements across the gutter. Big photos or illustrations will usually work best, since smaller elements (headlines, text, cutlines) seldom align successfully. Most readers are tolerant, but don't push your luck.

This photo spread from The Times (Beaverton, Ore.) ran on two facing pages — not a true double truck. We've printed it here the way many readers saw it: with the pages slightly out of alignment and a gutter opening up through the lead photo and headline. That's a problem, but not a serious one.

BAD JUXTAPOSITIONS

As newspaper designer Phil Nesbitt once said: People and puppies must both be trained to use a newspaper.

In olden days, readers were trained to read newspapers *vertically* — and since every story on every page ran vertically, readers were rarely confused about which photo went with which story.

Today, however, stories run in vertical and horizontal modules that change from page to page. And on every page — even with every story — we expect our readers to instantly deduce which photo belongs to which story.

We don't always make their choices easy (as in the example at right: Is Nixon the escaped lunatic? Is that gorilla photo a portrait of Nixon's new grandchild?) So it's especially important to analyze every page design as objectively as you can, to determine:

Ax-wielding lunatic escapes from asylum

By ROBIN FOX
Special writer, The Bugle Beacon

Non equidem insector delendave carmin Livi esse reor, memini quae

Non equidem insector delendave carmin Livi esse reor, memini.

Ex-president Nixon visits new grandchild

By ROBIN FOX
Special writer, The Bugle Beacon

Gorilla mom gives birth at city zoo

Non equidem insector dele ndave carmina Livi ess mundi.

Killer gorilla goes bananas, trashes tire store

By ROBIN FOX
Special writer, The Bugle Beacon

◆ If a photo sits at the intersection of two stories in a way that confuses or misdirects the reader.

◆ If two stories — or their headlines — seem inappropriate together on the same page. (Those two ape stories in the example above will seem related to many readers, thus creating a false impression.)

◆ If an advertisement seems to comment upon a neighboring news story.

It's easy to embarrass yourself, your readers and the subjects of your stories (both apes *and* humans) by dubious dummying. When in doubt, either *move* it or *box* it — whatever it takes to make your design perfectly clear.

THE PROBLEM: OVERLAPPING MODULES

To avoid blunders like that example above, beware of modules that overlap, whether horizontally (on both sides of a photo) or both vertically *and* horizontally (beside and below a photo):

Horizontally

Two stories, one photo — and the reader must guess where the photo belongs. To fix:
◆ *Box or screen one of the stories;*
◆ *Divide them with a cutoff rule; or*
  ◆ *Run a large headline across the top of the photo and its text.*

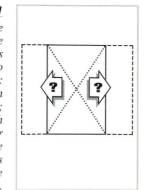

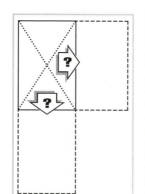

Horizontally and vertically

Dummying photos into corner intersections can be dangerous. To avoid confusion:
◆ *Box or screen one of the stories;*
◆ *Make sure any story below an unrelated photo is at least one column wider or narrower.*

RULES OF THUMB

LAYOUT & DESIGN

◆ All stories should be shaped like rectangles. Pages should consist of rectangles stacked together. **[40]**

◆ Avoid placing any graphic element in the middle of a leg of type. **[42, 126]**

◆ Avoid placing art at the bottom of a leg of type. **[42]**

◆ Text that wraps below a photo should be at least one inch deep. **[43]**

◆ In vertical layouts, stack elements in this order: *photo, cutline, headline, text.* **[42]**

◆ Every page should have a dominant piece of art. **[52]**

◆ A well-designed page is usually at least one-third art. **[68]**

◆ Avoid dummying a photo directly on top of an ad. **[83]**

◆ Avoid boxing stories just to keep headlines from butting; it's best to box stories only if they're special or different. **[70]**

TEXT

◆ The optimum depth for legs of text is from 2-10 inches. **[27]**

◆ Avoid dummying legs of text more than 20 picas wide, or narrower than 10 picas. **[27]**

◆ Use italics, boldface, reverses or any other special effects in small doses. **[26]**

◆ Type below 8 point is difficult to read. Use small type sparingly, and avoid printing it behind a screen. **[26, 181]**

HEADLINES

◆ Every story needs a headline.

◆ Headlines get smaller as you move down the page. Smaller stories get smaller headlines. **[25]**

◆ 5-10 words is optimum for most headlines. **[25]**

◆ Never allow an art element to come between the headline and the start of a news story. **[47]**

◆ Don't butt headlines. If you must, run the left headline several counts short, then vary their sizes and the number of lines. **[69]**

◆ Writing headlines: Avoid stilted wording, jargon, omitted verbs, bad splits; write in the present tense. **[69]**

PHOTOS

◆ Shoot photos of *real* people doing *real* things. **[92, 99]**

◆ Directional photos should face the text they accompany. **[46, 47]**

◆ When in doubt, run one big photo instead of two small ones. **[53]**

◆ When using two or more photos, make one dominant — that is, substantially bigger than any competing photo. **[53, 75]**

◆ Try to vary the shapes and sizes of all photos (as well as stories) on a page. **[74]**

CUTLINES

◆ To avoid confusion, run one cutline per photo; each cutline should touch the photo it describes. **[31, 111]**

◆ When cutlines run beside photos, they should be at least 6 picas wide. **[31]**

◆ When cutlines run below photos, square them off as evenly as possible on both sides of the photo. They should not extend beyond either edge of the photo. **[31]**

◆ Avoid widows in any cutline more than one line deep. **[31]**

JUMPS

◆ Run at least 4 inches of a story before you jump it. **[81]**

◆ Jump at least 6 inches of a story (to make it worth the reader's effort). **[81]**

◆ Jump stories once and once only. Whenever possible, jump to the same place.

EXERCISES

ANSWERS ▶ 201

1 You need to dummy text in a box that's 40 picas wide. How wide will each leg be if there are 4 legs? If there are 3 legs? If there are 2 legs?

2 You're laying out an inside page in a 5-column format. The ads stack up pretty high; your available space for news is 6 inches deep and the full page (5 columns) across. You need to dummy two stories: one 15 inches long, the other 10 inches. Neither has art. You can trim one inch out of either story, if necessary — but no more. How many design options do you have?

3 There are several things wrong with each of these three page designs. Like what, for instance?

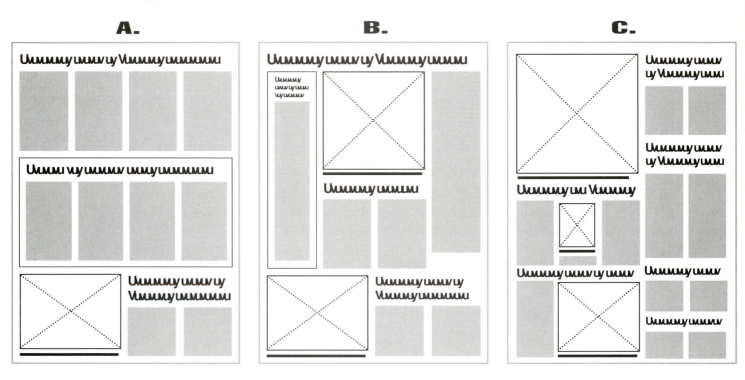

A.   **B.**   **C.**

4 The four layouts below all use the same story elements. Which one of the four layouts is the best, and why?

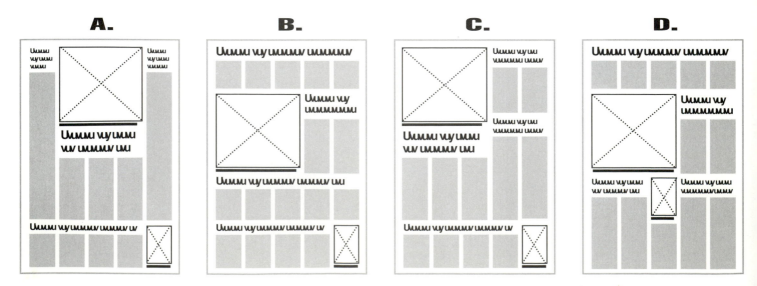

A.   **B.**   **C.**   **D.**

(Newspaper layout example at top showing The Oregonian front page with headlines: "Hyundai picks Portland as principal port", "CAMPAIGN '88", "3 hijackers, 1 hostage die in shootout after pope's visit", "'Human mouse' portends breakthroughs in medicine", etc.)

5 When the layout above ran in the newspaper, some editors complained that the Campaign '88 promo box was positioned poorly. It appears as if it's part of the Hyundai story to its left. How would you redesign this part of the page to avoid that problem, using the sizes shown here?

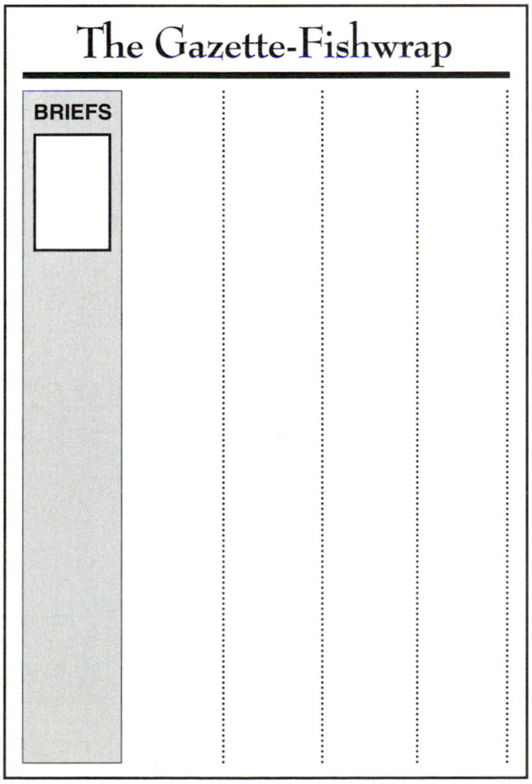

The Gazette-Fishwrap

BRIEFS

6 At left is Page One of a typical tabloid. It uses a 5-column format; the left-hand column is reserved for news briefs.

Design this page with the following three elements:

1) A 10-inch lead story with a good horizontal photo;

2) An 8-inch story with a horizontal photo; and

3) A 4-inch bright (an upbeat, offbeat feature).

7 Here's an inside page for a tabloid. Down the right side, there's a column of news briefs. Draw a dummy that shows how you'd design this page with the following elements:

◆ A lead story — about 15" long, but cuttable* — that uses a strong, deep vertical photo.

◆ A secondary story — about 12" long, but cuttable — with a mug shot.

◆ A short, bright feature story — about 4" long.

Note: There are two somewhat different, but acceptable, solutions for this page. Try your best to figure out both options.

* By "cuttable," we're talking a couple of inches, max — nothing too drastic.

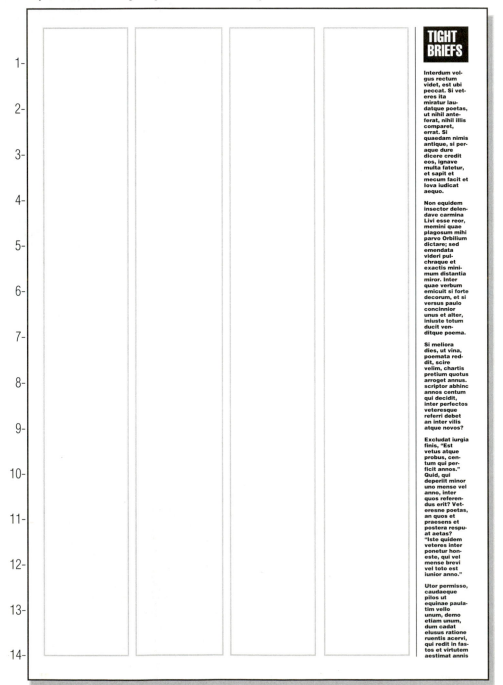

ANSWERS ▶ 201

On March 4, 1880, the New York Daily Graphic became the first newspaper to print a photograph. And from that day to this, newspaper photographers have constantly wondered: "Won't they *ever* give us any respect?"

You can't blame photographers for feeling paranoid. Newsrooms, after all, are dominated by editors who were once reporters, who believe news means *text,* who think photos make nice decoration — but if space gets tight, and they need to cut either the story or the photo, you know how they'll vote.

Trouble is, those editors are sadly mistaken. Our culture is becoming more and more *visual.* In today's media, images are strong; text, by comparison, is weak. If you want to convey information, photos can be as valuable as text. If you want to hook passing readers, photos are even *more* valuable than text.

Until now, this book has treated photos as boxes parked on the page. But there's more to it than that. Photographs are essential for good design, and good design is essential for photos.

In this chapter, we'll take a closer look at the art and science of photojournalism.

SOME PHOTO GUIDELINES

There's a lot to learn about shooting photos, cropping and sizing them, transforming them into halftones, designing them into photo spreads. . . but before we begin, let's summarize a few basic photojournalistic guidelines:

◆ **Every photo should have a clean, clear center of interest.** A good photo, like a well-written story, is easy to read. It presents information that's free of clutter and distractions. Every photo must be sharply focused and cleanly composed, so its most important elements stand out instantly.

◆ **Every photo should get a cutline.** It's surprising how often editors think, "Well, *everyone* knows who *that* is: It's Millard Fillmore!" Never assume readers are as smart as you are — or that they actually intend to *read the story*. Identify everything: all faces, places and activities .

◆ **Every photo should be bordered.** Don't allow the white tones of a photo to float into the whiteness of the page. Frame each image with a border — a plain, thin rule running along the edge of the photo (1-point is standard; in this book, we use .7 point). But don't overdo it. Fancy borders around photos and cutlines may separate them from each other — or from the stories they accompany.

◆ **Every photo should look natural.** In amateur snapshots, people smile stiffly at the camera; in professional news portraits, they're loose, relaxed, engaged in activities. Whenever possible, shoot *real* people doing *real* things, not gazing blankly into space or pretending to be busy.

◆ **Every photo should be relevant.** Readers don't have time for trivia in text; they don't want to see it in photos, either. Show readers images that have a direct connection to today's news (the movers & shakers, winners & losers — not squirrels playing in the park). Photos must provide information, not decoration.

◆ **Every face should be at least the size of a dime.** It's rare that photos are played too big in newspapers, but they often run too small — especially when the key characters shrink to the size of insects. If you want images with impact, shoot individuals, not crowds. Then size photos as big as you can.

This photo has a clean, clear center of interest: an old war veteran caught in a nostalgic salute. It's a sharp, strong image, with no background clutter to distract us. And it seems to be an honest portrait — not posed or artificial.

This high-contrast portrait of an urban gang member uses a compelling composition. But notice how the white background blends into the whiteness of the page. Without a border to frame this image, the crops at the top and bottom of the photo look awkward.

This news photo of Bill Clinton on the 1992 presidential campaign trail is interesting — but only if it runs HUGE. At the size shown here, all its impact is lost. The faces in the crowd blur together, and Clinton himself fades into the background.

GOOD PHOTOS

What makes a photograph good? In the pages that follow, five photographers from The Oregonian (Portland's daily paper) present their favorite images — and explain what makes these photos strong.

Kraig Scattarella:

"This is the aftermath of a fatal fire where a relative has just come on the scene and realized that her grandson was killed. The emotion overwhelmed her, and all she wanted to do was run inside and see the body. The fireman stepped in to hold her back and comfort her.

"The news editor was adamant about NOT using this picture.* He felt that it was an invasion of these people's privacy — which it is. It's their moment of grief. My selling point for this picture was that these people didn't have any smoke detectors in their house. In the story it mentions that; they had just moved into the house a day or two before. And anybody that sees that picture is going to think of himself in that situation and think, 'I don't want this to happen to me.'

"This is the picture you dream about, that all photojournalists strive for — when all the elements fall together to make a complete picture that can stand alone, without words. If you can capture a moment like this, then you've done your job 100%."

* The photo did run, though.

Randy L. Rasmussen:

"This is Patricia Kent. She was in her 70s or early 80s when I photographed her for a series The Oregonian did on poverty and unemployment in Oregon. For this series, I traveled throughout western Oregon for two weeks of shooting.

"She lived near Woodburn in a little one-room house that had no central heating system, no running water. . . . She had subsisted that way for years. When I met her, she was chopping her own firewood. She embodied a sort of pioneer spirit, yet she also symbolized the victimization of older people. She was a gutsy lady; she didn't want any help.

"I photographed her a couple different times. In this picture, she was standing in her doorway. She's out in the light, and the doorway falls off dark behind her. I think we were saying goodbye. It just seemed to characterize the loneliness and depression that was going on around the state at that time.

"The photo ran with the story in the opening of the series, then was picked up and incorporated in the logo for the series, which was called 'Sorrowful Spring.' It fit perfectly.

"It's one of the few assignments that's stuck with me through the years. To me, it's classic portraiture. It captures everything about this lady in a quick read. You can really see the suffering she's gone through."

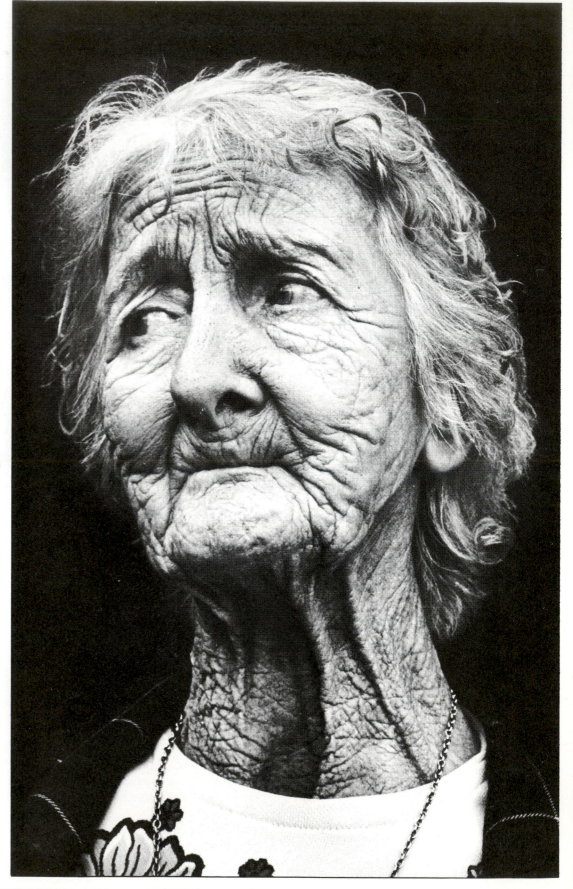

GOOD PHOTOS

Michael Lloyd:

"This picture is from the Portland State University women's volleyball championship — a successful defense of their national title for the second year in a row.

"A lot of sports action pictures — say, of the volleyball game itself — are quite ambiguous. Even a great action picture really doesn't tell you who wins or loses. But in this case, this moment said it all. It wasn't an action moment; it was after the game was over. It required a lot of quickness and preparation, to see this happening and get there in time to shoot it. Which all comes from experience, from covering a lot of things like this over a long time.

"When I shoot sports, I try to tell a story through the emotions of the people. Sometimes that's in action; a lot of times it's not.

"This ran real well (because I was picture editor for Sports). It ran at least three columns. One picture. Didn't need to clutter up the page with a lot of photos. This one said it all."

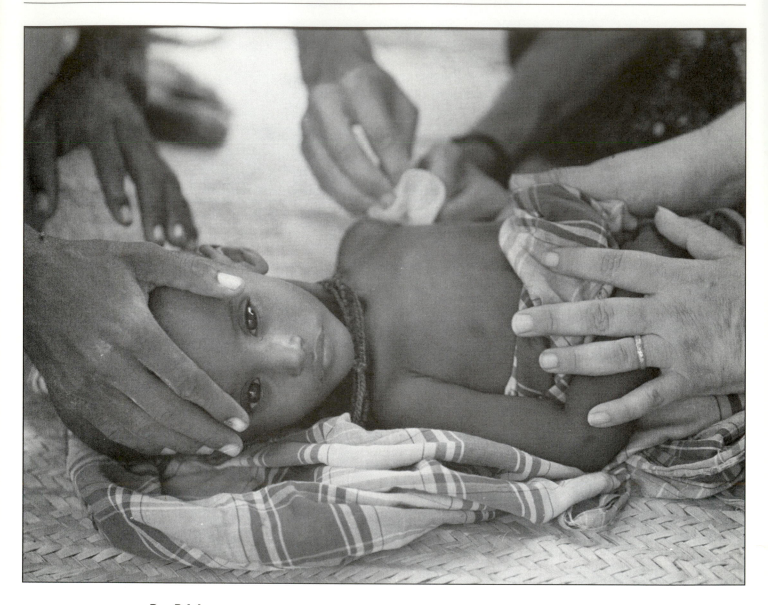

Ben Brink:

"We were in Wajir, a border town in northeast Kenya, back in the fall of '92. The situation in Somalia was a combination of war, drought and famine which caused hundreds of thousands of people to flee the country. I went over with the Northwest Medical Teams before the U.S. troops went in. And this clinic is right out on the desert floor, amongst the acacia trees, where these nomadic tribes set up their huts.

"This is a little boy from one of the tribes who was brought in by his mother. He was malnourished and dehydrated. At this point, the doctors are trying to rehydrate him with a mixture of salt and water. I'm across the clinic with a long lens. As I started to shoot, it was interesting how many sets of hands were attending to him: keeping him calm, keeping him down, keeping him from wiggling as needles went into him. He'd been thrashing around earlier, but at this particular moment he calmed down and seemed to be very serene. He couldn't fight it anymore.

"He's exhausted. His strength is gone. Yet his eyes are looking straight at you, so peaceful and calm and resigned. And now all these giving hands come in to do the best they can to save him.

"I was there for a couple weeks, and I saw him come back day after day. He looked a little better, but his body was ravaged by the dehydration. I don't know if he lived."

GOOD PHOTOS

Ross Hamilton:

"I've always been a boxing fan. And being able to appreciate an event has a lot to do with what you come up with.

"This is a perfect example of one of those sports shots you always hope for, where lots of elements come together: timing, luck, focus. Probably the same could be said for the guy hitting the other guy. It's a powerful shot. By me AND the boxer.

"Some of it is luck. But you have to be prepared to take advantage of lucky events. There was a photographer next to me, shooting the same stuff, and he didn't get that shot. He might have been changing film, or changing lenses, or changing cameras — he may even have shot it, and it was out of focus. But there I was. Lucky.

"We were both being sprayed with sweat, blood and water. We were constantly wiping off our lenses as we were shooting. So he might have been wiping sweat and blood off his lens while I got the shot.

"It wasn't until I got back and saw the shot that I went, 'Damn, I got one.' I remember feeling confident, but I didn't realize until I saw the film that I had such a crucial moment.

"I love the guy's face. I love the fact that he's just getting blasted. I love the swirl of sweat coming off his head. It's a successful, powerful sports image."

BAD PHOTOS

Light pole sticking out of subject's head (poor mix of foreground and background).

Harsh shadows on subject's face.

Subject is out of focus. And photo is underexposed (too dark).

Unflattering and unnatural pose.

Scratches and assorted darkroom crud.

Image is flopped (printed backwards) — note words on sign.

Distractions in the background.

Subject is off-center, awkwardly cropped; no strong center of interest.

Photos can be bad in a mind-boggling number of ways. They can be too dark, too light, too fuzzy, too tasteless, too meaningless or too *late* to run in the paper. They can, like the photo above, show blurry blobs of useless information — depicting, with frightening clarity, a person with a streetlight growing out of his head.

Be grateful, then, whenever a photographer hands you a sharp, dramatic, immaculately printed photograph. And avoid turning good photos into bad ones by cropping them clumsily. By playing them too small. Or by dummying them where they compete with another photo or intrude into the wrong story.

Remember, photographers often use terms like "hack," "mangle," "kill" and "bury" to describe what editors do to their photos. So be careful. People who talk like that shouldn't be pushed too far.

MAKING THE BEST OF BAD PHOTOS

What can you do to salvage a bungled photo assignment?

◆ **Edit carefully.** Find the most informative frame on the roll. Is there one successful image that shows more than the rest? A telling face, gesture, action?

◆ **Crop aggressively.** Focus our attention on what works in the photo — not what doesn't. Play up what's important and eliminate the rest.

◆ **Run a sequence.** Sometimes two small photos aren't as bad as one big weak one. Consider pairing a couple of complementary images.

◆ **Reshoot.** Is there time? A willing photographer? An available subject?

◆ **Try another photo source.** Was there another photographer at the scene? Would older file photos be appropriate?

◆ **Use alternative art.** Is there another way to illustrate this story? With a chart? A map? A well-designed mug/liftout quote? A sidebar?

◆ **Retouch mistakes.** With a grease pencil, airbrush or photo-retouching program, tone down distracting backgrounds, sharpen contrast, add highlights.

◆ **Bury it.** By playing a photo small, you can de-emphasize its faults. By moving it further down the page, you can make it less noticeable.

◆ **Mortise one photo over another.** It's risky, but may help if there's an offensive element you need to eliminate or disguise. (See page 179.)

◆ **Do without.** Remind yourself that bad art is worse than no art at all.

BAD PHOTOS

Photojournalistic cliches have plagued editors for decades. Some, like "The Mayor Wears a Funny Hat," have a *little* merit (either as entertainment or as a peculiar form of revenge).

Others, like the examples shown below, have almost no redeeming value — except to friends, relatives and employees of those in the photo. Shoot these space-wasters if you must, but look for alternatives (for instance, *real* people doing *real* things) every chance you get.

THE "GRIP & GRIN"

Usual victims: Club presidents, civic heroes, honors students, school administrators, retiring bureaucrats.

Scene of the crime: City halls, banquets, school offices — anyplace civic-minded folks pass checks, cut ribbons or hand out diplomas.

How to avoid it: Plan ahead. If someone *does* something worth a trophy, take a picture of him (or her) *doing* it. Otherwise, just run a mug shot.

THE EXECUTION AT DAWN

Usual victims: Any clump of victims lined up against a wall to be shot: club members, sports teams, award winners, etc.

Scene of the crime: Social wingdings, public meetings, fund-raisers — usually on a stage or in a hallway. Also occurs, pre-season, in the gym.

How to avoid it: Same as the Grip & Grin — move out into the real world, where these people actually *do* what makes them interesting.

THE GUY AT HIS DESK

Usual victims: Administrators, bureaucrats, civic organizers — anybody who bosses other people around.

Scene of the crime: In the office. Behind the desk.

Variations: The Guy on the Phone. The Guy on the Computer. The Guy in the Doorway. The Guy Leaning on the Sign in Front of the Building.

How to avoid it: Find him something to *do*. Or shoot a tighter portrait.

THE BORED MEETING

Usual victims: Politicians, school officials, bureaucrats — anybody who holds any kind of meeting, actually.

Scene of the crime: A long table in a nondescript room.

How to avoid it: Run mug shots and liftout quotes from key participants. Better yet: find out in advance what this meeting's *about*, then go shoot a photo of *that*. Illustrate the topic — not a dull discussion about it.

CROPPING PHOTOS

Most photographers shoot 35mm film, which produces a frame like the one at left. But that doesn't mean all your photos must be shaped like that — or that you're required to use the entire image a photographer shoots.

To get the most out of a photograph, you *crop* it. Cropping lets you re-frame the image, creating a new shape that emphasizes what's important — and deletes what's not.

Three ways to crop the same photograph:

◆ *Full frame (left), we see the full photo image. By showing us the entire stage, Eddie Van Halen's leap looks truly dramatic — but would this image lose impact if the photo ran small?*

◆ *A moderately tight crop (above) focuses tightly on Eddie. By zeroing in this closely, we've eliminated all those background distractions.*

◆ *An extremely tight crop (below) turns the photo into an attention-getting mug shot. We've tilted the image, too, to make it vertical. But does this crop destroy the integrity of the original?*

CROPPING PHOTOS

Yes, a photo can be cropped to fit any space, regardless of its original shape. But designers who do that are insensitive louts. That's like taking a 20-inch story and cramming it into a 10-inch hole: not a smart move.

Always try to edit and crop photos *first,* before you dummy the story. Once you've made the strongest possible crop, *then* create a layout that plays off the photo cleanly and attractively.

To do all that, you must learn where to crop — and where to stop:

This is the photograph as originally shot, full frame. Notice the excessive amount of empty space surrounding the central action.

Here's the proper crop. Notice how it focuses tightly on the action without crowding — and without cropping into the hoop, ball or feet.

This is a bad crop. It's too tight. We've chopped off the top of the ball, amputated feet and jammed the action against the edge of the frame.

A GOOD CROP:
◆ **Adds impact.** It finds the focal point of a photo and enhances it, making the central image as powerful as possible.
◆ **Eliminates what's unnecessary:** sky, ground, people, distractions in the background.
◆ **Leaves air where it's needed.** If a photo captures a mood (loneliness, fear, etc.), a loose crop can enhance that mood. If a photo is active and directional, a loose crop can keep action from jamming into the edge of the frame.

A BAD CROP:
◆ **Amputates body parts** (especially at joints: wrists, ankles, fingers) or lops off appendages (baseball bats, golf clubs, musical instruments, etc.).
◆ **Forces the image into an awkward shape** just to fit a predetermined hole.
◆ **Changes the meaning of a photo** by removing information. By cropping someone out of a news photo or eliminating an important object in the background, you can distort the meaning of what remains.
◆ **Violates works of art** (paintings, drawings, fine photography) by re-cropping them. Any artwork not printed in full should be labeled "detail."
◆ **Damages the original photo.** Never cut photographs or mark them with ink. Instead, make crop marks with a grease pencil, write notes in the margins, or attach a sheet of paper with cropping instructions.

SIZING PHOTOS

The original print •••••••••••
is this size. All enlarge-
ments and reductions are
measured as percentages
of the original.

20%

30%

40%

50%

75%

100%

125%

300%

Cropping photos is one way to create new shapes. You can also *resize* (or *scale)* photos: enlarging them *up* or reducing them *down*.

When you change the size of a photo, you measure its new size as a percentage of the original. As you see here, a photo that's half the size of the original is called a 50% reduction; a photo three times the size of the original is a 300% enlargement. You determine these percentages by using rulers and proportion wheels (see next page) or by importing images electronically into a page-layout program and letting the computer do the math for you.

It's also possible — though not advisable — to alter an image in weird, wacky ways by changing just one of its dimensions: i.e., enlarging it *horizontally* while reducing it *vertically.* This sort of gimmickry is easy to do with computers, either deliberately or accidentally, so be careful. By distorting a photo's true proportions, you damage its credibility.

A little knowledge is a dangerous thing — and once you learn how to squish and stretch images electronically, you might be tempted to try these kinds of effects. As a rule, avoid this (whether intentionally or by accident) .

30% *width,*
60% *depth*

150% *width,*
60% *depth*

THE PROPORTION WHEEL

Before there were computers, there were pica poles and proportion wheels. And if you don't use a computer — or if, say, you're trapped in the newsroom during a power failure — here's how to resize photos the traditional way:

THE PROBLEM: HOW DO YOU CALCULATE NEW PHOTO SIZES?

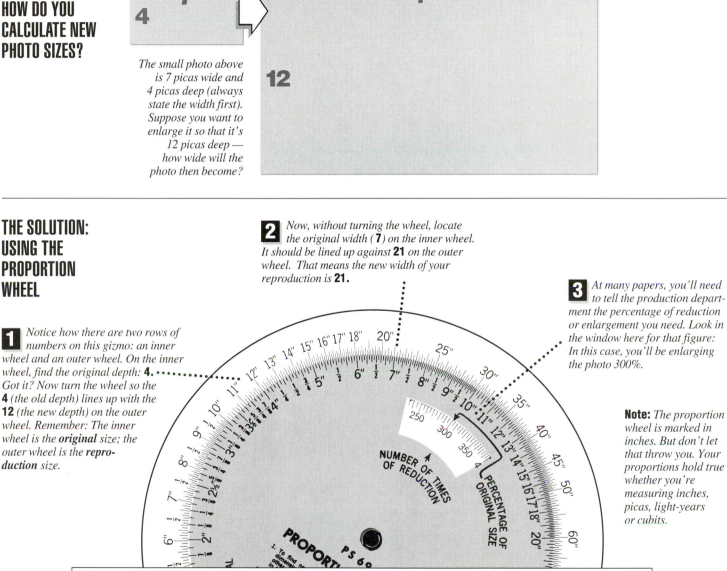

7
4
?
12

The small photo above is 7 picas wide and 4 picas deep (always state the width first). Suppose you want to enlarge it so that it's 12 picas deep — how wide will the photo then become?

THE SOLUTION: USING THE PROPORTION WHEEL

1 *Notice how there are two rows of numbers on this gizmo: an inner wheel and an outer wheel. On the inner wheel, find the original depth:* **4.** *Got it? Now turn the wheel so the* **4** *(the old depth) lines up with the* **12** *(the new depth) on the outer wheel. Remember: The inner wheel is the* **original** *size; the outer wheel is the* **reproduction** *size.*

2 *Now, without turning the wheel, locate the original width (* **7** *) on the inner wheel. It should be lined up against* **21** *on the outer wheel. That means the new width of your reproduction is* **21.**

3 *At many papers, you'll need to tell the production department the percentage of reduction or enlargement you need. Look in the window here for that figure: In this case, you'll be enlarging the photo 300%.*

Note: *The proportion wheel is marked in inches. But don't let that throw you. Your proportions hold true whether you're measuring inches, picas, light-years or cubits.*

OR IF YOU'D RATHER USE A CALCULATOR . . .

A proportion wheel is just a mathematical short-cut, a way of showing that the *original width* is to the *original depth* as the *new width* is to the *new depth*. If you'd rather do the math by hand or on a calculator, use this formula:

$$\frac{original\ width}{original\ depth} = \frac{new\ width}{new\ depth}$$

For our example above, you'd use this equation to find the new width:

$\dfrac{7}{4} = \dfrac{x}{12}$ *7 is to 4 as **what** is to 12? To find the missing number, multiply the diagonals (7 X 12 = 84) . . .*

$4x = 84$ *. . . then divide that total by the remaining value (84 ÷ 4) . . .*

$x = 21$ *. . . to find the missing width.*

HALFTONES & SCREENS

PHOTO HALFTONES

Once a photo has been cropped, it still needs to be reprocessed before it's printed in the paper. There are three reasons for this:

1) The photo may need to be reduced or enlarged to a new size.

2) The contrast or exposure of the original photo may need fine-tuning to improve the way it reproduces on newsprint.

3) Printing presses cannot print gray. They can only create the illusion of gray by changing the photo into a pattern of dots called a *halftone*.

Halftone dots are created by re-shooting the original photo through a halftone screen. Those dots usually run in diagonal rows or lines (as you can see in the enlargement at right). The density of a halftone screen is measured by the number of lines per inch.

MORE ON ▷

◆ **Screens & reverses:**
How dot screens are used with type 180

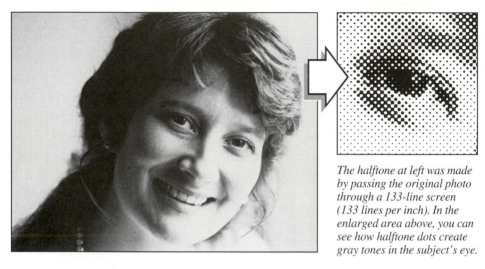

The halftone at left was made by passing the original photo through a 133-line screen (133 lines per inch). In the enlarged area above, you can see how halftone dots create gray tones in the subject's eye.

SCREEN DENSITIES

The finer the dot screen, the smaller the dots. The smaller the dots, the less visible they are. The less visible they are, the more realistic the photo appears.

For realistic-looking photos, then, you should use the finest dot screen your paper can handle. Newspapers, unfortunately, often use rather coarse screens — one reason their photos don't look as slick as those in books and magazines.

65-line screen: *This is a very coarse screen, with only 65 lines of dots per inch. The dots are quite apparent, but at least they won't smudge into each other when printed on rough newsprint by an unreliable printing press.*

85-line screen: *This is the most common screen density newspapers use — again, that's because of the limitations of newsprint. With a finer screen, the ink would smudge and the spaces between the dots would fill in.*

133-line screen: *This is one of the finer halftone screens printers use. Because books and magazines use smooth paper and high-quality presses, the dots will hold — and the results show crisp, clean detail.*

HALFTONES & SCREENS

LINE SHOTS

As we've learned, halftone screens are necessary to preserve gray tones when photos are printed on newspaper presses. But what would happen if you printed a photo without using a halftone screen?

You'd create something called a line conversion or *line shot*. All dark tones turn black, while light tones turn white — and as you can see, the result is a dramatic, high-contrast image.

Line shots are used to copy any art that uses no gray tones (pen-and-ink drawings, type treatments, etc.) But since line shots distort the honesty and integrity of photo images, it's best to reserve them for features, not hard news.

Compare this image to the halftone treatment on the facing page. Notice how the lighter gray tones have turned white; the darker grays turned black. A line shot, then, is just a high-contrast image without grays.

SCANNING PHOTOS ELECTRONICALLY

Until recently, converting photos to halftones and line shots was an expensive, time-consuming process that required professional technicians. Today, it's easy to do. All you need is a computer, the right software, and a *scanner,* a machine that captures images electronically — *digitizes* them — then lets you store, transmit and dummy them via computer.

Scanners belong to the family of computer hardware called *input devices,* which process text and graphics *into* your computer (a printer, on the other hand, is an *output device.)* Most scanners look and perform like photocopying machines. Here's how the process works:

1 **Preparing to scan:** *Take your original image — a photo, a drawing, some type — and lay it face-down on the scanner's glass surface. Special software will allow you to crop the image, resize it — even adjust its contrast.*

2 **Scanning the image:** *The scanner lights up like a photocopying machine as it duplicates the image electronically, converting it into microscopic dots or pixels (picture elements). The more dots the scan uses, the finer the resolution will be.*

3 **Importing the image:** *Once it's scanned, the electronic image can be transmitted into a page-layout program, where you can further adjust its size and shape. The image can then be printed alone or as part of a finished design.*

STAND-ALONE PHOTOS

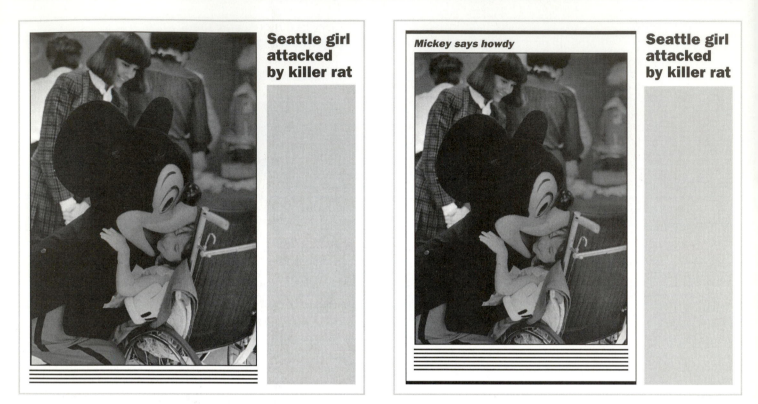

Seattle girl attacked by killer rat

Mickey says howdy

Seattle girl attacked by killer rat

In the example at left, you'd assume that's an actual photo of the Seattle girl being attacked by a rat, like the headline says. But no — it's actually a sweet, funny, *stand-alone photo* that's completely unrelated to the story. In the layout at right, the photo is boxed separately, to show readers it's a separate element. (You could argue that it's in poor taste to dummy these two items alongside each other *at all,* but we're trying to make a point here.)

The point is this: Photos often run independently. You don't need text or a newsworthy hook to justify printing a strong photo image. These photos, sometimes called "wild" art because they're so free-form and unpredictable, can add life to pages where stories are dull and gray (sewer commission meetings, budget conferences, etc.). Stand-alone photos should be encouraged, but they must be packaged in a consistent style that instantly signals to readers that the photo stands alone.

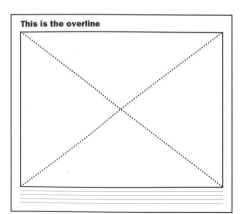

This is the overline

Some papers create a stand-alone photo style using an overline (a headline over the photo). The text, below, is larger than a standard cutline.

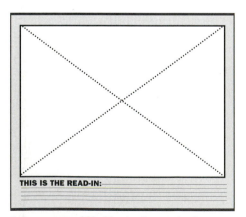

THIS IS THE READ-IN:

Some papers add bold rules for emphasis or run a screen in the background. Some start cutlines with boldface read-ins instead of using overlines.

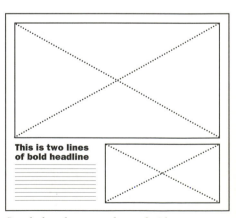

This is two lines of bold headline

Stand-alone boxes can be used with two or more photos. But as boxes grow bigger, you'll need to follow the guidelines for photo spreads.

PHOTO SPREADS

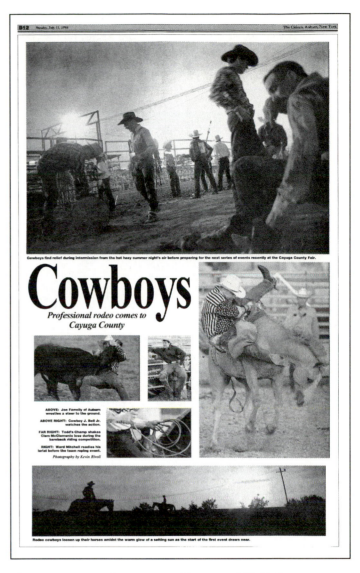

This photo page from The Citizen in Auburn, New York, tells a story of professional rodeo cowboys. Note the variety of shapes and sizes; note the balance and flow of the layout. As this paper's photo editor puts it: "Compelling, high-impact images help readers not only understand the story, but feel it."

Unlike the rest of the newspaper, where photos compete for space with text (and usually lose), photo spreads are self-contained visual packages that give special photos the big, bold play they deserve. They're usually used for:

◆ **Covering a major event** (a disaster, election night, The Big Game) from a wide variety of angles — often from several photographers.

◆ **Exploring a topic or trend** (the homeless, neo-Nazis, a skateboarding craze), taking readers on a tour of people and places they've never seen.

◆ **Profiling a personality** (an athlete, a disease victim, a politician), painting a portrait by capturing a person's moods, activities and surroundings.

◆ **Telling a story** with a definite beginning, middle and end (the birth of a baby, a Marine's ordeal in boot camp, an artist in the act of creation).

◆ **Displaying objects/places** (a tour of a new building, fall fashions, hot toys for Christmas), where photos catalog an inventory of items.

Photo spreads are different from standard news layouts. They bend and break the rules. They let you play with headlines and decks. They let you use unorthodox widths for cutlines and text. Text, in fact, often becomes a minor element on photo pages. Some pages use just a short text block; others use long stories, but jump most of the text to another page to maximize the photo display.

This Halloween page from The Oregonian displays an assortment of customized pumpkins and their creators. Since there's no storytelling here — no dramatic beginning, middle or end — the main design consideration is fitting all the photos onto the page in an orderly, attractive way.

PHOTO SPREADS

At many papers, photographers shoot special assignments, then design their own photo pages. Usually, however, the layout is done by an editor or designer who's handed some photos, given a headline and asked to leave room for a certain amount of text. Here's a typical example of how it works:

DESIGN EXERCISE: PHOTO SPREADS

Using these four photos, let's design a photo page for a tabloid. The photos were shot at a folk music festival, so the headline can simply say "Folk Fest." There's no story, but let's assume someone will write a short text block (3-4 inches) to describe the event. Cutlines can be written later.

This shot is the photographer's favorite. He wants it to be the dominant image on the page. And this is the way he'd like the photo cropped. You can make slight cropping changes to suit your layout, but you should always try to respect the composition suggested by the photographer.

Another nice shot. This little girl was a real crowd-pleaser, so be sure to run this photo big enough that we can see her.

This shot provides "color," showing the types of folks attending the folk festival. It's an appealing alternative to the performance shots. And besides, it's a vertical, and the layout needs at least one alternative to those other three horizontals.

This is the scene-setter (sometimes called an "establishing shot") showing the stage platform. As these four photos demonstrate, a good photo layout combines close-up, midrange and wide-angle shots to tell the whole story.

Here are six layouts using those photos from the facing page:

This layout alternates the sizes of photos — big, small, big, small — to achieve balance. Note how the page is bordered by two sets of outer margins: 1) a thin margin around the entire page, and 2) a wider indent beside the text and that vertical photo. Balancing two sets of indents gives you more flexibility in sizing photos and keeps pages from getting too dense.

FOLK FEST

Photos by Tim Jewett

FOLK FEST

Photos by Tim Jewett

This layout is a flopped variation (with minor changes) of the page at far left. The text runs in two legs instead of one, and there are now two pairs of shared cutlines. Notice how, of all the layouts on this page, this one is the most tightly packed. The rest all allow more air in their outer margins.

This layout treats the headline as an independent art element, placing it squarely in the center of the page, aligned with the two photos below it. The leg of text then runs beside it — an arrangement that might not work in a standard news story, but fits neatly here. Note how all the open space runs along the left edge of the page.

FOLK FEST

Photos by Tim Jewett

FOLK FEST

Photos by Tim Jewett

This page moves the text into a bottom corner. Since there's not enough text to fill the hole, it's indented (to match the photo indents on the right side of the page), and the photo credit pads the remaining space. Note how the text is indented more than the headline — a kind of hanging indent. A final note: Placing cutlines in a top corner sometimes looks awkward, but here it balances the cutline in the bottom corner of the page.

This design is a variation on the layout directly above. Placing the headline and text in the center of the layout divides the photos into two separate groups. Is that a problem? Regardless, the page looks well-balanced and appealing.

FOLK FEST

Photos by Tim Jewett

FOLK FEST

Photos by Tim Jewett

This approach is an old favorite: Park the scene-setter beside the headline at the top of the page, then smack readers with the loud lead photo. The text begins below the lead photo, directly beneath the headline. That breaks the usual rule about keeping headlines with text — but it works here. Note how the elements above and below the lead photo align with each other; all are indented equally along the edges of the page.

PHOTO SPREAD GUIDELINES

The following guidelines apply not just to photo pages but to feature sections and special news packages as well. You'll find that most of these principles hold true whether you're using photos, illustrations, charts or maps.

Note: You don't have to design picture pages with gray background screens; we just added screens to these examples to make the photo shapes easier to see.

PHOTO GUIDELINES

◆ **Talk to the photographer (and the reporter).** Learn about the story so you can prioritize the photos. Find out what's dominant, what's secondary, what's expendable. Make sure the page displays material fairly and accurately.

◆ **Mix it up.** Use different shapes. Different sizes. Different perspectives. Tell the story with a variety of visuals: horizontals and verticals, tight close-ups and wide-angle scene-setters. Keep things moving. Surprise our eyes.

 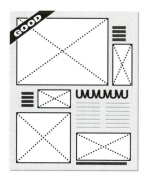

The layout at left looks static and dull because the photos are all similar in shape and size. Nothing grabs your eye. The page at right mixes shapes and sizes, and, as a result, looks interesting and inviting.

◆ **Design for quality, not quantity.** Yes, you want variety — but one good picture played well is worth two small ones played weakly. Mix it up, but be a tough judge. If you overcrowd the page, all the photos lose impact.

◆ **Position photos carefully.** Are photos strongly directional? (Don't let them collide or face off the page.) Are they sequential or chronological? (Give the page order — a beginning and an end, a setup and a punchline.)

◆ **Make one photo dominant.** Play it big. Give it clout. Anchor it solidly, *then* play the other photos off of it. And remember: Dominant photos usually work best in the top half of the layout:

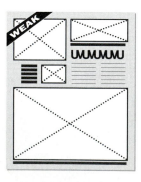 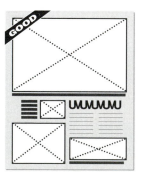

The layout at left seems bottom-heavy and poorly balanced. Compare that to the effect of the page at right. It uses the same elements, but here the lead photo has been dummied on top.

HEADLINE GUIDELINES

◆ **Write your headline first.** Pages look better and come together more easily if you have a headline *before* you start designing. If you leave a hole for someone to fill later, you may get a dull headline that doesn't quite fit.

◆ **Use a display headline (with a deck) if appropriate.** Don't limit yourself to standard banner headline styles. Try something with personality: a clever, punchy phrase with a descriptive deck below it. Create something bold. Don't be shy.

PHOTO SPREAD GUIDELINES

TEXT GUIDELINES

◆ **Don't run too much text — or too little.** Most photo pages need text to explain why they're there. But anything under 3 inches may get buried; huge text blocks, on the other hand, turn the page gray and crowd out photos.

◆ **Keep text blocks modular.** Never snake text over, around and through a maze of photos. Keep text rectangular. Park it neatly in a logical place.

◆ **Ask for leeway on story sizes.** Sure, you dummy as closely as you can, but those 17.3-inch stories sometimes *have* to be cut — or padded — to fit. Make sure writers and editors give you a little flexibility on story lengths.

CUTLINE GUIDELINES

◆ **Give every photo a cutline.** Two photos may share a cutline if the layout requires it, but make sure it's clear which description fits which photo.

◆ **Add flexibility by running cutlines beside or between photos.** But don't float them loosely — plant them flush against the photo they describe. If cutlines use ragged type, run ragged edges *away* from the photo.

◆ **Push cutlines to the outside.** In weak designs, cutlines butt against headlines or text. In strong designs, cutlines move to the outside of the page, where they won't collide with other type elements:

   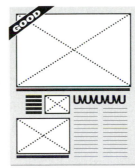

In the layout at left, one set of cutlines butts against the headline; another bumps into the bottom of a leg of text. Both problems have been fixed in the layout at right, where the cutlines have been moved to the outside.

◆ **Credit photos properly.** You can do this by dummying a credit line along the outer edge of the design, or by attaching credit lines to each photo (or just to the lead photo, if they're all shot by the same photographer).

OTHER DESIGN ADVICE

◆ **Add a little white space.** Don't cram text and photos into every square pica. Let the page breathe with what's called "white space" or "air." But don't trap dead space between elements; push it to the outside of the page:

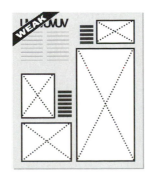   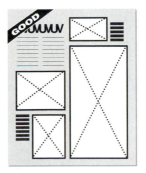

Note how pockets of dead space seem scattered through the page at left. At right, all the extra space has been pushed to the outer edges of the layout. As a result, the elements fit more neatly.

◆ **Use an underlying grid.** Don't just scatter shapes arbitrarily. A good grid aligns elements evenly and maintains consistent margins throughout the page.

◆ **Use screens sparingly.** A gray background screen can help organize and enhance layouts. But too much gray makes pages drab — so be careful.

STUDIO SHOTS

Photojournalism is an honest craft. It records real people in real situations, without poses or props. But suppose you need a photo of a hot new bikini. A plate of food. An album cover. Will that photo be *real, honest* photojournalism?

Not exactly. It's a studio shot. And unlike news photos, where photographers document events passively, studio shots let photographers manipulate objects, pose models, create props and control lighting.

Studio shots — or any other set-up photos, whether they're shot in a studio or not — are used primarily in features, and primarily for:

◆ **Fashion.** Clothes by themselves are dull; clothes worn by a model who smiles, struts or flirts will yank readers into the page.

◆ **Food.** Making food look delicious in a 2-column black-and-white photo is tougher than you think, but absolutely necessary for food stories.

◆ **Portraits.** Special faces deserve special treatment. Studio shots let you glamorize the subjects of those in-depth personality profiles.

◆ **Incidental objects.** Remember, it's important to show readers the actual album covers, book jackets and new products mentioned in features and reviews. *Show* — don't just tell.

MORE ON ▶

◆ **Photo cutouts:** *How to turn studio shots (like the fashion model at left) into silhouettes* **178**

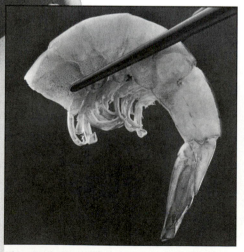

This simple yet striking shrimp-and-chopsticks photo was shot against a black background.

A portrait of Bud Clark, former mayor of Portland (the Rose City — hence the flower).

PHOTO ILLUSTRATIONS

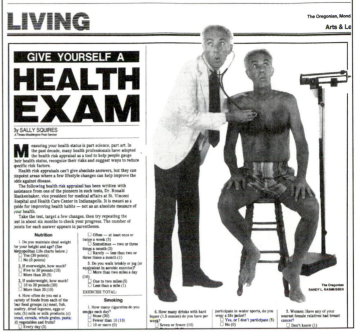

This award-winning photo (by T. J. Hamilton of The Grand Rapids Press) illustrates a feature story on the parental pressures of raising children. It's cute and compelling — and it perfectly complements the story's "Handle With Care" headline.

Sometimes the best way to illustrate a feature story is to create a photograph where actors or props are posed to make a point — as if it were a drawing. The result is called a *photo illustration.*

Photo illustrations are usually studio shots (see previous page). But unlike fashion photos or portraits, photo illustrations don't simply present an image; they express an idea, capture a mood, symbolize a concept, tell a visual joke.

Photo illustrations are often excellent solutions for topical features where the themes are abstract — depression, love in the workplace, junk-food junkies — stories where real photos of real people would be too difficult to find or too dull to print.

A good photo illustration:

◆ **Instantly shows what the story's about.** A photo illustration shouldn't confuse or distract readers. It should present one clean, clear idea that requires no guess-work (and avoids misleading meanings). And it *must* match the tone and content of the text.

◆ **Should never be mistaken for reality.** Most newspaper photos are honest: They show real people doing real things. Readers expect that. So if you're going to change the rules and present a false image, make it immediately obvious. Distort angles, exaggerate sizes, manipulate lighting, use odd-looking models — do *something* to cue the reader that this photo isn't authentic. It's dishonest to pass off a posed photo (someone pretending to be a drug addict) as the real thing. Even warning readers in a cutline isn't good enough; once a photo makes its impact on a reader, the damage is done.

◆ **Works with the headline.** The photo and the headline must form a unit. They must work together to convey *one* idea, not two.

◆ **Performs with flair.** A good photo illustration displays the photographer's skill and cleverness with camera angles, lighting, special effects, poses and props. In a world where newspaper graphics compete against slick TV and magazine ads, you either excel or you lose. If your photo illustration looks bland and uninspired, you lose.

This photo-illustration is a humorous depiction of the story's headline. To exaggerate the point, the head of the seated model has been pasted onto the doctor's body (note the comical expression on the model's face). Computer programs now make this kind of image manipulation easy.

ILLUSTRATIONS

Newspapers are packed with illustrations. Some aim to amuse (comics, for instance). Some appear in ads, selling tires and TVs. Some promote stories in teasers. Some jazz up graphics and logos.

And then there are more ambitious illustrations, the ones that (like photos) require more space, more collaboration between writers, editors and designers — and bigger budgets.

Here's a quick look at the most common types of newspaper illustrations:

COMMENTARY & CARICATURE

The first illustration ever printed in an American newspaper was an editorial cartoon in Ben Franklin's Pennsylvania Gazette. It showed a dismembered snake, with each section representing one of the 13 colonies. It carried the caption "JOIN or DIE".

Editorial cartoons have gotten a lot funnier since then. Today, they're expected to be humorous, yet thoughtful; provocative, yet tasteful; far-fetched, yet truthful. That's why editorial cartooning is one of the toughest jobs in journalism — and why successful editorial cartoonists are rare.

This editorial cartoon, by Jack Ohman of The Oregonian, relies on a hip drawing style, crisp hand lettering and a wicked sense of satire.

A similar type of illustration, the commentary drawing, also interprets current events. Like editorial cartoons, commentary drawings usually run on a separate opinion page. Unlike editorial cartoons, commentary drawings accompany a story or analysis, rather than standing alone. They don't try as hard to be funny, but still employ symbols and caricatures to comment on personalities and issues.

A goofy caricature of goofy comedian David Letterman. Artist Ron Coddington has exaggerated Dave's gap-toothed grin to an absurd extreme (and note bandleader Paul Shaffer tucked beneath Dave's arm).

Caricatures, however, aren't limited to opinion pages. They're often used on sports or entertainment pages to accompany profiles of well-known celebrities. A good caricature exaggerates its subject's most distinctive features for comic effect. Like editorial cartooning, it's a skill that's difficult to master, and should be avoided if:

◆ The subject's face isn't very well-known.
◆ The story is too sensitive or downbeat for a brash style of art.
◆ The artist's ability to pull it off is doubtful.

ILLUSTRATIONS

**FLAVOR
DRAWINGS**

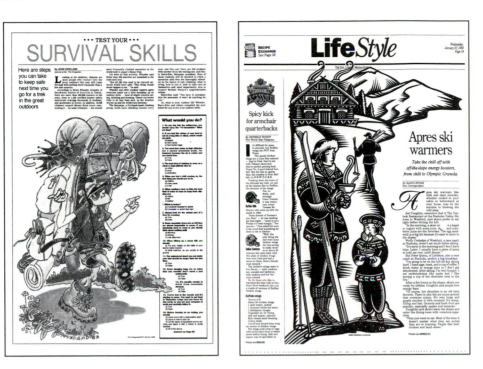

This comical cartoon of a happy hiker ran in The Oregonian. It immediately clues readers what the story's about: an upbeat IQ test for campers heading to the woods. A realistic hiking photo wouldn't have been as appealing as Pat McLelland's drawing.

The lead story on this food page (from The Sun in Lowell, Mass.) discusses the diets of skiers — and this illustration captures the flavor of traditional New England with a woodcut-style drawing of a mother and child sharing steaming bowls of soup.

Feature pages often focus on abstract concepts: drugs, depression, dreams, diets, and so on. Many of those concepts are too vague or elusive to capture in a photograph.

That's where illustrations can save the day. Flavor drawings — drawings that interpret the tone of a topic — add impact to the text while giving focus to the design.

Finding the right approach to use in an illustration takes practice — both for artists and editors. But flavor drawings can be silly or serious, colorful or black-and-white. They can dominate the page or simply drop into a column of text to provide quick diversion.

Be careful, however, not to overload your pages with cartoons. Readers want *information,* not decoration. They can sense when you're simply filling space.

**CLIP
ART**

Illustrations are terrific — *if* you have the budget to hire artists or pay for free-lance artwork. But what if you don't?

Advertisers have had that problem for years. And when they need images of generic-looking people and products to spruce up their ads, they often use *clip art:* copyright-free cartoons and drawings.

Clip art is popular and cheap. You can buy catalogs and computer disks containing hundreds of, say, holiday images (Santas, turkeys, pumpkins and valentines) at ridiculously low prices.

For a classier look, you can "borrow" historic old engravings, like the one at right, from books that call themselves "pictorial archives." And those classic images can be evocative and effective.

But be careful. Clip art usually looks lowbrow. At its worst, it's *extremely* cheesy. You want your stories to look like news, not like ads for pizzas and power tools.

A CHECKLIST: FINDING FEATURE ART

Feature pages require good art. To produce good art, you need good ideas. And you need those good ideas *before* stories are written, *before* photos are shot, *before* you start to design the page. Begin searching for ideas before deadline pressures force you to take shortcuts.

Stumped on how to illustrate a page? The following checklist can help guide you to the graphic heart of a feature story:

PHOTO SOLUTIONS

■ Can we <u>shoot</u> photos?

Can we illustrate this story photojournalistically — showing real people in real situations? Look for:

❏ Events:
What events or actions are connected with this story? What do the main characters *do* that's interesting? (A reminder: Talking, thinking and sitting at a desk are *not* interesting.) What can readers do after they've finished the story?

❏ People:
Who is the key player? Are there several? What kind of portrait shows us the most about them? What emotions do they experience in this story? Can one mood-oriented portrait convey the idea? Is there a situation where emotions and actions intersect?

❏ Places:
Can location/setting help tell the story, either:
• With a main character posed in a dramatic location?
• With several main characters working or interacting?
• Without people (focusing instead on buildings or scenery?

❏ Objects:
What items are integral to the story? Examples:
• Machines
• Tools & equipment
• Works of art
• Vehicles
• Clothing
Can they be used as lead art? Turned into a diagram? Explained in detail in a sidebar?

■ Can we <u>obtain</u> photos (from an outside source)?

❏ A wire service?

❏ Other media (TV networks, professional or student newspapers, film studios)?

❏ Organizations (government offices, museums, clubs, stores, companies mentioned in the story)?

❏ The newsroom library? A local library?

❏ The personal archives of people in the story?

❏ Books or magazines (with approval from the publisher or copyright holder)?

❏ Stock photo services?

If photos won't tell the story, then you should consider:

ART SOLUTIONS/PHOTO ILLUSTRATIONS

■ Does the story focus on an abstract topic? Can one strong image capture that topic and anchor the page? Or are several smaller images needed?

■ Should we create a:

❏ *Drawing?* (Is an artist available? Or do we prefer the realism of a photo?)

❏ *Photo illustration?* (Is a photographer available? Or do we want a freer, more fanciful solution?)

To pull strong images out of the story, try to:

■ Write a headline. A clever headline will often inspire a graphic hook. Before you begin sketching art ideas, wander through the story and look for key words and phrases. Loosen up and noodle around with:

❏ Puns. *Give Peas a Chance. The Noel Prizes. Art and Sole.*

❏ Alliteration and rhyme. *FAX Facts. High-Tech Home Ec. Tool Time.*

❏ TV, movie or song titles. *Born to Run. The Right Stuff. All in the Family. Rebel Without a Clue. Running on Empty. Home Alone.*

❏ Popular quotes, proverbs or slang expressions.

❏ A quote or phrase lifted from the text of the story.

❏ A key word from the story: A name *(Skipper).* A place *(Gilligan's Island).* An emotion *(The Crying Game).* A sound or feeling *(Yum!).*

A CHECKLIST: FINDING FEATURE ART

No headline yet? Or is it clever, but still vague?

■ **Brainstorm images.** Wander through your topic again, but this time compile a list of concepts, symbols, visual cliches. Analyze the story in terms of:

❏ **Who.** What personality types (or stereotypes) are involved? How can you exaggerate their personalities? Are there victims? Villains? Can you use props or symbols to represent people in the story?

❏ **What.** What objects, feelings or actions are involved? What cliches or symbols come to mind? Isolate them. Mix 'n' match them. What happens if you exaggerate or distort them? See anything humorous? Dramatic?

❏ **When.** When does the action occur? Are there moments when the topic is most dramatic or humorous? At what times does the topic begin or end? What was the history of this topic?

❏ **Where.** Where does this topic occur? Where does it start? Finish? If you were filming a movie, what dramatic angles or close-ups would you use?

❏ **Why.** What does this story mean? What's the end result, the ultimate effect? What's the reason people do it, dread it, love it? And why should we care?

Once you've compiled a list of images, try to combine them in different ways. View them from different angles. Or try these approaches:

❏ **Parody.** There's a world of symbols and cliches out there waiting to be recycled. Some are universal: an egg (frailty, rebirth), a light bulb (creativity), a test tube (research), a gun (danger), an apple (education). You can play with the flag, dollar bills, road signs, game boards. Or parody cultural icons: The Statue of Liberty. The Thinker. Uncle Sam. "American Gothic."

❏ **Combination.** Two images can combine to form a fresh new idea. If your story's about people trapped by credit cards, create a credit-card mousetrap. If your story's about some puzzle at City Hall, create a City Hall jigsaw puzzle. And so on.

❏ **Exaggeration.** Distort size, speed, emotion, repetition. Is there a BIG problem looming? Is something shrinking? Fading? Taken to an extreme, what would this subject look like? How would affected people look?

❏ **Montage.** Arrange a scrapbook of images: photos, artifacts, old engravings from library books. Try to create order, interplay or point of view.

OTHER GRAPHICS SOLUTIONS

By now, you may have found a solution that seems like pure genius to you. But beware: Ideas don't always translate into reality. Your solution must work instantly for hundreds of readers. So before you proceed, run a rough sketch past your colleagues to test their reactions. If it doesn't fly, drop it.

Remember, too: Informational art is usually better than decorational art. Will your illustration inform, or is it just a silly cartoon? Does it make a point, or convey fuzzy emotion? Is it big simply because you need to fill space?

You can still salvage your idea — but consider using it along with:

❏ **Infographics.** Dress up charts, graphs, maps or diagrams as lead or secondary art. Show your readers how things work, what they mean, where they're headed. Use the design to teach — not just entertain.

❏ **Sidebars** (with or without art). You can create lists, glossaries, how-to's, polls (see our list on page 145). If you add enough art (mug shots, diagrams, book jackets, products, etc.) you can make a sidebar carry the whole page.

❏ **Big, bold type effects.** Often a display headline that's big and bold enough can serve as a page's dominant element — you could even work a piece of art *into* the headline. Or how about starting the text with a jumbo initial cap?

❏ **Mug shots and liftout quotes.** Drop these in wherever pages look gray. Or play them up as dominant elements by adding rules, screens, shadows. Or group a series of mug/quotes in a bold, colorful way.

If you're still trying to dress things up, try a combination of boxes, screens or background wallpaper effects. This is just fancy footwork, however — a way of distracting the reader to disguise your lack of art.

■ **A FINAL WARNING:** If you've come this far and still don't have a solid solution, re-think your story. If it's too vague for you, it's probably too vague for readers.

RISKY BUSINESS

*In your search for
The Ultimate Page Design,
you may be tempted to try
some of these effects.
But before you do, read on.*

 STEALING ▶

Before you "borrow" an image from an outside source, be sure you're not violating copyright laws. Old art (like the Mona Lisa) is safe; copyrighted art can be used if it accompanies a review or a breaking news story. But copyright laws are complex — as are laws governing the reprinting of money* — so get good advice before you plunge into unfamiliar territory.

◀ FRAMING

There are dozens of decorative border tapes. Books full of fancy frames. Computer programs loaded with clip art. Someday, you'll succumb to temptation and destroy an elegant image with a gaudy, glitzy frame. Don't do it. Art and photos should be bordered with thin, simple rules. Anything thick, ornate or colorful just distracts readers' attention from what's important.

FLOPPING ▶

Printing a photo backward, as a mirror image of itself, is called *flopping.* Usually, it's done because a designer wants a photo facing the opposite direction, to better suit a layout. But that's dangerous. It distorts the truth of the image. *Never* flop news photos; flop feature photos or studio shots *only* as a last resort, and only if there's no way to tell you've done it.

◀ RESHAPING

As we've learned, photos work best as rectangles with right-angle corners. Cutting them into other "creative" shapes distorts their meaning, confuses readers and clutters up the page. Put simply: Slicing up photos is the mark of an amateur. There's rarely a valid reason for doing it, so put the idea right out of your mind.

TILTING ▶

Sometimes you get art that's so wild, so wacky, you just *must* give it an equally nutty layout. OK — but beware. Unless you choose appropriate art, tilt it at just the right angle and skew the type smoothly, you'll trash the page. Even though pros try it once in a while (see page 182), remember: Tilting can be treacherous.

◀ SILHOUETTING

If a photo is weakened by a distracting background, you may consider cutting out the central image and running it either against the white page or with a new background. That works well with some photos, poorly with others — but should be considered *only* for feature pages. For more advice and warnings, see page 178.

**For instance,
dollar bills can only
be reproduced with black ink; they
must be enlarged to 150% or more,
or reduced to 75% or less.*

EXERCISES

ANSWERS ▶ 204

1 Below are four photos that accompany a story about a woman jockey. Using all four, create a full-page photo spread for a broadsheet feature section, with the headline "On the fast track" (and you'll need to add a deck below the headline, as well). The story is very long, so assume you can jump as much text as you need.

Crop the photos as you see fit. But before you begin, ask yourself: Which photo should be dominant?

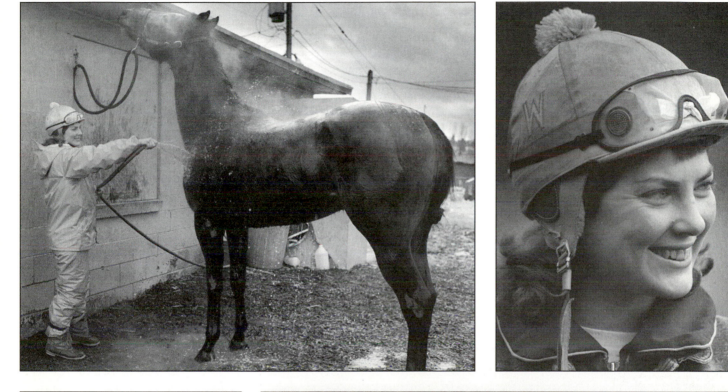

EXERCISES

2 The photos for that woman jockey spread (previous page) were good, both in content and technical quality. But if you were the photo editor for that page, and there was time to go back and shoot more photos, what might you ask for? What's missing?

3 The three layouts below were created from those jockey photos. Can you find at least three things wrong with each of these page designs?

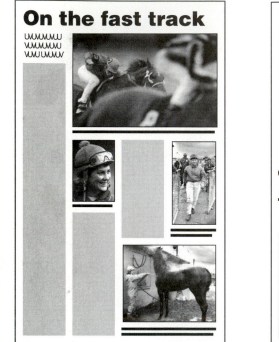

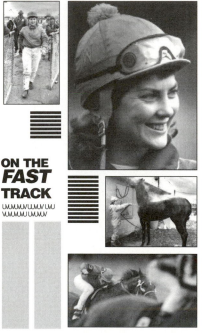

4 **A.** At left is a full-frame photo from a local drug bust. How would you crop this shot if you were using it as a horizontal lead photo?

B. Now that you've cropped it, what will its new depth be if its width becomes 45 picas?

ANSWERS ▶ 204

A newspaper is a product — like corn flakes. Like corn flakes, newspapers are good for you. Like corn flakes, newspapers are a part of America's breakfast routine. And like corn flakes, newspapers seem pretty similar from one brand to another.

So how do you make *your* brand of corn flakes tastier to consumers? You dress it up in a colorful box. Design a snappy-looking name. Play up a catchy promotion *(FREE WHISTLE INSIDE!)* or lift out some quotable phrase ("High-fiber nutrition with real blueberry goodness") to catch the eye of passing shoppers. Finally, you stick in all the extras that are required to be there — ingredients, the date, the company address — as neatly and unobtrusively as you can.

All that holds true for newspapers, too. And in this chapter, we'll examine the graphic nuts and bolts used to assemble newspapers: logos, flags, bylines, decks, teasers, liftout quotes and more.

Previously, we looked at ways to design individual stories. In this chapter, we'll explain how to label and connect related stories. How to break up deep columns of gray text. How to add graphic devices that sell stories to readers.

In other words, how to pack more real corn goodness into every bite.

Weather

Partly cloudy. Winds NW 10-15 mph. High 70, low 40. Details on **2A**

THE FLAG

It's one of journalism's oldest traditions: centering the *flag* (or *nameplate*) at the very top of Page One. And though newspapers often search for alternatives — boxing it in a corner, flipping it sideways, floating it partway down the page — most papers choose the simplest solution: Anchor the flag front and center, and hope it lends the page a little dignity.

Most designers have little input when it comes to flags, which get overhauled maybe once every few decades, if that often. (Flags, incidentally, are often mistakenly called "mastheads." But a masthead is the staff box full of publication data that usually runs on the editorial page.)

There are two contrasting philosophies of flag design. One insists that flags should evoke a sense of tradition, trust, sobriety — and indeed, most Old English flags look downright *religious*. But others argue that flags are like corporate logos and should look fresh, innovative, graphically sophisticated. (Some try to play it both ways: conservative, yet a bit hip.)

Ponder the flags below. Do they offer clues to their papers' personalities?

Some papers float their flag in white space to give it prominence. Others add *ears* (text or graphic elements in the corners beside the flag) to fill the space. Papers stick a variety of items in their ears: weather reports, slogans ("All the News That's Fit to Print") or teasers promoting features inside the paper:

What's essential in a flag? The name of the paper. The city, school or organization it serves. The date. The price. The edition *(First, Westside, Sunrise),* if different editions are printed. Some papers include the volume number — but though that may matter to librarians, readers don't keep score.

LOGOS & SIGS

STANDING HEADS & SECTION LOGOS

As you journey through a newspaper, you pass signposts that tell you where you are. Some are like big billboards ("Now entering **LIVING**"). Others are like small road signs ("Exit here for *Movie Review*").

Every paper needs a well-coordinated system of signposts — or, as they're often called, *standing heads* or *headers*. Just as highway signposts are designed to stand apart from the scenery, standing heads are designed to "pop" off the page. They can use rules, bold type, extra leading, screens or reverses — but it's essential that they project a personality that differs from the ordinary text and headlines they accompany.

Compare, for example, these two headers or *section logos:*

This section logo uses the same typeface as the headlines — they're both the same size and weight, too. There's nothing to set the headers apart from the day's news; the logos don't "pop" off the page.

WEAK

Living & Life

Oat bran: the silent killer?

GOOD

LIVELY LIVING

Oat bran: the silent killer?

Here, the section logo looks entirely different from the headline below. It uses a condensed serif font, all caps. It's screened, with a thin drop shadow. And a thick rule sets the header apart from the live stories downpage.

A *logo* is a title or name that's customized in a graphic way. Logos can be created with type alone, or by adding rules, photos or other art elements.

Section logos, like those above, help departmentalize the paper. In small tabloids, they should appear atop the page each time the topic changes (from Features to Opinion, for instance). Bigger papers use section logos to identify each separate section, often adding teasers to promote what's inside:

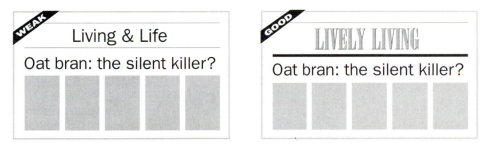

Some papers use standing heads to label the content on every page. Others reserve that treatment for special themed pages or feature packages (*Super Bowl XXXIV Preview* or *AIDS in Our Schools: A Special Report*).

Either way, those added signposts guide readers most effectively when they're designed and positioned consistently throughout the paper, in a graphic style that sets them apart from the "live" news.

LOGOS & SIGS

As we've just seen, section logos and page headers label entire sections and pages. But labels are necessary for special stories, too. And these labels for stories are simply called *logos, sigs* or *bugs.*

Story logos are usually small enough to park within a leg of text. But whatever their size, they need to be designed with:

◆ A graphic personality that sets them apart from text and headlines;

◆ A consistent style that's maintained throughout the paper; and

◆ Flexible widths that work well in any design context.

It's important to dummy logos where they'll label a story's content without confusing its layout — which means they shouldn't disrupt the flow of text or collide against other elements.

Here are some of the most common ways to dummy logos with stories:

In multi-column layouts, sigs and logos are usually dummied at the top of the second leg so they won't interrupt the flow of the text. Avoid running mug shots or photos in that second leg — the logo will look odd whether dummied above or below other art, and both images will fight for the reader's attention.

In vertical layouts, sigs and logos are either dummied above the headline or indented a few inches down into the text. Indenting logos is tricky, though, since text should be at least 6 picas wide — which doesn't leave room for long words in a logo.

Instead of placing sigs and logos down in the text, some papers use headers that stretch above the headline, usually running the full width of the story. This is a very clean, clear way to label special features, but it takes up more space than the other formats — and doesn't do much to break up gray legs of text.

COLUMN LOGOS

Column logos are a way to label special writers, those regularly appearing personalities whose names and faces deserve prominent display. These logos (also called *photo sigs*) are usually reserved for writers who express opinions — writers whose columns, for whatever reason, create a reader habit. (To support that reader habit, then, it's important to dummy the column in the same style and the same place each time it runs.)

Column logos usually consist of:

◆ The writer's name.

◆ The writer's likeness (either a photo or a sketch).

◆ A catchy title: *Dear Abby, Screen Scene* or (yawn) *On the Town.*

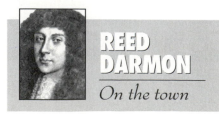

LOGOS & SIGS

SIGS & BUGS

Column logos promote the personalities of *writers*. Sigs and bugs, on the other hand, identify *topics*. They're a functional yet decorative typographic treatment that's used to label:

◆ Briefs and non-standard news columns *(Business Notes, People, World Roundup).*

◆ Opinion pieces that appear on news pages *(News Analysis, Movie Review).*

◆ Regularly appearing features *(NBA Notebook, Letter to the Editor, Money Matters, Action Line!).*

At some papers, there's even a trend toward labeling more and more stories by topic *(City Council, Medicine, Tennis).* That's difficult to do consistently throughout the paper — quick, what's a one-word label for a story about two jets that nearly collide? — but when it works, it's a helpful way to guide busy readers from topic to topic.

Other papers use sigs that refer to stories on other pages or include fast facts (as in that bottom movie review sig at right).

Sigs can be designed in a variety of sizes and styles, adding rules, screens or graphic effects to catch readers' eyes. But every paper should use a consistent graphic treatment for all its logos. That means the style you use for POP MUSIC should also be appropriate for OBITUARIES.

MOVIE REVIEW

Ghostbusters 3
★★★

Starring: Bill Murray, Dan Aykroyd, Sigourney Weaver
Director: Ivan Reitman
Rating: PG for language, nudity, slime
Now showing at: Mall City Octoplex

MORE ON ▶

◆ **Fast-fact boxes:** *Ideas for capsulizing information like that movie review box below* **146**

SERIES LOGOS

Series logos are a way to label special packages (a five-day series on *Racism in the Classroom*) or stories that will continue to unfold over an extended period (like *Election '96* or *Revolt in China.*)

Series logos (called icons at some papers) usually consist of:

◆ A catchy title that creates instant reader familiarity.

◆ A small illustration or photo that graphicizes the topic.

◆ Optional refer lines to other pages or to tomorrow's installment.

Logos are usually one column wide or indented into the text — and as these examples from The Detroit Free Press show, they come in a variety of styles:

LIFTOUT QUOTES

" I don't care what is written about me, so long as it isn't true.

— KATHARINE HEPBURN

"

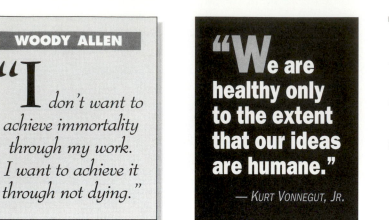

WOODY ALLEN

"*I don't want to achieve immortality through my work. I want to achieve it through not dying.*"

"**W**e are healthy only to the extent that our ideas are humane."

— KURT VONNEGUT, JR.

"If I repent of anything, it is very likely to be my good behavior. What demon possessed me that I behaved so well?"

— Henry David Thoreau

"The surest way to make a monkey of a man," said Robert Benchley, "is to quote him." And a sure way to make readers curious about a story is to insert a wise, witty or controversial quote into a column of text.

As the examples above show, liftout quotes can be packaged in a variety of styles, enhanced with rules, boxes, screens or reverses. (They're known by a variety of names, too: *pull quotes, breakouts, quoteblocks, quote sandwiches,* etc.) But whether simple or ornate, liftout quotes should follow these guidelines:

◆ **They should be quotations.** Not paraphrases, not decks, not narration from the text — but complete sentences spoken by someone in the story.

◆ **They should be attributed.** Don't run "mystery quotes" that force us to comb the text for the speaker's identity. Tell us who's doing the talking.

◆ **They should be bigger and bolder than text type.** Don't be shy. Use a liftout style that pops from the page to catch the reader's eye— something distinctive that won't be mistaken for a headline or subhead.

◆ **They should be 1-2 inches deep.** Shallower than that, they seem too terse and trivial; deeper than that, they seem too dense and wordy.

COMBINING QUOTES & MUGS

Words of wisdom are attractive. And when we see the speaker's face, we're attracted even more. That's why mug/quote combinations are among the best ways to hook passing readers.

Quotes with mugs can be boxed or unboxed, screened or unscreened. Whatever style you adopt, adapt it to run both horizontally (in 2- or 3-column widths) and vertically (in 1-column widths or indented within a column). Be sure the format's wide enough, and the type small enough, to fit long words without hyphenation.

"*People have got to know whether or not their President is a crook. Well, I am not a crook.*"

— RICHARD NIXON

sound bites

"It's been an extraordinary life. I just wish that I had been there to enjoy it."

SYLVESTER STALLONE

LIFTOUT QUOTES

GUIDELINES FOR DUMMYING LIFTOUTS

◆ Be sure you have a quote worth lifting *before* you dummy it in. You can't expect great quotes to materialize automatically — some stories, after all, don't even *use* any quotations.

Read the story first. Or talk to the reporter. Remember, once you develop the habit of promoting great quotes, it encourages reporters to *find* more great quotes. As a result, both stories and readers will benefit.

◆ Don't sprinkle liftouts randomly through the text just to kill space:

That's too distracting. For maximum impact and better balance, dummy quotes symmetrically (below left). Or create a point/counterpoint effect with two mugs (center). Or combine multiple liftouts into an attractive quote package (right).

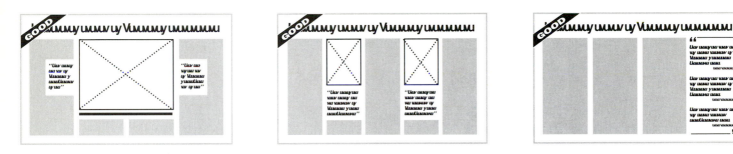

◆ Never force readers to read around *any* 2- or 3-column impediment; text that jumps back and forth like that gets too confusing (below left). It's OK to interrupt a leg of text with a 1-column liftout, but use 2-column liftouts *only* at the top of the text (center). As an alternative, you might try indenting a window for the liftout, then wrapping the text around it (right).

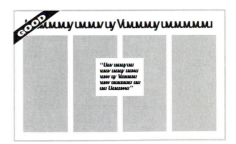

◆ Keep liftout quotes as typographically tidy as you can. Avoid partial quotes, parentheses, hyphenation, ellipses and widows.

The liftout below actually ran in a student newspaper. The editors probably thought they were keeping the quote accurate, but the distracting typography killed the quote's readability:

"... possible enhancements (such as) ... an essay as a direct measurement of writ-ing skill..."

MORE ON ▶

◆ **Making stories fit**
by adding liftout quotes 80

◆ **Quote packages:**
Special treatments for collections of quotes 150

◆ **Skews and text wraps:** *Guidelines for dummying special type effects* 176

DECKS & SUMMARIES

One of the most persistent problems in all of newspapering is The Headline That Doesn't Exactly Make Sense:

Schools bill falls

Copy editors are only human, usually, so headlines like that are inevitable. But one way to make headlines more intelligible — especially on important stories — is to add a *deck* below the headline to explain things further:

Schools bill falls
Senate vetoes plan to finance classes by taxing cigarettes

This example uses a 36-point boldface headline and an 18-point lightface deck. Decks are most effective in lightweight or italic faces that contrast with the main headline. In news stories, they're usually set flush left in the first leg of text.

Quite often, decks make more sense than headlines. Which shows you how valuable they can be.

Years ago, papers stacked decks in deep rows (see example, page 24). Today, most use only one deck per story. Decks for news stories are often 3-4 lines (6-12 words); decks for features are generally longer (10-30 words).

Some editors think decks are a waste of space and use them only as filler when stories come up short. That's a mistake. Since most readers browse the paper by scanning headlines, it's easy to see that a good head + deck combination adds meaning — and increases readership.

BASIC DECK GUIDELINES

◆ **Use decks for all long or important stories.** Remember, readers are more likely to plunge into a gray sea of text if they know in advance what it's about.

◆ **Use decks with all hammer or display headlines.** It's fine to write a clever feature headline like "Heavy Mental." But if you don't add a deck to explain what that *means,* readers may not appreciate your cleverness.

◆ **Give decks contrast — in size and weight.** By sizing decks noticeably smaller than headlines, they'll be easier to write. They'll convey more information. And they'll look more graceful (as magazines discovered long ago). Though most papers devise their own systems of deck sizing, decks generally run from 14 to 24 points, depending on the size of the headline they accompany.

For added contrast, most papers use either italic decks (with roman heads) or lightface decks (with regular or boldface heads). Whatever your paper's style, it's important to set the deck apart — with both spacing and typography — from the headline and the text.

◆ **Stack decks at the start of the story.** Don't bury them in the text, stick them in some corner or banner them across the full width of the page. Decks are functional, not decorative. Put them to work where they'll lead readers into the text — usually in the first leg (though in wider layouts, 2-column decks work fine).

In fancy feature layouts, you can be more creative. But that comes later.

DECKS & SUMMARIES

SUMMARY DECKS

Some papers call them *summaries*. Others call them *nut grafs*. Either way, they're more than just downsized decks. They're a response to busy readers who say, *I'm in a hurry — why should I care about this story?*

In 1987, The Oregonian became the first major U.S. daily to add summaries to all key stories on section fronts. Today, hundreds of papers use them on all their stories, as a way to distill the content of the text into 20-30 words:

MORE ON ▶

◆ **Headlines:** *Different styles of headlines and how to size them* **24**

◆ **Display headlines:** *How to add variety to feature headlines ...* **84**

◆ **Fast-fact boxes:** *How they summarize stories for readers in a hurry* **142**

Compare this headline/ deck combination with the one on the facing page. Which offers more information at a glance? This example uses 13-point type. It begins with a dingbat to catch your eye (and to distinguish the summary from the text that follows).

Schools bill falls

■ By a 78-12 vote, the Ohio Senate rejects a plan to finance classes by adding a 10-cent tax on each pack of cigarettes sold this year

The simplest way to create a summary is to write a longer-than-usual deck using smaller-than-usual type. But some papers try more creative approaches, both in the typography they use and in the way they highlight information:

This summary uses a boldface lead-in to highlight key words — followed by more detailed summary material in contrasting lightface type.

TAX PLAN DEFEATED: By a 78-12 vote, the Ohio Senate rejects a plan to finance classes by adding a 10-cent tax on each package of cigarettes sold this year

BRIEFLY

Background: To compensate for a projected $3 million budget shortfall, the Ohio Senate debated a plan to finance classes by adding a 10-cent tax on each pack of cigarettes you buy.

What it means: By rejecting the bill 78-12, the Senate may force drastic school budget cuts.

This summary reverses BRIEFLY in a bar, then uses boldface key words to set up a detailed summary of the story. The type is 9-point — which may be a bit small for a deck like this.

SUMMARY GUIDELINES

◆ **Don't rehash the headline and the lead.** Each element — the main headline, the summary and the lead of the story — should add something different to the reader's overall understanding. That means you should avoid repeating words or phrases; more importantly, it means writing those three elements as a single unit, with a flow of logic that leads the reader smoothly into the text.

In many newsrooms, the writer of the story contributes the wording for the headline and summary. That's an excellent way to maintain accuracy and avoid redundancy.

◆ **Use conversational language.** Summaries should be complete declarative sentences in the present tense. Unlike traditional decks, summaries are couched in a reader-friendly, conversational style. As the examples above show, there's no need to eliminate articles *(a, an, the)*, relative pronouns or contractions.

Don't be stodgy or pretentious. Avoid obscure words or jargon. Simple words always work best — and short words will make hyphenation unnecessary.

◆ **Don't worry about bad breaks.** Those traditional rules of headline-writing don't apply here. A subject can be on one line, a verb on the next. Nobody will care if an infinitive is split between lines. But *do* avoid leaving a widow on that last line.

◆ **Feel free to improvise.** Many papers add quotes or mug shots to summaries, transforming them into graphic elements. How far is *your* paper willing to go?

BYLINES

To reporters, bylines are the most important graphic element in the entire newspaper. What a shame, then, that readers rarely give bylines a glance as their eyes leap from the end of the headline to the start of the story.

It's necessary, though, to give credit where credit is due (especially when readers have complaints or questions about a story). Papers differ on byline policies, but most put reporters' names on stories of any substance — i.e., stories more than 6 inches long.

Bylines generally run at the start of the story in a style that sets them apart from the text (often achieved with boldface, italics, or one or two rules). The first line gives the reporter's name; a second line tells whether he or she writes for an outside organization (The Associated Press, for example), works as a free-lancer (often labeled a "special writer" or "correspondent") or belongs on the staff (most papers run either the name of the paper or the writer's title).

Every newspaper should adopt one standard byline style. Some examples:

By MOE HOWARD
The Daily Planet

By Larry Fine
THE DAILY PLANET FILM CRITIC

By CURLY HOWARD
Staff writer

Student newspapers often use loud, eye-catching byline styles, perhaps as a bribe to lure reporters onto the staff. Screened, reversed or indented bylines can be fun, but they risk calling too much attention to themselves — and they can get awfully difficult to read. Proceed with caution.

BY HARPO MARX

By CHICO MARX
of the Times

By GROUCHO MARX

For short sidebars or columns of briefs, credit is often given in the form of a flush-right tag line at the end of the text. As with bylines, these credit lines need spacing and typography that sets them apart from the text:

— The Associated Press

— Compiled from staff reports

Some papers now run *all* bylines at the end of the story — and some even include the reporter's phone number (!). At the start of the story, the logic goes, bylines just add clutter amid the headlines and decks; since the writer's name is optional information, it can come later.

On photo spreads and special features, newspapers often use a more prominent byline style to credit the writer, the photographer, or both (page designers, sad to say, rarely receive printed credit for their work). These special credits are either parked at the edge of the design or indented into a wide column of text (like the Laurel & Hardy credit above).

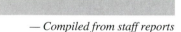

Story by
STAN LAUREL

Photos by
OLIVER HARDY

CREDIT LINES

Artwork, like stories, should be credited — whether the art comes from staffers, free-lancers, wire services or library files. Different styles of credit lines serve different functions:

◆ For photos and illustrations, they provide the name and affiliation of the photographer or artist who produced the image.

◆ For old, historic photos or maps, they tell readers where the documents come from (i.e., The Bozoville Historical Society). Often, credit lines include the date a photo was taken, which is necessary for any photo that could mistakenly be considered current.

◆ For charts or diagrams, an additional "source" line tells readers where the artist obtained the data that was graphicized. Citing such sources is just as important for artists as it is for reporters.

◆ For copyrighted material, they provide the necessary legal wording (*Reprinted with permission of . . .* or *© 1994 by . . .*).

Not all papers credit all photos, however. Most papers, for instance, don't bother crediting run-of-the-mill mug shots. And publicity handouts — movie stills, fashion shots, glossies of entertainers — usually run uncredited, too (probably because editors resent giving away all that free publicity).

Most papers run credits in small type (below 7-point), in a font that contrasts with any cutlines nearby. Some papers still run photo credits at the *end* of their cutlines, like this —

Tokyo citizens scream in terror Friday as Godzilla destroys the city. (Staff photo by Dan Gustafson).

— but that credit style isn't as effective as it could be. Ideally, there should be a clear distinction between cutlines and credit lines, just as there's a distinction between text and bylines.

Most papers run credit lines flush right, just a few points below the bottom edge of the art and a few points above the cutline. Some papers run them flush left; some run them on top; some have even tried running them sideways along the right edge, though that's difficult to read and tends to jam up against any adjacent leg of text. (When graphics use both a source line *and* a credit line, they should be dummied in two separate positions to avoid confusing readers.)

Below, you can gauge the effectiveness of each location:

MORE ON ▶

◆ **Photo spreads:**
Tips on designing photo pages — and positioning photo credits **110**

Some papers run credit lines above the photo, flush right — though many readers habitually look for them down around the cutline.

Many magazines run credit lines sideways — but even if the type is tiny, it risks crowding into adjacent columns of text.

Not many papers run credit lines in the lower left corner. Instead, it's common to run the **source line** *here — that's the line in a chart, map or diagram that tells the source of the data being used. Putting that information here (or inside the box) keeps it separate from other credit lines.*

The Oregonian/JOEL DAVIS

The Oregonian/JOEL DAVIS

Most papers run credit lines flush right, a few points below the photo. Whatever you choose to do, keep it consistent — pick one position and run all credits there.

Source: Department of Redundancy Department   The Oregonian/JOEL DAVIS

This is the cutline (or caption). Cutlines usually run a few points below the credit line and use a font that's bigger and bolder than the credit.

SPACING

Every paper should standardize its spacing guidelines. Here, for example, is how one typical newspaper might space story elements on a typical page:

Friday, April 14, 1994 **5B**

in 9th inning

The Oregonian/STEVE NEHL

e run as the Dodgers rallied in the ninth inning to win.

tcher threw,
us terrified
ball game."

— Joe Spooner

rs." That was a signal ized, although it had ssed between him and

s saying, "Pitch to the

big bum if he hammers every ball in the park into the North River."

And so, at Snyder's request, Bentley did pitch to Ruth, and the Babe drove the ball deep into right center; so deep that Casey Stengel could feel the hot breath of the bleacherites on his back as the ball came down and he caught it. If that drive had been just a shade to the right it would have been a third home run for Ruth. As it was, the Babe had a great day, with two home runs, a terrific long fly, and two bases on balls.

Ump claims
new balk rule
may be unfair

By EAMONN HUGHES
Sports editor

For the first time since the American League instituted its

SECTION LOGOS & HEADERS

Above: *Allow 3 points between logos and the folio line.*
Inside: *Maintain 8-point margins between logo type and the edge of the box.*
Below: *Allow 18 points between logos and headlines or photos.*

HEADLINES

Above: *Allow 18 points between logos or unrelated stories and the top of the headline.*
Below: *Allow 1 pica between descenders and text/photos below.*
Roundups and briefs: *When compiling packages of briefs that use small headlines (12- or 14-point), use tighter spacing: one pica of space above the headline and 6 points below.*

PHOTOS

Credit line: *Allow 3 points between photos and credit lines.*
Cutline: *Allow 3 points between credit lines and cutlines. Allow 3 points between photos and cutlines if there's no credit line.*

TEXT

Above: *Allow 1 pica between cutlines and text.*
Gutters: *All vertical gutters are 1 pica wide.*
Graphic elements: *Allow 1 pica between all graphic elements (liftout quotes, refers, etc.) and text.*
Below: *Allow 18 points between text and unrelated stories.*

BOXED STORIES/GRAPHICS

Margins: *Allow 1 pica between outside rules and all headlines/text/photos.*

BYLINES

Above: *Allow 1 pica between headline descenders and bylines.*
Below: *Allow 1 pica between bylines and text.*

RULES & BOXES

Newspapers use rules both functionally (to organize and separate elements) and decoratively (to add contrast and flair). Notice, for instance, how the rules in this sig and byline are both functional and decorative:

NFL ROUNDUP

By ROBIN FOX
Bugle-Beacon staff writer

Rule thickness, like type size, is measured in points. That "NFL Roundup" sig uses a 4-point rule above the type and a 1-point rule below, while the byline uses a hairline rule (that's the thinnest rule available). With so many thicknesses to choose from, most papers limit rule usage to just one or two sizes — say, 1-point and 4-point: one thin, one thick.

Rules are most commonly used in the following ways:

◆ To build logos, bylines and other standing elements.
◆ To create boxes (for stories, graphics, ads, etc.).
◆ To build charts & graphs.

◆ To embellish feature designs and display headlines.
◆ To separate stories and elements from each other.
◆ To border photos.

This page from The Portland Press Herald uses boxes and rules to organize story elements.

Decades ago, newspapers commonly used rules to separate stories from each other. Some ran vertically in the gutters (called *column rules*), while others ran horizontally beneath stories (called *cutoff rules*). That trend faded in the '60s, but it's been making a comeback recently in newspapers like the one at left. As Harold Evans, editor of The Sunday Times in London, once said: "The most backward step, under the flag of freedom, has been the abandonment of column rules and cutoffs which so usefully define columns and separate stories."

Most modern papers run most stories unruled and unboxed, reserving box treatments for big news packages, sidebars, stand-alone photos, etc. As we've said before, it's best to box stories only if they're special or if they need to be set apart from other stories on the page. Rules and boxes can produce handsome designs, but they shouldn't be used to compensate for butting headlines or poorly placed photos. A weak design is a weak design, regardless of whether rules are used to soften the impact of colliding elements.

You'll often be tempted to use decorative rules or borders for special effects. But like other graphic gimmicks, it's easy to use them clumsily or excessively — so go easy.

A SAMPLING OF RULES & BORDERS

Hairline

1 point

2 point

4 point

6 point

12 point

Decorative borders

This box is bordered with a plain .5-point rule.

Thick frames and fat shadows add too much noise and clutter. Avoid them. It's best to use thin rules to build boxes and bor-

Underscoring

Someday, you'll get bored with news headlines and decide they look better with a rule (called an *underscore*) beneath them. But avoid doing that. Save rules for kickers or display headlines (see page 184 for more details).

Rounded corners and decorative borders were stylish 20 years ago, but they're corny and old-fashioned today. Gimmicks like these just call attention to themselves.

REFERS, TEASERS & PROMOS

REFERS

Throughout this book, we've cross-referenced material by adding "INSIDE" boxes at the top of many pages. Those boxes are a handy way to show you where to find related information elsewhere in this book.

Newspapers need to cross-reference their stories, too. And they do that by using lines, paragraphs or boxes called *refers* (see examples below). Some refers are simple; others, with art, are more elaborate. Whatever style your paper uses, refers should:

◆ **Stand out typographically** from the surrounding text. That's why refers often include rules, bullets, boldface or italic type.

◆ **Be tightly written.** Refers are signposts, so they should simply point — not pontificate.

◆ **Be specific.** Refers should index all related items — on the TV page, the opinion page, wherever — not just say, "Other stories inside."

◆ **Be consistently positioned** every time they're used— i.e., above the byline, at the top of a column, at the end of the story — whatever is most appropriate and unobtrusive.

Refer line:

❏ **How Perot views the tax plan,** Page 5A.

Refer paragraph:

NAVY ALERT: Turkish destroyers were placed on red alert Wednesday as Iran prepared to launch its first nuclear submarine / **Page 4A**.

Refer box (with art):

INSIDE

▶ *Why Kraft was forced to resign* **A5**

▶ *Reaction from other board members* **A7**

▶ *Highlights of Kraft's stormy career* **A7**

TEASERS & PROMOS

A refer is a signpost that guides readers to stories inside the paper. A *teaser* is another kind of signpost — actually, it's more like a billboard. Where refers advise, teasers advertise. They say **"BUY ME: HOT STORY INSIDE."**

The covers of most supermarket tabloids are loaded with titillating teasers. Most newspapers, by comparison, use a more refined approach for their teasers (also called *promos, skylines* or *boxcars*). Teasers are usually boxed in an eye-catching way at the top of Page One. Some are bold and simple —

The Sun (in Lowell, Mass.) assembles a variety of promos — they call them "windows" — above the flag on Page One. These promos aren't all light and breezy — note how two of them refer to murders.

SPOONER'S GRAND SLAM WINS IT FOR DODGERS/D1

— but the question is: Do readers even *notice* these text-only teasers? A better idea is to combine a catchy headline phrase, a short copy blurb and *art,* since an arresting image is the surest way to grab readers' attention.

Here are two examples of aggressive front-page teasers:

The Oregonian runs teasers below the flag — an unorthodox location which makes them a more active part of the page. Note the huge word WEDNESDAY, which accents the timeliness of the day's news.

BREAKING UP TEXT

Reading long columns of text is a tiring chore. But if you break up the gray with occasional subheads, initial caps or dingbats, you can better organize your material — and, at the same time, provide rest stops for the reader's eye.

SUBHEADS

Subheads are the most common way to subdivide long stories (i.e., features or news analyses that run over 30 inches). They're usually inserted every 8-10 inches, wherever there's a shift of topic or a logical pause in the commentary. Avoid inserting them at random (which won't help the reader's understanding of the material) or at the very bottom of a leg of type.

Subheads come in a variety of styles, but they're usually bolder than text type:

without first having his wife brought to see him; and they had sent an escort for her, which had occasioned the delay.

Under the guillotine

He immediately kneeled down, below the knife. His neck fitting into a hole, made for the purpose, in a cross plank, was shut down, by

This is a typical style for news subheads: bold type, centered, a few points larger than text.

Sutherland's trip at 7 p.m. Thursday at Pioneer Courthouse Square. The program is free.

■ **Africa preview:** A slide presentation on Kenya and Tanzania will be shown at 10:30 a.m. Wednesday at Weststar Tour and Travel, 19888 S.E. Stark. The show is a preview of a February trip to desert

This format is used to change topics in stories that consist of short, assorted bits and pieces.

$50 for Oslo, but a seven-day second-class rail pass can be bought for about $70 at rail stations.

WHERE TO STAY

The Fjord Pass program offers discounts on rates at 200 hotels. The pass costs $10 and comes with a list of hotels offering discounts for

This reversed subhead helps organize catalog-style stories into clearly labeled sections.

INITIAL CAPS

Initial caps are a classy way to begin features, columns or specially packaged news stories. They're also a decorative (though non-informational) alternative to subheads for breaking up long columns of text.

Be sure the large cap letter is neatly spaced and aligned, whether it's indented into the text or raised above it:

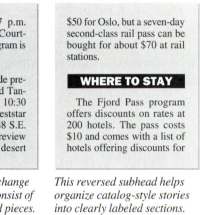

This is an example of a dropped initial. These are usually tucked into the first three or four lines of the text.

Here is a raised initial, which sits above the first line of the text.

Even small graphics and sidebars can begin with initial caps to give the text extra typographic emphasis. Use them sparingly, though, as a way to anchor text blocks.

DINGBATS

Dingbat is the ridiculous-sounding term used to describe typographic characters like these:

✔ ❑ ❒ ■ ○ ▲ ❈ ● ✛ ◆ ❀ ♥ ♣ ↔ ◆ ☞ ✜ ★ ✂ ✪

Most dingbats are too silly to use in a serious-minded newspaper. Some, however, are handy for relieving long legs of text (see example at right).

Others, like bullets (●) and squares (■), can help itemize lists within text. Remember, however:

◆ Use bullets or squares for three or more related items. Fewer than that, it looks odd.

◆ Keep bullet items short and punchy. Like this.

◆ Don't overdo it. Use bullets only for emphasis.

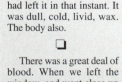

had left it in that instant. It was dull, cold, livid, wax. The body also.

❑

There was a great deal of blood. When we left the window, and went close up to the scaffold, it was very dirty; one of the two men who were throwing water

Continued from page 81

and 4.

◆ **Avoid jumping orphans.** An *orphan* (sometimes called a *widow*) is a short word or phrase that's carried over to the top of a new column or page. Like the first line in this column: "and 4."

Orphans look clumsy — like typographical errors, even if they aren't. And, as you may have just experienced, it's aggravating enough to reach the end of a column, then be told to turn to page 136, then fumble around trying to *find* page 136, then, when you get to page 136, read something cryptic like "and 4" — at which point you discover you've forgotten the rest of the sentence back on page 81.

And that's why readers dislike jumps.

◆ **Label jumps clearly.** Since jumping is so distasteful, use typography to make it easier. There are two ways to do this:

1) Run *continuation lines* (the lines that tell you where a story is continued) flush right, since that's where your eye stops reading at end of a column. Run *jump lines* (the lines that tell you where a story has been jumped from) flush left, since that's where your eye begins reading at the top of a column.

2) Give each jump a key word or phrase, then highlight it typographically.

Suppose, for instance, you're jumping a story on oat bran. You could run a continuation line that simply says **Turn to page 6.** But that's not too friendly — and it's not very informative. When readers get to page 6, how will they spot the jump?

You'd be wiser to run a continuation line like **Please see OAT BRAN, page 6.** And when readers arrived at page 6, they'd find a jump headline like one of these:

Oat bran: Study proves it prevents heart attacks

Continued from Page One

This is a popular treatment for jump headlines. It treats the key word (or phrase) as a boldface lead-in, then follows with a lightface headline written in standard style. Since the key word is played so boldly, jump stories are easy to spot when readers arrive at the new page. To be effective, jump lines should be set apart from text by both extra spacing and type selection.

Oat bran *Continued from Page One*

This is another common style for jump headlines. It uses only the key word (or phrase) to catch readers' eyes, then adds a rule both for emphasis and to separate the text from any columns running above. One problem: Readers encountering this jump story for the first time won't have any idea what it's about if all the headline says is something like "SMITH."

Study proves oat bran can prevent heart attacks

■ OAT BRAN, from Page One

This treatment is rather straightforward: a standard banner headline followed by a boldface key word in the jump line. But is it obvious enough to readers that this is the oat bran story they're searching for? Some would argue that unless the jump headline boldly proclaims a key word or phrase, too many readers may get lost.

◆ **Give jumps design attention.** Remember to package jumps as attractively as you'd package any other story. Many newspapers regard jumps as mandatory blocks of gray slop — ugly leftovers from nice-looking pages. And if your deadlines are tight, you may be forced to blow off jump-page designs. But if there's time, add photos. Create mug-quote blocks. Pull out charts or maps.

To summarize: Jumps will never be popular. But if you can devise a clear, consistent format for packaging jump stories, readers will regard them as minor detours — not major roadblocks. And their benefits to designers (higher story counts and increased layout options on key pages) far outweigh the annoyance they cause readers.

W e live in a visual age. We're bombarded with movies, videos, ads, photographs, charts, diagrams. We're spoiled. And we've gotten lazy. When we want information, we say *show* me — don't tell me.

Images are strong and seductive. Words take work. So most of us prefer images over words. We'd rather scan the pictures on that page at right than read this column of text. So what does that mean for newspapers? It means we've entered the age of informational graphics (or *infographics* for short). With infographics, newspapers can combine illustration and information into colorful, seductive packages. Infographics can be maps. Charts. Lists. Diagrams. They can be created as tiny insets. Or as entire full-color pages.

Do infographics junk up journalism? Some critics of TV and USA Today think so; cartoony charts and goofy graphs just trivialize the news, they say.

But remember: true journalism is *teaching.* You have information; your readers need it; you must teach it to them as quickly and clearly as you can. Sometimes words work best. Other times, information transmits best *visually,* not verbally.

Your job, as a newspaper designer, is to choose the best possible approach. This chapter will show you some of your options.

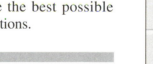

WRITING FOR NON-READERS

It's the first day of a new school year. You're about to begin a tough new class — say, Advanced Biology. You're holding a copy of the textbook you'll be using this term. On the cover, there's a cute photo of a red-eyed tree frog. But when you turn inside, page after page after page after page after page after page after page looks like this:

Your heart sinks. Your intestines churn. "Hoo boy," you groan. If only they'd used maybe a *little* art to break up all that gray — you know, something like this:

The fact is, you've come face to face with a cruel and ancient law of publication design:

IN VAST QUANTITIES, TEXT LOOKS AWFULLY DULL.

Yes, deep in the childish recesses of our brains, we all share the same throbbing dread of text. It's like math anxiety: *text anxiety.* In small doses, text is tolerable. But when we're wading through deep heaps of it, we hate it. Even worse, we hate *writing* it.

And yet we all need to communicate, to share information, to express ideas. It's a primal urge — one that has evolved over the ages. In ancient, prehistoric times, our ape-like ancestors struggled to piece together this primitive kind of narrative:

> Me hungry! Kill moose! Eat meat!

As the centuries dragged by, early humans polished their delivery. After eons of practice, they became skilled storytellers:

> . . . So there I was, trapped in the Cave
> of Death, staring into the drooling jaws
> of Mongo, The Moose From Hell . . .

This narrative style reached a climax with the invention of the romance novel:

> . . . Helga, the voluptuous Moose Queen, slowly peeled off her gown
> and uttered a moan as the mighty Ragnar clenched her in his tawny arms.
> "Be gentle, my warrior," she sighed as he ran his tongue down her neck.
> "Yaarrrrrgggh!" he grunted. Helga's bosom heaved with desire as
> Ragnar's hungry kisses grew ever more furious. *"Yes!"* she cried. *"Yes!"*

WRITING FOR NON-READERS

So far, so good. And perhaps that kind of narration is what the written word does best — storytelling that transports us *emotionally* from one place to another. As opposed to this type of narration:

> Consumption of moosemeat declined significantly during the first three decades of the 9th century. Marauding hordes of Vikings averaged 14.3 pounds per capita of moosemeat monthly during that period, while consumption among Druids climbed to 22.8 pounds (for males) and 16.3 pounds (females) during winter months, up from 15.5 pounds in summer.

"Yaarrrggh," as Ragnar might say. For most folks, data turns deadly dull in narrative form. Our eyes glaze. Our bosoms heave. It feels like we're staring into the drooling jaws of The Statistician From Hell.

Such data might work better as a chart or graph:

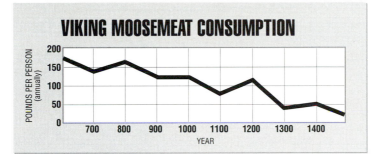

That's a fine match of medium and meaning. It's quick. It's visual. It's precise. And best of all, it's interesting — almost interactive.

It's *non-text,* a form of writing that's — well, a kind of *non*-writing. Which is perfect for today's generation of non-readers.

Now, these *non-text* formats work fine for business reports, government statistics, news features and so on. But they won't work for everything. Take Helga the Moose Queen; something's missing when you write her love scene like this:

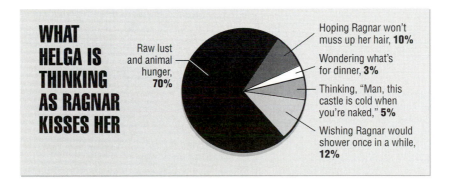

Obviously, some types of information are best expressed in narrative form. And that's fine. Usually.

But pause for a moment and ponder these past two pages. Notice how *visually* we presented our material. Would we have held your interest if we'd explained it all with normal narrative text?

WRITING FOR NON-READERS

So what's it all mean to newspapers? It means that editors, writers and designers *must* realize that today's readers are visual. Impatient. Easily bored. Readers absorb data in a variety of ways: through words, photos, charts, maps, diagrams. They want their news packaged in a sort of "information mosaic": a combination of text, data and images that approaches complex issues from fresh new angles.

Years ago, when big stories broke, editors assigned reporters to write miles and miles of pure text. (And yes, readers would read it.) Today, when big stories break, editors assign reporters, photographers *and* graphic artists to make concepts understandable in both words *and* pictures.

For instance, when the Hindenburg crashed in 1937, most newspapers ran a photo or two, but relied upon yards of text to describe the tragedy. If that disaster struck today, you'd see pages like the one at right below. Which do you prefer?

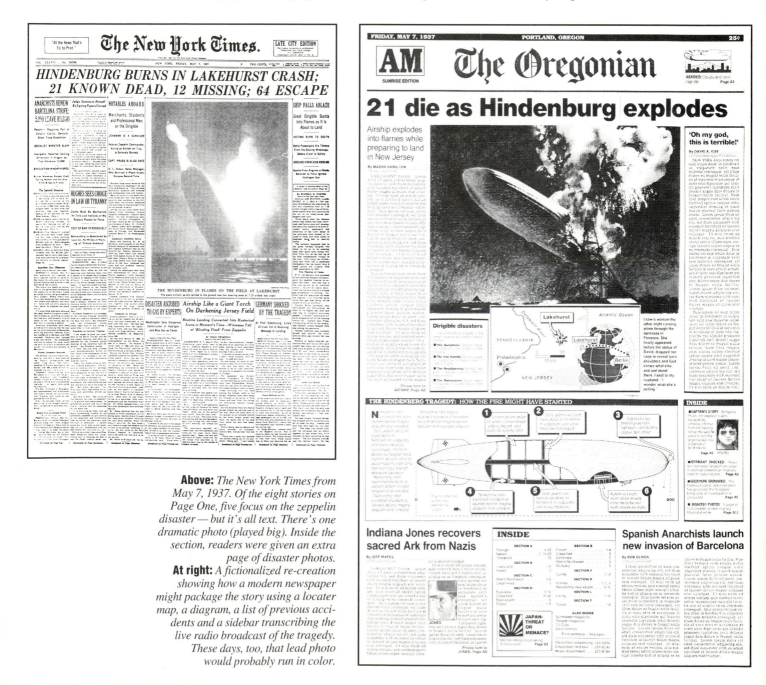

Above: *The New York Times from May 7, 1937. Of the eight stories on Page One, five focus on the zeppelin disaster — but it's all text. There's one dramatic photo (played big). Inside the section, readers were given an extra page of disaster photos.*

At right: *A fictionalized re-creation showing how a modern newspaper might package the story using a locater map, a diagram, a list of previous accidents and a sidebar transcribing the live radio broadcast of the tragedy. These days, too, that lead photo would probably run in color.*

SIDEBARS & INFOGRAPHICS

A *sidebar* is any short feature that accompanies a longer story. An *infographic* (short for "informational graphic") blends text and illustrations to convey information visually — clarifying the facts with charts, maps or diagrams.

Years ago, sidebars and infographics were considered optional. Nowadays, they're essential for effective newspaper design. Why?

◆ They carve up complicated material into bite-size chunks.

◆ They offer attractive alternatives to gray-looking text.

◆ They let writers move key background information, explanations or quotes out of the narrative flow of the text and into a separate, highly visible spot.

◆ Because they're tight, bright and entertaining, they add reader appeal to any story, whether news or features. In fact, they often attract higher readership than the main story they accompany.

Sidebars are usually specially packaged — boxed or screened — to help them stand apart from the main story. Notice how that's true for our sidebar below: a visual index to all the sidebars and infographics we'll explore in the pages ahead.

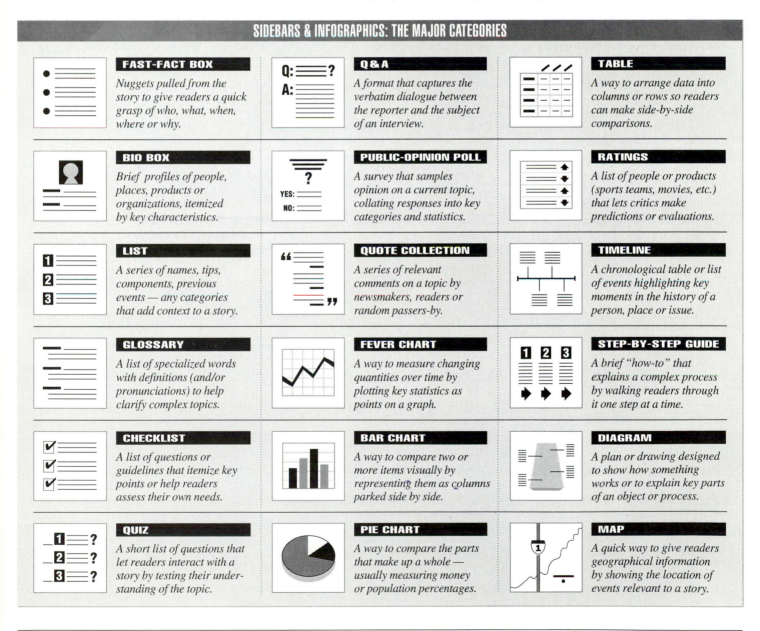

SIDEBARS & INFOGRAPHICS: THE MAJOR CATEGORIES

FAST-FACT BOX
Nuggets pulled from the story to give readers a quick grasp of who, what, when, where or why.

Q & A
A format that captures the verbatim dialogue between the reporter and the subject of an interview.

TABLE
A way to arrange data into columns or rows so readers can make side-by-side comparisons.

BIO BOX
Brief profiles of people, places, products or organizations, itemized by key characteristics.

PUBLIC-OPINION POLL
A survey that samples opinion on a current topic, collating responses into key categories and statistics.

RATINGS
A list of people or products (sports teams, movies, etc.) that lets critics make predictions or evaluations.

LIST
A series of names, tips, components, previous events — any categories that add context to a story.

QUOTE COLLECTION
A series of relevant comments on a topic by newsmakers, readers or random passers-by.

TIMELINE
A chronological table or list of events highlighting key moments in the history of a person, place or issue.

GLOSSARY
A list of specialized words with definitions (and/or pronunciations) to help clarify complex topics.

FEVER CHART
A way to measure changing quantities over time by plotting key statistics as points on a graph.

STEP-BY-STEP GUIDE
A brief "how-to" that explains a complex process by walking readers through it one step at a time.

CHECKLIST
A list of questions or guidelines that itemize key points or help readers assess their own needs.

BAR CHART
A way to compare two or more items visually by representing them as columns parked side by side.

DIAGRAM
A plan or drawing designed to show how something works or to explain key parts of an object or process.

QUIZ
A short list of questions that let readers interact with a story by testing their understanding of the topic.

PIE CHART
A way to compare the parts that make up a whole — usually measuring money or population percentages.

MAP
A quick way to give readers geographical information by showing the location of events relevant to a story.

FAST FACTS

THE KLAMATH FALLS QUAKE

◆ **MAGNITUDE:** 5.4 on the Richter scale
◆ **TIME:** 8:29 p.m. Monday
◆ **EPICENTER:** About 15 miles northwest of Klamath Falls, Ore.
◆ **DEATHS:** One person died when boulders crushed his car on U.S. 97 near Chiloquin
◆ **AFTERSHOCKS:** 5.2 and 4.5

This fast-fact box accompanied a long news story on an Oregon earthquake, delivering essential facts at a glance.

SUPER BOWL XXVIII

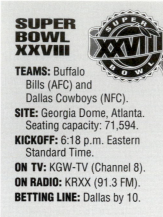

TEAMS: Buffalo Bills (AFC) and Dallas Cowboys (NFC).
SITE: Georgia Dome, Atlanta. Seating capacity: 71,594.
KICKOFF: 6:18 p.m. Eastern Standard Time.
ON TV: KGW-TV (Channel 8).
ON RADIO: KRXX (91.3 FM).
BETTING LINE: Dallas by 10.

Boxes like these could accompany any sports, entertainment or political event — and you can add art, as well.

One of the best ways to present news in a hurry is to distill the *who-what-when-where-why* of a story into a concise package. By creating fast-fact boxes, you add graphic variety to story designs, introduce basic facts without slowing down the text, and provide entertaining data for those who may not want to read the text at all.

The average full-time salary of a black female college graduate is less than that of a white male high-school dropout.

Fast-fact boxes can deliver statistics. History. Definitions. Schedules. Trivia. They can update readers on what just happened — or try to explain what'll happen next.

They can even display stand-alone "factoids" — like the one at left — that lure readers into the story in the same way that liftout quotes do.

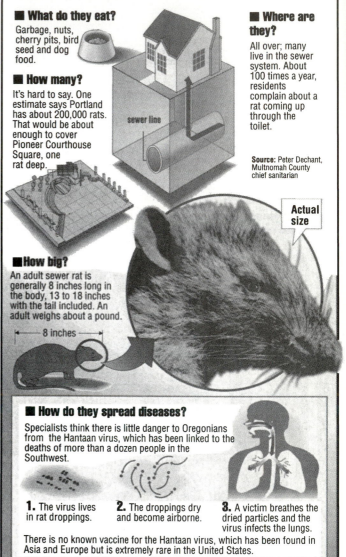

RAT SNAPSHOT

Nobody likes to admit to having rats, but Multnomah County has them. Here's a snapshot of the rat population.

■ **What do they eat?**
Garbage, nuts, cherry pits, bird seed and dog food.

■ **How many?**
It's hard to say. One estimate says Portland has about 200,000 rats. That would be about enough to cover Pioneer Courthouse Square, one rat deep.

■ **How big?**
An adult sewer rat is generally 8 inches long in the body, 13 to 18 inches with the tail included. An adult weighs about a pound.

← 8 inches →

■ **Where are they?**
All over; many live in the sewer system. About 100 times a year, residents complain about a rat coming up through the toilet.

Source: Peter Dechant, Multnomah County chief sanitarian

sewer line

Actual size

■ **How do they spread diseases?**
Specialists think there is little danger to Oregonians from the Hantaan virus, which has been linked to the deaths of more than a dozen people in the Southwest.

1. The virus lives in rat droppings.
2. The droppings dry and become airborne.
3. A victim breathes the dried particles and the virus infects the lungs.

There is no known vaccine for the Hantaan virus, which has been found in Asia and Europe but is extremely rare in the United States.

WORM FARMING AT A GLANCE

Want to start your own worm farm? It's easy. Just dig these earthy facts:

◆ An earthworm can eat half its weight in food each day.
◆ People are either boys or girls, but earthworms are both male and female.
◆ An earthworm matures to breeding age in 60-90 days given proper food, care and environmental quality.
◆ A mature breeding worm can produce an egg capsule every 7-10 days.
◆ An egg capsule will hatch in 7-14 days.
◆ An egg capsule contains 2-20 baby earthworms, with an average of 7 per capsule.
◆ One breeder can produce 1,200-1,500 worms per year; 2,000 breeders can produce 1 billion worms in two years.

FOR MORE INFO:

◆ *Worm Digest* is published four times a year. To subscribe, send $4 to Worm Digest, Box 544, Eugene, OR 97440.
◆ For tips on building a wormbox, call Metro Recycling Information at 234-4000.

The fast-fact box above tells you everything you need to know about urban rats: their diet, their size, their location, etc. Notice how tightly written the text is. The worm-farming sidebar at left offers a variety of "worm trivia" — but the box that tells readers where to go for more information is a helpful addition.

BIO BOXES

The 19th-century philosopher Karl Marx wrote a revealing self-portrait while playing a Victorian parlor game called "Confessions." Here's what he confessed:

Favorite virtue in a man: *Strength*
Favorite virtue in a woman: *Weakness*
Your idea of happiness: *To fight*
Your idea of misery: *Submission*
Favorite occupation: *Bookworming*

Favorite poet: *Shakespeare, Aeschylus, Goethe*
Favorite hero: *Spartacus*
Favorite color: *Red*
Favorite motto: *De omnibus dubitandum*
("You must have doubts about everything")

You can gain surprising insights through biographical bits like these. By listing facts in a *bio box,* you can quickly profile almost any person, place or thing. Bio boxes can stick to a strict *who-what-when-where-why* — or they can spin off on specialized (or humorous) tangents, as these examples show:

in your face

Joe Spooner
Cartoonist

Age: 48.
Hometown: Portland.
Bats: Right.
Writes: Left.

Occupation: Cartoonist and bon vivant.

Heroes: Gary Larsen, Dave Barry, Paul Rubens.

Ambition: To have someone else pay my health-insurance premiums.

Motto: "Je n'ai pas m'empecher de rire — ha-ha-ha!" *(I cannot stop myself from laughing.)*

Forms of exercise: Running and limping.

Favorite spouse: Patti.

Favorite food: Turkey pie.

Favorite drink: Guinness Stout.

Favorite dessert: Gobi.

Favorite subject in school: Spelling.

All-time favorite album: *Abbey Road.*

Favorite new music: *Abbey Road* the CD.

Person whose lifestyle I'd most like to emulate: Ernest Hemingway, except for that part about the shotgun.

Proudest feat: Getting through five years of flying in the Air Force without killing myself.

Bedside book: American Heritage Dictionary.

Last words: "Couldn't I just stay until the next commercial?"

Above all else, bio boxes must contain tightly written and meaningful information. But as this sidebar shows, they can also use humor to capture the true spirit of their subject.

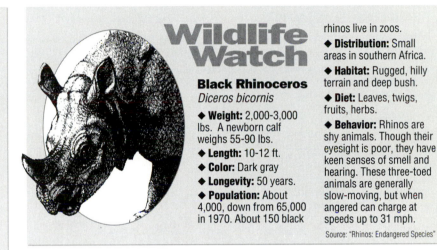

Wildlife Watch

Black Rhinoceros
Diceros bicornis

◆ **Weight:** 2,000-3,000 lbs. A newborn calf weighs 55-90 lbs.
◆ **Length:** 10-12 ft.
◆ **Color:** Dark gray
◆ **Longevity:** 50 years.
◆ **Population:** About 4,000, down from 65,000 in 1970. About 150 black rhinos live in zoos.
◆ **Distribution:** Small areas in southern Africa.
◆ **Habitat:** Rugged, hilly terrain and deep bush.
◆ **Diet:** Leaves, twigs, fruits, herbs.
◆ **Behavior:** Rhinos are shy animals. Though their eyesight is poor, they have keen senses of smell and hearing. These three-toed animals are generally slow-moving, but when angered can charge at speeds up to 31 mph.

Source: "Rhinos: Endangered Species"

When it comes to bio boxes, animals can enjoy the same treatment as people. Above, this tightly-written "Critter of the Week" profiles a celebrity from the animal kingdom.

ESTONIA: FACTS AND FIGURES

■ **AREA:** At 45,000 square kilometers (about the size of New Hampshire and Vermont combined), Estonia is one of the smallest states in Europe.

■ **HISTORY:** Estonia was dominated by Germans since the 13th century and by Swedes in the 16th-18th centuries. Later ruled by Russia, Estonia became independent after 1917 and was forcibly annexed by the Soviet Union in 1940. It won independence from the Soviet Union in 1991.

■ **POPULATION:** About 30 percent of Estonia's 1.6 million people are ethnic Russians, many of whom moved to Estonia after its annexation by the Soviets.

■ **RUSSIAN TROOPS:** 2,400 Russian soldiers remained in Estonia as of December.

■ **ECONOMY:** Estonian currency, the kroon, has held relatively steady since its introduction in 1992. The GNP rose 3 percent in 1992, making the Estonian economy one of the fastest-growing in Europe.

FINLAND
Baltic Sea
★ Tallinn
ESTONIA
RUSSIA
LATVIA
LITHUANIA
BELARUS
RUSSIA
EUROPE
0   100
miles
POLAND
AFRICA

Source: The Associated Press

This type of fast-facts treatment has appeared in almanacs and encyclopedias for years, summarizing the who-what-when-where of countries around the globe. When used to accompany new stories, these sidebar boxes give readers background data at a glance.

LISTS

What are the most popular movies of all time? The largest fast-food chains? The best-selling Christmas toys? The most prestigious universities?

Ours is a culture obsessed with keeping score. We're *dying* to know who's the richest, the biggest, the fastest, the best. And often the fastest and best way to convey that information is by compiling lists like these.

Lists can be used to chart rankings. To itemize tips or warnings. To summarize critical opinions. And as David Letterman has shown, they can even get laughs as a comedy bit on late-night talk shows *(". . . and the Number One Least Popular Fairy Tale: Goldilocks and the Tainted Clams!")*.

GOT ANY BANANA PUDDING, ELVIS?

These items were to be kept at Graceland "for Elvis — AT ALL TIMES — EVERY DAY":

Fresh ground round
One case regular Pepsi
One case orange drink
Six cans of biscuits
Hamburger buns, rolls
Pickles
Potatoes and onions
Assorted fresh fruit
Cans of sauerkraut
Wieners
Milk, half and half
Lean bacon
Mustard
Peanut butter

Banana pudding
Ingredients for meat loaf
Brownies
Chocolate ice cream
Fudge cookies
Gum (Spearmint, Juicy Fruit, Doublemint — three packs each)
Cigarettes
Dristan
Super Anahist
Contac
Sucrets
Feenamint gum

Source: The Associated Press

Random lists: *These items run in no particular order, but stacking them in rows makes them more interesting (and easier to read) than if they'd run in the middle of a paragraph of text.*

HOW TO STAY YOUNG
by Leroy "Satchel" Paige

Satchel Paige, the first black pitcher in major-league baseball, was 59 when he played his final game. Here are his tips for staying youthful:

◆ Avoid fried meats, which angry up the blood.

◆ If your stomach disputes you, lie down and pacify it with cool thoughts.

◆ Keep the juices flowing by jangling around gently as you move.

◆ Go very lightly on the vices, such as carrying on in society. The social ramble ain't restful.

◆ Avoid running at all times.

◆ Don't look back. Something may be gaining on you.

Source: The People's Almanac

Lists itemized with bullets: *Here, we use a combination of dingbats, a hanging indent and extra leading to separate items. Note, too, how the introduction is written in smaller italic type.*

1993 OSCAR WINNERS

BEST PICTURE
Schindler's List

BEST ACTOR
Tom Hanks, *Philadelphia*

BEST ACTRESS
Holly Hunter, *The Piano*

BEST SUPPORTING ACTOR
Tommy Lee Jones, *The Fugitive*

BEST SUPPORTING ACTRESS
Anna Paquin, *The Piano*

BEST DIRECTOR
Steven Spielberg, *Schindler's List*

Lists arranged by categories: *Note the typographic elements at work here: boldface caps, italics, extra leading between items. Lists can often be centered (like this) rather than flush left.*

THE ESSENTIAL CYBERPUNK LIBRARY

Cyberpunk: Think of the movie "Blade Runner." If you're unfamiliar with this futuristic literary genre, these books will get you started:

AMY THOMSON, *"Virtual Girl":* A lovely woman from a Virtual Reality landscape is forced to survive in an alien environment.

K.W. JETER, *"Farewell Horizontal":* A rebel in a horizontal world seeks to attain status by achieving a vertical existence.

ORSON SCOTT CORD, *"Ender's Game":* A civilization under siege breeds a race of military geniuses to battle invading aliens.

WILLIAM GIBSON/BRUCE STERLING, *"The Difference Engine":* The 19th-century Victorian world is moved by a huge steam-powered computer.

— Paul Pintarich

Lists with commentary: *Any subjective Top 10 list — whether it ranks pop tunes or presidents — will benefit by adding bite-size evaluations that analyze each entry or offer advice to readers.*

MOST COMMON LAST NAMES IN THE U.S.

1. *Smith*
2. *Johnson*
3. *Williams*
4. *Jones*
5. *Brown*
6. *Miller*
7. *Davis*
8. *Anderson*
9. *Wilson*
10. *Thompson*

Top 10 lists: *Notice how the numbers are boldface — and how the periods following the numbers are all vertically aligned.*

THE WORLD'S 10 DEADLIEST DISEASES
(with annual deaths)

1	Cardiovascular diseases	12 million
2	Diarrheal diseases	5 million
3	Cancer	4.8 million
4	Pneumonia	4.8 million
5	Tuberculosis	3 million
6	Chronic Lung Disease	2.7 million
7	Measles	1.5 million
8	Hepatitis B	1.2 million
9	Malaria	1.2 million
10	Tetanus (neonatal)	560,000

Source: World Health Organization

Top 10 lists with data: *Often it's not enough simply to show rankings — you need statistical support. Here, the death totals run flush right alongside the disease names. Rules and reversed numbers add graphic organization.*

LISTS

THE HARPER'S INDEX

Back in 1984, Harper's Magazine began publishing an addictingly clever page near the beginning of each issue. As editor Lewis Lapham described it, the Harper's Index offers "numbers that measure, one way or another, the drifting tide of events." A typical Harper's Index might include such items as:

> Number of Americans who drink Coca-Cola for breakfast: 965,000
> Price of a 1909 Honus Wagner baseball card: $32,000
> Average weight of a male bear in Alaska: 250 pounds
> In Pennsylvania: 487 pounds
> Chance that a female graduate student in psychology has had sex with one of her professors: 1 in 6
> Abortions per 1,000 live births in New York City: 852
> Astronomers in the United States: 3,650
> Astrologers: 15,000

As you can see, the basic index format is consistent: a setup (in text) followed by a punchline (a number). But what makes these lists fascinating are the strange, curious, often surprising combinations of random factoids — some of which, when juxtaposed like those astronomer/astrologer statistics, raise provocative cultural questions.

As with most sidebars, the juicier your facts, the more entertaining your list.

GLOSSARIES & DICTIONARIES

Think of dictionaries as immensely long lists. While ordinary dictionaries compile alphabetical lists of words in general use (along with their pronunciations and meanings), specialized dictionaries, or *glossaries,* zero in on subjects that may be unfamiliar to readers. And since every subculture — from skateboarders to Pentagon generals to newspaper designers — has its own lingo, by compiling lists of new or unusual words you can help readers expand their vocabularies while deciphering complex topics.

THAT SLANG THANG
Hot buzzwords on college campuses

Bank: money
Benzo: a Mercedes-Benz
Be sprung on: to like someone
Blaze: to leave
Blizz: a crazy, unrestrained act
Booty: drunk
Buckled: ugly
Bump: to skip or drop ("I *bumped* the class.")
Circle of death: a bad pizza
Coldblooded: very cool
Couch commander: a TV remote control
Crib: someone's home
Dog: a friend, buddy
Duggy: stylishly dressed

Filthy: Cool
Five-0: police officers
Frontin': to lie
Hane: heinous or gross
I'm sideways: goodbye
Jag: a loner or nerd
Juice: power, respect
Knuckle up: to fight
Lamo: a weird person
Lampin': relaxing
Loopy: drunk
Mad: good
Phat: good or cool
Reality impaired: an "airhead"
Scam: to cruise for girls or guys

Source: Los Angeles Daily News

This glossary offers outsiders — that is, most of us "normal" folks — a glimpse of the jargon used by college-going insiders. Though most slang terms are short-lived and regional, some occasionally slip into the mainstream. And they certainly paint a colorful cultural portrait.

FAKING FRENCH
A quick guide to common words and phrases

bon appetit (*BOH* nap-uh-teet): good appetite; a toast before eating.
carte blanche (kart *BLAHNSH*): full discretionary power.
c'est la vie (say la *VEE*): that's life.
déja vu (*DAY*-jah *VOO*): the sensation that something has happened before.
faux pas (fowe *PAW*): a social blunder.
je ne sais quoi (zhu nu say *KWAH*): I don't know what; the little something that eludes description.
joie de vivre (zhwah duh *VEEV*-ruh): love of life.
raison d'etre (*RAY*-zone *DET*-ruh): reason for being.
vis-à-vis (vee-zuh-*VEE*): compared to.

Source: The World Almanac

News stories often introduce readers to foreign words, names, and phrases. And whether a story discusses Russian politicians or Chinese athletes, pronunciation guides increase our word power.

HOORAY FOR HOLLYWOOD!

Number of movies where we've seen the naked posterior of:
◆ Al Pacino: **2**
◆ Mel Gibson: **3**
◆ Rob Lowe: **5**
◆ Dennis Quaid: **5**

Amount Humphrey Bogart bequeathed in his will to anyone claiming to be his heir: **$1**

Pairs of sunglasses owned by Jack Nicholson: **15**

Of actors getting top billing, the percentage that were women in:
◆ 1920: **57**
◆ 1990: **18**

Number of people killed by Santa Claus in the 1984 film *Silent Night, Deadly Night:* **9**

Number of heads smashed against walls in *Terminator 2: Judgment day:* **26**

Budget per episode of *Miami Vice:*
$1.5 million

Annual budget of the Miami Vice Squad:
$1.2 million

Estimated value of an 8x10 photo signed by:
◆ Mel Gibson: **$60**
◆ Mother Teresa: **$175**
◆ Marilyn Monroe: **$7,500**

Of the world's 10 all-time highest-grossing films, the number made by George Lucas, Steven Spielberg, or both: **7**

Percentage of airline passengers who say their favorite part of a flight is:
◆ the movie: **25**
◆ the in-flight magazine: **27**
◆ the peanuts: **19**

Number of minutes Zsa Zsa Gabor swims nude every day: **30**

Sources: Premiere Magazine, Entertainment Weekly, Willamette Week, Harper's Magazine.

CHECKLISTS

HOW YOU CAN HELP THE EARTH

It's never too late to change your habits, to begin making Earth-saving choices every day. Ordinary people CAN make a difference. And here are a few ways you can help.

WHEN YOU DRIVE

❏ Save gas by avoiding sudden stops and starts. If idling for more than a minute, turn off your engine.

❏ Avoid jackrabbit starts. Better yet, don't speed at all.

❏ Avoid air conditioning. The largest source of ozone-depleting CFC emissions in this country is car air-conditioning.

❏ Buy a fuel-efficient car. Increasing fuel-efficiency standards by a single mile per gallon would save 5.9 billion gallons of gas a year.

❏ Try to get there *without* driving: walk, bicycle, take the bus. Carpool.

WHEN YOU SHOP

❏ Bring your own reusable shopping bag.

❏ Buy organically grown food and favor locally grown products.

❏ Buy in bulk. Repackage in smaller portions with reusable storage containers for pantry or freezer.

❏ Look for unbleached paper versions of coffee filters, milk cartons, toilet paper and paper towels.

❏ Avoid products using excessive packaging. Tell store managers how you feel about over-packaging.

❏ Avoid products made from endangered species of taken illegally from the wild. Before buying a pet or plant, ask the store owner where it came from.

❏ Instead of buying them, rent or borrow items you don't use often, and maintain and repair the things you own to make them last longer.

WHEN YOU DO LAUNDRY

❏ Use detergents without phosphates. Better yet, use soap flakes.

❏ Use chlorine bleach sparingly. Or switch to a non-chlorine bleach.

❏ Only run full loads. Set up a rack to dry small loads (socks or underwear). Consider drying with solar power on an outdoor clothesline.

❏ Keep your dryer's lint trap clean.

❏ When buying a new washing machine, consider a front-loading washer. They use 40 percent less water. When buying a new dryer, consider an energy-efficient gas model, or an electric model with energy-saving features.

Most lists are passive — that is, they itemize information in a concise way, but they don't really ask readers to *do* anything.

But suppose you want to engage readers more actively? To force them to grab a pencil and *interact*? That's dynamic newspapering. And that's what we'll explore in the pages ahead.

Checklists, for instance, are instantly interactive. They can be simple, like this checklist of Macaroni & Cheese ingredients:

❏ **Macaroni**   ❏ **Cheese**

Or they can be complex and decorative, compiling tips, asking questions, encouraging responses. The important thing is to *get the reader involved* — to make information as accessible and relevant as you can.

CHILD-CARE CHECKLIST

Not sure what to look for at day-care centers? Here are questions to ask.

■ **How long has this center been operating?**

■ **What kind of training have staff members had?**

■ **What is the child-to-teacher ratio?** Experts say it should be no more than 4:1 for infants, 10:1 for toddlers.

■ **How are children disciplined?**

■ **Are meals provided?** If so, what's on the menu?

■ **Are facilities clean and well maintained?** Are child-safety precautions observed: heat covers on radiators, safety seals on electrical outlets, etc.

■ **Is there plenty of room for children to work and play?** Are play materials available and appropriate for different age levels?

■ **Are there facilities for taking care of sick children?**

■ **Most important: Do the children look happy and occupied?** Trust your instincts.

IS YOUR HOME BURGLAR-PROOF?

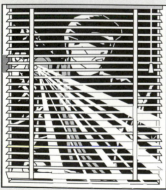

Knight-Ridder Tribune News

	YES	NO
1. Are exterior doors able to withstand excessive force?	☐	☐
2. Are exterior doors secured with deadbolt locks?	☐	☐
3. Do all exterior doors fit snugly in their frames?	☐	☐
4. Are door hinges pinned to prevent their removal?	☐	☐
5. Are garage doors and windows secured with locks?	☐	☐
6. Does your basement door have extra protection?	☐	☐
7. Is there a wide-angle viewer on the entrance door?	☐	☐
8. Are sliding-glass doors secure against forcing?	☐	☐
9. Are double-hung windows secured with extra locks?	☐	☐
10. Do basement windows have metal screens or locks?	☐	☐
11. Are trees & shrubs trimmed from doors & windows?	☐	☐
12. Are all entrances well-lighted at night?	☐	☐

All three checklists on this page strive to be interactive, either by offering user-friendly tips, by asking a series of questions, or by letting readers quiz themselves with check-off boxes for their answers.

Q&As

Q: **What's the deal here? Why is this sentence in boldface? And what's with that little "Q" in the black box?**

A: Good questions. *Journalistically,* we've changed our editorial approach. Rather than conveying information in the usual way — as narrative text in monologue form — we're printing a verbatim transcript of a conversation. *Typographically,* we're giving each voice in this dialogue a distinct identity. The interviewer speaks in boldface sans-serif, while the interviewee speaks in serif roman. And *legally,* I'm interviewing myself because my original plan for this page went down the toilet. I was going to reprint a juicy Q&A with a famous rock star, but the legal clearances got all mucked up. So you'll have to settle for *me* instead.

Q: **A famous rock star? Really? Which one?**

A: Forget it. It's just not gonna happen. I tried, but some editors can be real tightwads when it comes to *sharing old material they're never going to use again anyway.*

Q: **Was there anything, uh, *juicy* in that interview you'd like to share with us?**

A: No. Something about sleeping with Madonna, as I recall. But let's get back to our discussion of infographics, shall we? When you run a Q&A, you want to make sure each voice gets proper spacing, leading and—

Q: **Madonna? Really? Who slept with Madonna?**

A: Look, I'd rather not *discuss* it now. Let's talk about Q&As. Like, how effectively they can capture the spirit of an interview, making you feel as if you're actually *eavesdropping* on someone else's conversa—

Q: **Was it Meat Loaf? Charles Barkley — wait, no… he's not a rock star… Hey! I know: Sting!**

A: Huh?

Q&A: INDIVIDUAL RETIREMENT ARRANGEMENTS

What is an IRA?
It's an "individual retirement arrangement" that allows you to save up to $2,000 annually in a special account for your later years. You can then postpone paying taxes on your earnings until you begin making withdrawals at age 59½. You can set up an IRA at a bank, thrift or brokerage.

What are its tax advantages?
You can fully deduct your $2,000 contributions from your income on your tax return if you aren't covered by a retirement plan at work. If you *are* covered by earn less than $35,000 for single or $50,000 for married taxpayers, you may be able to deduct all or part of your contribution.

What if I can't deduct any part of my contribution?
They still are tax-advantaged; earnings on your money accumulate on a tax-deferred basis. That means faster accumulation and more money in the pot at the end.

Q&A formats capture the flavor of actual conversations, as shown above. They can answer hypothetical questions, too. At left, a small "explainer" sidebar poses typical questions readers might ask — an effective way to decode confusing subjects. At right, another type of Q&A — a stand-alone special feature — gives bold display to a single reader query.

THE STRAIGHT **POOP** BY WALT POOPUS

Does Coca-Cola contain actual cocaine? Was there ever a time when it did?
— **Pat Minniear, Boulder, Colo.**

When druggist John Pemberton brewed his first batch of "French Wine Coca (Ideal Nerve and Tonic Stimulant)" back in 1885, it contained both wine *and* cocaine. A year later the wine was removed, caffeine and cola nuts were added — and Coca-Cola was born. The original Coke contained (and presumably still contains) three parts coca leaves to one part cola nut. It was advertised as a medicine that would cure headaches, hysteria and melancholy.

Over the years, Coca-Cola quietly switched from fresh to "spent" coca leaves (minus the actual cocaine). Coke's true formula, however, remains a mystery — and its secret ingredient *7X* is known to only a handful of Coke employees.

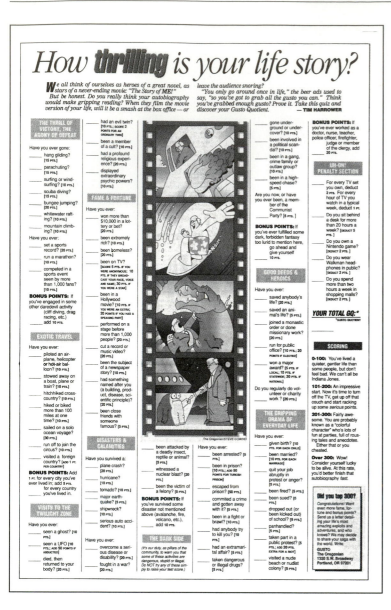

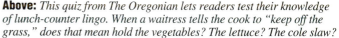

Above: *This quiz from The Oregonian lets readers test their knowledge of lunch-counter lingo. When a waitress tells the cook to "keep off the grass," does that mean hold the vegetables? The lettuce? The cole slaw?*

Left: *This full-page quiz asks, "How thrilling is your life story?" You earn points if you've seen a ghost, survived a plane crash, spent time in jail, etc. — and by totaling your points, you can gauge your "gusto quotient." This feature was enormously popular with readers, largely because it's so offbeat and interactive.*

Most newspaper stories are written in third-person past-tense: THAT GUY over THERE did THAT THING back THEN. As a result, readers often feel disconnected. Uninvolved. Aloof.

That's why quizzes are so successful. They're a quick way to let readers participate in a story, whether the topic is health *(Are You a Candidate for a Heart Attack?)*, sports *(The Super Bowl Trivia Test)* or hard news *(Are You Prepared for an Earthquake? Test Yourself)*. Quizzes, after all, are a kind of game, and readers love games. Feature pages, in fact, sometimes use game-board parodies *(How to Win the Diet Game)* to analyze and satirize topics.

Most of the time, you'll need to provide quiz answers somewhere in the paper. But if you're running a contest or reader poll, you'll need to include a mail-in address and formulate a system for processing masses of entries — as well as a plan for a follow-up story that tabulates survey results.

As any student knows, tests and quizzes come in a wide variety of formats: true/false, multiple choice, matching and so on. On the next page, we've displayed the most popular quiz formats for newspapers:

QUIZZES

SHORT ANSWER TESTS

1. How many Elvis albums reached Number One?
2. What was Elvis' major in high school?
3. In 1955, Elvis and his group were rejected when they auditioned for *Arthur Godfrey's Talent Scouts.* Who went on to win that competition?
4. What was Elvis' middle name?
5. What was Elvis' ironclad rule during concerts?
6. Who was Elvis' favorite movie actor as a teenager?
7. Which of Elvis' records was his own favorite?
8. What was the name of Elvis' flamboyant manager?
9. How much did Elvis weigh when he died?
10. What was Elvis doing when he died?

ANSWERS

1) None. 2) Shop. 3) Pat Boone. 4) Aron. 5) He never took requests. 6) Tony Curtis. 7) *It's Now or Never.* 8) Col. Tom Parker. 9) 255 pounds. 10) He was in his bathroom reading a book on the Shroud of Turin.

This is a typical format for a short trivia test. Note the boldface numbers, the hanging indent, the extra leading between questions. To conserve space, we've run the answers in paragraph form in the answer key. Are they easily readable?

MULTIPLE CHOICE TESTS

1. Which uses the most energy?
a) Stove
b) Refrigerator
c) Washing machine

2. Which form of energy is most environmentally friendly?
a) Nuclear power
b) Natural gas
c) Coal

3. What percentage of tropical rain forests still remain?
a) 80
b) 50
c) 20

4. How long does it take an aluminum can to decompose?
a) 50 years
b) 150 years
c) 500 years

5. What state has the highest level of carbon dioxide emissions?
a) California
b) New Jersey
c) Texas

6. Which consumes the most water?
a) Washing machine
b) Dishwasher
c) Toilet

ANSWERS

1. (a) But gas stoves are more efficient than electric models. 2. (b) 3. (b) They originally covered 12 percent of the earth; today they cover 6 percent. 4. (c) 5. (c) 6. (c)

Another familiar quiz format. Here, we've boldfaced the questions and aligned everything flush left. The answer box has been printed upside-down to keep readers from cheating — and also because many readers don't WANT to be able to peek at the answers.

SELF-APPRAISAL TESTS

Is your job burning you out? For each "yes" answer, give yourself the number of points shown, then add your total.

	SYMPTOM POINTS
1. My job consists of boring, repetitive tasks	2
2. It's not likely that I'll be promoted anytime soon	2
3. When I'm overloaded with work, there's no one to help me	3
4. I have more work to do than I could possibly finish	3
5. My boss and colleagues are extremely critical of my work	4
6. I've been getting sick more frequently lately	4
7. I'm using more alcohol/tranquilizers than I probably should	5
8. I've lost all sense of commitment and dedication to my job	5
9. I act depressed and irritable around friends and family	5
10. I fantasize acts of violence against my boss	7

SCORING YOURSELF

0-10 points: Your job stress is relatively normal. **10-20:** Moderate stress. Cultivate healthy habits to keep yourself optimistic. **20-30:** Stress is affecting your life negatively. Time to consider a change. **30-40:** Get some relief before your job seriously undermines your health.

Unlike the quizzes above, self-appraisal tests have no right or wrong answers. Rather, these tests are checklists which allow readers to evaluate their behavior. Like other exercises in pop psychology, these tests often try to point out problems readers may be unaware of.

FILL-IN-THE-BLANK SURVEYS & CONTESTS

1. **Favorite TV comedy** _____
2. **Favorite TV drama** _____
3. **Favorite TV actress** _____
4. **Favorite TV actor** _____
5. **Favorite TV theme song** _____
6. **Favorite TV news anchor** _____
7. **Favorite TV talk-show host** _____
8. **Favorite TV commercial** _____

MAIL TO:
Television Survey
The Bugle-Beacon
P.O. Box 1162
Portland, OR 97207

FAX TO:
(503)221-8069

Entries must be received by noon Monday, April 14. One entry per family, please.

You don't need to add fill-in blanks for most quiz answers, because they take up too much space. But if you want readers to DO something with their answers — add up scores, participate in a survey, enter a contest — then a format like this is helpful. If you want readers to respond, be sure to give them enough room to write.

SURVEYS & POLLS

WHERE DO *YOU* STAND ON FAMILY VALUES?

Test your own views with this cross section of questions from our family values poll, then see how your answers compare to the 400 statewide residents we surveyed last week.

Do you agree or disagree with the following statements:

1. In general, fathers do not make children as much of a priority as mothers do.
☐ Agree   ☐ Disagree

2. Businesses should offer flexible work schedules to accommodate the needs of families.
☐ Agree   ☐ Disagree

3. Families where Dad works and Mom stays home with kids just aren't realistic any more.
☐ Agree   ☐ Disagree

4. One of the biggest causes of teen problems is that parents don't spend time with their kids.
☐ Agree   ☐ Disagree

5. One family arrangement is as good as another, as long as children are loved and cared for.
☐ Agree   ☐ Disagree

6. Two-income families tend to place material needs ahead of family values.
☐ Agree   ☐ Disagree

7. Two-parent families are the best environment in which to raise children.
☐ Agree   ☐ Disagree

8. When parents can't get along, they should stay together for the sake of the children.
☐ Agree   ☐ Disagree

9. A parent should stay home with preschool children even if it means financial sacrifice.
☐ Agree   ☐ Disagree

10. I've seen just as many problems in two-parent families as in single-parent families.
☐ Agree   ☐ Disagree

STATEWIDE RESULTS

1. 58% agree.
2. 77% agree.
3. 63% agree.
4. 84% agree.
5. 76% agree.
6. 48% agree.
7. 79% agree.
8. 25% agree.
9. 67% agree.
10. 67% agree.

Source: The Oregonian

Checklists and quizzes ask readers questions. But when you want to know their answers, you conduct a poll.

Taking the public's pulse can be fascinating. Frightening. Time-consuming. But it's vital, whether the survey poses a question as simple as this —

If you had $100 million to spare, would you feed the poor or buy a pro baseball team?

Feed the poor	**69%**
Buy a team	**31%**

— or asks a series of questions like the chart below. As you can see, a variety of design options are available, from plain text to decorative logos, photos and graphics. The crucial thing is to keep data accurate by surveying as wide a sample as possible — and by avoiding biased or misleading questions.

CONGRESS: FIRST DISTRICT

If the primary election were held today, who would you vote for?

DEMOCRATS

Gary Conkling	**28%**
Elizabeth Furse	**39%**
Undecided	**33%**

REPUBLICANS

Tony Meeker	**58%**
Rick Rolf	**19%**
Undecided	**23%**

CHEATING: HOW COMMON IS IT?

A majority of high-school high achievers (students who maintain an A or B average) admit they cheat. Most say they've copied someone else's homework, but a surprising 40% confess to cheating on a test or quiz.

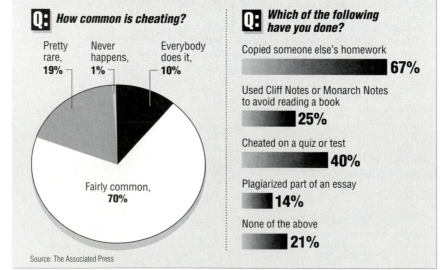

Q: How common is cheating?

Pretty rare, **19%**
Never happens, **1%**
Everybody does it, **10%**
Fairly common, **70%**

Q: Which of the following have you done?

Copied someone else's homework **67%**
Used Cliff Notes or Monarch Notes to avoid reading a book **25%**
Cheated on a quiz or test **40%**
Plagiarized part of an essay **14%**
None of the above **21%**

Source: The Associated Press

WHO WOULD YOU RATHER BE?

**BILL CLINTON
62%**

**BILLY IDOL
38%**

Survey results can run as plain text — or you can dress them up with graphic extras like these. At left, an election logo identifies this poll as part of a series; above, pie charts and bar charts help quantify poll results; at right, small mug shots add instant reader appeal.

QUOTE COLLECTIONS

STREET TALK: DO YOU SUPPORT THE PRESIDENT'S NEW TAX PLAN?

"The president's plan sounds fair to me. It's time for people to stop whining and start paying their fair share."

KRYSTYNA WOLNIAKOWSKI,
Lake Oswego

"No. Enough is enough. I don't think I should be penalized for running an honest, profitable business."

MIKE MORGER,
Wilsonville

"I don't mind being a bread-winner, but why do politicians eat such a big slice?"

BILL CANAVER,
Wilsonville

Roone Arledge, president of ABC News, allegedly quipped that when gathering public-opinion quotes, you need only three: one *for,* one *against* and one *funny.*

We've tested that maxim in our man-in-the-street quote sequence above. And whether you agree with Arledge or not, you must admit that those talking heads are both visually appealing *and* user-friendly — after all, readers love hearing their own voices in their newspaper.

Even without accompanying mug shots, quote collections are entertaining and informative. They generally follow one of two formats: a sampling of opinions on one topic from a variety of sources (below left), or a sampling of one person's opinions on a variety of topics (below right).

Either way, a few well-chosen remarks can give any story extra quotability.

FAMOUS LAST WORDS

Some fond farewells and deathbed wisdom from historical figures as they made their final exits:

"I wonder why he shot me?"
Huey Long, Louisiana governor (1935)

"My fun days are over."
James Dean, actor (1955)

"The earth is suffocating.
Swear to make them cut me open, so I won't be buried alive."
Frederic Chopin, composer (1849)

"Who the hell tipped you off? I'm Floyd, all right.
You got me this time."
Charles "Pretty Boy" Floyd, gangster (1934)

"I have a terrific headache."
Franklin Delano Roosevelt, U.S. president (1945)

"I am dying like a poisoned rat in a hole. I am what I am!"
Jonathan Swift, satirist (1745)

"I love you, Sarah. For all eternity, I love you."
James Polk, U.S. president (1849)

"I've had 18 straight whiskeys. I think that's the record."
Dylan Thomas, poet (1953)

THE WIT & WISDOM OF MARK TWAIN

Some wry observations from the writings of American humorist Samuel Clemens (1835-1910):

"When I was a boy of fourteen, my father was so ignorant I could hardly stand to have the old man around. But when I got to be twenty-one, I was astonished at how much he had learned in seven years."

"To cease smoking is the easiest thing I ever did. I ought to know because I've done it a thousand times."

"When your friends begin to flatter you on how young you look, it's a sure sign you're getting old."

"The secret source of humor itself is not joy, but sorrow. There is no humor in heaven."

"Good friends, good books and a sleepy conscience: this is the ideal life."

"Life would be infinitely happier if we could only be born at the age of eighty and gradually approach eighteen."

"Loyalty to a petrified opinion never yet broke a chain or freed a human soul."

"There is no sadder sight than a young pessimist."

This quote collection focuses on a single subject — famous last words — though the quotes originated from a wide variety of historical sources . . .

. . . while here, quotes cover a wide range of topics, but all originate from a single source. Either option is an effective sidebar for a longer feature.

CHARTS & GRAPHS

News is full of numbers: dollars, debts, crime statistics, budget percentages, election results. And the more complicated those numbers get, the more confused *readers* get. Take this brutal chunk of text, for instance:

> In 1968, 34,500 units were imported each year, comprising 16 percent of the annual total. By 1978, that number had risen to 77,400, and by 1988 more than 17,000 units were arriving monthly, representing an increase of 591 percent over 1967, the first full year of operation.

Huh? You see the problem. When math gets heavy, charts and graphs come in handy. They present numerical data in a simple, visual way — and the simpler they are, the better they work. On these pages, we'll look at the three basic types of numerical graphics: line charts, bar charts and pie charts.

The bars in most bar charts stack vertically — but they're equally effective when running horizontally, as they do above. Bar sizes and angles are often determined by the overall shape of the box, and here, that's how they fit best.

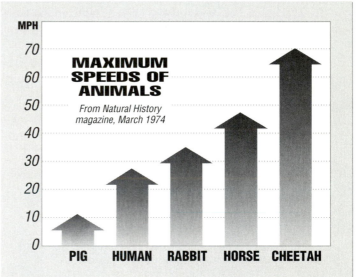

This bar chart adds a few extra graphic elements. Those dotted rules were added to help you gauge animal speed. The arrows atop the bars imply motion — as does the graduated tint in the arrows' screen.

BAR CHARTS

The bar chart *compares two or more items by sizing them as columns parked side by side.* It uses two basic components:

1) a scale running either horizontally or vertically showing data totals;
2) bars extending in the same direction representing the items being measured.

Bars are usually stacked in a logical order: either alphabetically, chronologically or ranked by size.

In simple bar charts, each item may be labeled either inside the bar or at either end (as in the examples above). The bars may be screened or given 3-D shadow effects, as long as the data isn't distorted.

In more complex bar charts — where the same items are compared to each other in different times or situations — each item is assigned its own color or screen pattern, which is then explained in a key or legend.

Background grids can be added to help readers track measurements. But though they're usually essential for fever charts, they're optional for bar charts.

CHARTS & GRAPHS

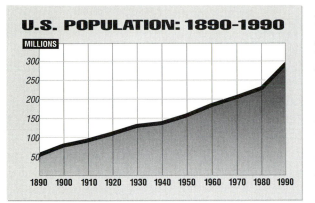

U.S. POPULATION: 1890-1990

MILLIONS

300
250
200
150
100
50

1890 1900 1910 1920 1930 1940 1950 1960 1970 1980 1990

Line charts work best when tracing one simple statistic over time — such as a growing population measured every decade (at left). The shading is an optional element. But you can also plot additional lines to compare different trends — as long as you clearly label which line represents which trend (at right).

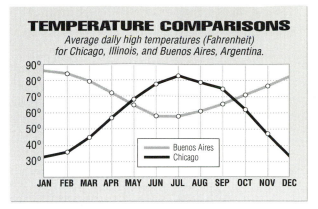

TEMPERATURE COMPARISONS

Average daily high temperatures (Fahrenheit) for Chicago, Illinois, and Buenos Aires, Argentina.

90°
80°
70°
60°
50°
40°
30°

Buenos Aires
Chicago

JAN FEB MAR APR MAY JUN JUL AUG SEP OCT NOV DEC

FEVER OR LINE CHARTS

The line chart (also called a fever chart) *measures changing quantities over time.* It uses three basic components:

1) a scale running vertically along one edge, measuring amounts;

2) a scale running horizontally along the bottom, measuring time; and

3) a jagged line connecting a series of points, showing rising or falling trends.

Line charts are created by plotting different points, then connecting the dots to draw a curve. (Charts often include a background grid to help readers track the numbers.) Obviously, a line that rises or falls dramatically will impress readers more than one that barely shows a blip.

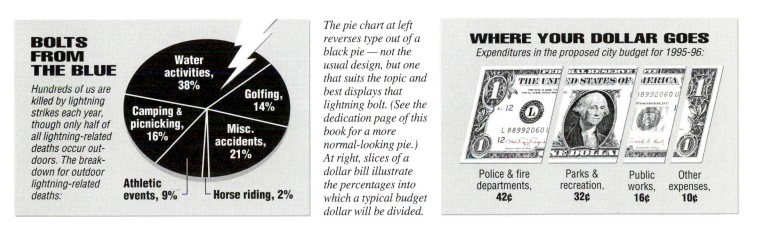

BOLTS FROM THE BLUE

Hundreds of us are killed by lightning strikes each year, though only half of all lightning-related deaths occur outdoors. The breakdown for outdoor lightning-related deaths:

Water activities, 38%

Golfing, 14%

Camping & picnicking, 16%

Misc. accidents, 21%

Athletic events, 9%

Horse riding, 2%

The pie chart at left reverses type out of a black pie — not the usual design, but one that suits the topic and best displays that lightning bolt. (See the dedication page of this book for a more normal-looking pie.) At right, slices of a dollar bill illustrate the percentages into which a typical budget dollar will be divided.

WHERE YOUR DOLLAR GOES

Expenditures in the proposed city budget for 1995-96:

Police & fire departments, 42¢

Parks & recreation, 32¢

Public works, 16¢

Other expenses, 10¢

PIE CHARTS

The pie chart *compares the parts that make up a whole.* It usually consists of:

1) a circle that represents 100% of something, and

2) several wedges (like slices of a pie) that divide the circle into smaller percentages. Each "slice" of the pie is an accurate proportion, which means that a segment representing 25% of the total would be one-quarter of the pie.

Figures for each slice are labeled either inside the slice (if there's room) or by scattering type, with pointers, around the outside of the pie. Slices are often shaded or color-coded for clearer distinction (or to emphasize a significant segment). As a rule of thumb, pies should be divided into no more than eight segments; beyond that, the slices get annoyingly thin.

To add impact, you can sometimes create pie charts from drawings or photos of the items being measured. For example, you can slice a dollar bill into sections to show where your tax dollar goes, or draw rings around a oil drum to break down the profits from a barrel of oil.

TABLES

CELEBRITIES AND THEIR REAL NAMES

WOODY ALLEN	ALLEN KONIGSBERG
TOM CRUISE	THOMAS MAPOTHER
JUDY GARLAND	FRANCES GUMM
WHOOPI GOLDBERG	CARYN JOHNSON
CARY GRANT	ARCHIBALD LEACH
ADOLF HITLER	ADOLF SCHICKLGRUBER
HARRY HOUDINI	EHRICH WEISS
BORIS KARLOFF	WILLAM PRATT
BEN KINGSLEY	KRISHNA BANJI
TINA TURNER	ANNIE MAE BULLOCK
JOHN WAYNE	MARION MORRISON

Tables using only text: *We've stacked two columns of names side by side to allow quick before-and-after comparisons. No headings or explanations are needed.*

THE U.S. & CANADA: HOW THEY COMPARE

	U.S.	Canada
AREA	3,618,770 sq. miles	3,849,672 sq. miles
POPULATION	256,561,239	27,351,000
POPULATION DENSITY	70 per sq. mile	7 per sq. mile
LARGEST CITY	New York (14,625,000)	Montreal (3,100,000)
GROSS DOMESTIC PRODUCT	$5.6 trillion	$521 billion
PER CAPITA INCOME	$22,470	$19,400
LIFE EXPECTANCY (at birth)	72 male, 79 female	74 male, 81 female
LITERACY RATE	97%	99%

Source: The World Almanac

Tables mixing text and numbers: *This simple table stacks two bio boxes side by side — one for the U.S., one for Canada — to allow readers to compare statistics. Note how the columns align with the left edges of the flags. Note, too, how the flags substitute for the names of the countries.*

A table is an age-old graphic device that's really half text, half chart. But unlike other charts, tables don't use bars or pie slices to make their point; instead, they stack words and numbers in rows to let readers make side-by-side comparisons.

Tables usually consist of: 1) headings running horizontally across the top of the chart; 2) categories running vertically down the left side; and 3) lists grouped in columns reading both across and down.

In short, tables are smartly stacked lists. They can compare two aspects of a topic (*WHAT'S IN & WHAT'S OUT*) or analyze a variety of categories:

WORLD RECORDS: TRACK AND FIELD

EVENT	RECORD	HOLDER	COUNTRY	DATE
100 meters	9.86 seconds	Carl Lewis	U.S.	Aug. 25, 1991
1 mile	3:44.39	Noureddine Morceli	Algeria	Sept. 5, 1993
High jump	8 ft., ½ in.	Javier Sotomayor	Cuba	July 27, 1993
Long jump	29 ft., 4½ in.	Mike Powell	U.S.	Aug. 30, 1992
Pole vault	20 ft., 1½ in.	Sergei Bubka	Ukraine	Sept. 19, 1992

To keep tables as neat as possible, carefully align all rows and columns. Though text usually works best flush left, numbers often align better flush right:

AMAZING BIBLE FACTS

Dr. Thomas Hartwell Horne (1780-1862), a student of the King James Version of the Bible, published these statistics in his book, *Introduction to the Study of the Scriptures:*

	OLD TESTAMENT	NEW TESTAMENT	TOTAL
Books	39	27	66
Chapters	929	260	1,189
Verses	23,214	7,959	31,173
Words	593,493	181,253	774,746
Letters	2,728,100	838,380	3,566,480

In small tables, hairline rules between rows may help alignment; in bigger tables, too many lines can look dizzying, so screen effects or occasional rules — every 5 lines, for example — may work better (see the tables at the top of this page). But for best results, remember: Keep all wording crisp and tight.

RATINGS

REALITY BITES *(PG-13)* Ben Stiller directs this charming and funny Generation X comedy about a young TV executive (Winona Ryder) torn between a grunge-rocker (Ethan Hawke) and a music-video executive (Stiller). The script captures some good, juicy twentysomething generational slang and cultural touchpoints. ★★★★

The most common way to rate movies, records, TV shows and restaurants is to assign from one (poor) to four or five stars (excellent).

REALITY BITES *(PG-13)* Ben Stiller directs this charming and funny Generation X comedy about a young TV executive (Winona Ryder) torn between a grunge-rocker (Ethan Hawke) and a music-video executive (Stiller). The script captures some good, juicy twentysomething generational slang and cultural touchpoints. **A-**

Many newspapers (and magazines such as Entertainment Weekly) assign letter grades — instantly decodable by anyone who's ever been a student.

REALITY BITES *(PG-13)* Ben Stiller directs this charming Generation X comedy about a young TV executive (Winona Ryder) torn between a grunge-rocker (Ethan Hawke) and a music-video executive (Stiller). The script blends juicy generational slang and cultural touchpoints.

Other papers, such as The San Francisco Chronicle, use a series of icons. For good films, the little man applauds; for bad ones, he falls asleep.

Journalists are trained to be objective. Impartial. Evenhanded. Fair.

Sure, that's one way to look at it. We could also argue that bland, impartial reportage puts readers to *sleep* — and that what readers *really* want is a guidebook to help them navigate through their world, a user's manual full of inside tips on what's good, what's bad and what's ugly.

Some parts of the paper have traditionally run consumer-friendly ratings and reviews: on editorial and entertainment pages, for instance. But ratings can also apply to politicians, hiking trails, stocks and bonds — nearly *anything*. Just choose the right device (stars, grades, thumbs) and label your package clearly.

THUMBS

◆ To the courage of the Magic Man.

◆ To Louisiana's voters, for having the sense to choose a scoundrel over a Nazi.

◆ To the continued dominance of the CHS cross country teams.

◆ To the cast of "Charlotte's Web" for an excellent performance.

◆ To the natural high gained from outwitting the hall monitor.

◆ To people in Spandex.

◆ To people who say that a *Terminator* costume promotes violence. They should be shot.

◆ To vandals who can't spell.

◆ To the clumps of freshmen that clog the 3rd floor hallway. Sort of like hairballs in a drain.

◆ To *New Kids On The Block* action figures. Good thing plastic melts in the microwave.

This table runs on the editorial page of The Little Hawk, allowing editors to hurl quick brickbats and bouquets.

RATING THE NINTENDO FOOTBALL GAMES

NAME OF THE GAME	GRAPHICS	PLAYING EASE	SOUND EFFECTS	SPECIAL FEATURES	OVERALL SCORE
10-YARD FIGHT	★	★★★★★	★	★	★★
JOHN ELWAY	★★	★★	★	★★	★
N.E.S.	★★★	★★	★★	★★	★★
JOHN MADDEN	★★★★★	★★★	★★★★★	★★★★	★★★★
TECMO BOWL	★★★★	★★★	★★	★★★	★★★

KEY If playing these games was like going to a real football game, this is how we'd rate them:

★ Kicked out for throwing weiners.
★★ That drunk, fat, shirtless guy in front of you.
★★★ You're there, but you're Bob Uecker.
★★★★ Like your own personal skybox.
★★★★★ On the sidelines, official waterboy.

This table from The Little Hawk rates five football games according to five sets of criteria. Stars indicate ratings, but we could just as easily have used icons, grades or descriptive text.

PIGSKIN PICKS

Our proud panel of prognosticators predicts this weekend's scores

	MADISON at LINCOLN 7:30 p.m. Friday	WILSON at JEFFERSON 2 p.m. Saturday	MONROE at ADAMS 1 p.m. Saturday	FILLMORE at JOHNSON 7 p.m. Friday
Bud Werner Sports editor, *The Times*	MADISON 21-14	WILSON 45-0	ADAMS 21-20	JOHNSON 7-0
Nick Kennedy Commentator, KXX Radio	LINCOLN 35-7	JEFFERSON 28-21	ADAMS 14-3	FILLMORE 21-14
Wally Benson Former Mudhog coach	MADISON 21-3	WILSON 45-7	ADAMS 35-7	FILLMORE 10-7

Another table: Here, a panel of sports experts predicts winners (and scores) for upcoming football games. Once created, this graphic format is easy to recycle week after week.

TIMELINES

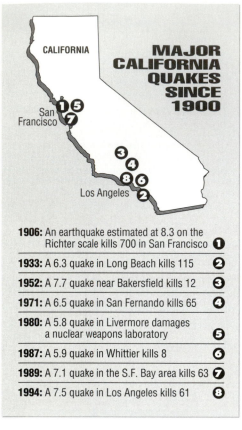

MAJOR CALIFORNIA QUAKES SINCE 1900

CALIFORNIA

San Francisco ①⑤⑦

Los Angeles ③④⑧⑥②

1906: An earthquake estimated at 8.3 on the Richter scale kills 700 in San Francisco ❶

1933: A 6.3 quake in Long Beach kills 115 ❷

1952: A 7.7 quake near Bakersfield kills 12 ❸

1971: A 6.5 quake in San Fernando kills 65 ❹

1980: A 5.8 quake in Livermore damages a nuclear weapons laboratory ❺

1987: A 5.9 quake in Whittier kills 8 ❻

1989: A 7.1 quake in the S.F. Bay area kills 63 ❼

1994: A 7.5 quake in Los Angeles kills 61 ❽

MILESTONES IN MACHINE INTELLIGENCE

1943: Do mathematics

1950: Large memories

1958: Play decent chess

1959: Beat humans at checkers

1965: First expert system

1976: Read printed text to blind

1975: Understand limited English

1979: Translate foreign language

1980: Beat world backgammon champion

1981: Synthesize speech

1983: Recognize restricted speech

1986: Beat human at ping pong

1988: Beat grand master at chess

1989: Read handwriting

1993: Recognize continuous speech

2000: Beat world chess champion

2005: Translate international phone call

2010: Understand unlimited English; serve dinner, clean house

2015: Use common sense

1940 1950 1960 1970 1980 1990 2000 2010 2020

SOURCE: Raymond Kurzweil, Maureen Caudill, American Association for Artificial Intelligence

Knight-Ridder Tribune News

Above: *This 1990 timeline chronicles key dates in computer history. Note how the scale turns gray in 1990, signaling a shift from historical events to projections.*

Left: *This California earthquake timeline is keyed to a map. Readers can either read the timeline first, then check the map, or study the map and then consult the timeline.*

Right: *When investigating a crime, it's essential to reconstruct the exact sequence of events. This minute-by-minute chronology paints a clear picture of the action.*

A CHRONOLOGY OF THE BEATING

Here's how events unfolded in Friday's beating of Tony Hewlitt at Lloyd Center:

9:05 p.m. Vice Principal Ted Brooks calls school police to report 40 to 50 "unwanteds" trying to get into a dance at Adams High School.

9:08 p.m. Lt. Steve Hodges of the school police arrives and requests backup from Portland police. Units are sent from North precinct.

9:35 p.m. The dance is shut down.

9:40 p.m. A number of youths drift toward Lloyd Center as police disperse the crowd from the dance.

10 p.m. The crowd of youths arrives at Lloyd Center as Hewlitt and his fiancee, Tara White, wait for their ride. Hewlitt is beaten by two youths. Police arrive minutes later.

When we write fiction, we plot the story chronologically: *Boy meets girl in spring, boy marries girl in summer, boy gets hit by a bus in fall,* and so on. But when we write newspaper stories, we often bounce back and forth through time: *Yesterday's meeting discussed tomorrow's vote to repeal a 1987 tax to fund a domed stadium by 2001. . .* and so on.

Time gets tangled up in text. That's why timelines (or chronologies) are so effective. They put topics in perspective by illustrating, step by step, how events unfolded.

The most graphically ambitious timelines combine images and text to create a pictorial recap of past events. Here, mug shots of musicians help to reconstruct the year's musical highlights. (Keep in mind that faces in photos should always be at least the size of a dime; this timeline, like many of the graphics on these pages, has been slightly reduced.)

PORTLAND: THE YEAR IN ROCK

From Tina Turner to Tom Petty, 1994 was a stellar year for local music-lovers. A few selected highlights:

April 14: Despite constant rain and thunder, 120,000 gather in Hebb Park for the Spring Fling Wingding featuring Toejam and Ducks Deluxe.

Aug. 10: The Grateful Dead play a surprise gig at Mummy's Cabaret Lounge. Opening the show is controversial rapper Ice-9.

Oct. 17: Tina Turner energizes a crowd of 22,000 at the Schnitz, performing such deathless classics as "Proud Mary" and "Lover Man."

JAN. | FEB. | MARCH | APRIL | MAY | JUNE | JULY | AUG. | SEPT. | OCT. | NOV. | DEC.

Feb. 17: Kurt Cobain smashes his guitar to protest the war in Bosnia during Nirvana's sold-out show at Civic Auditorium.

May 20: Billy Idol causes a near-riot when he incites fans to storm the Memorial Coliseum stage; four are injured, 22 arrested in the stampede.

Sept. 3: Tom Petty and the Heartbreakers headline a benefit performance for Greenpeace in Pioneer Courthouse Square.

Nov. 25: Local rock legend Elvis King stuns fans by announcing he's retiring from the stage to pursue a newspaper career.

STEP-BY-STEP GUIDES

HOW TO RESUSCITATE A LIZARD

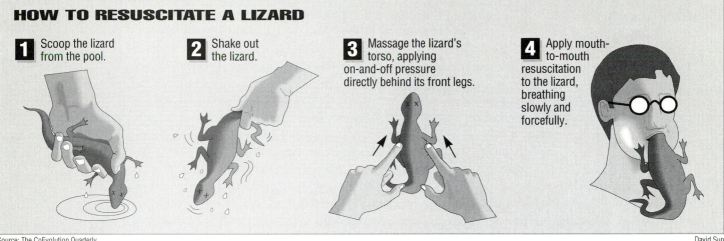

1 Scoop the lizard from the pool.

2 Shake out the lizard.

3 Massage the lizard's torso, applying on-and-off pressure directly behind its front legs.

4 Apply mouth-to-mouth resuscitation to the lizard, breathing slowly and forcefully.

Source: The CoEvolution Quarterly   David Sun

Life is full of complex procedures, from changing a tire to baking a cake to — well, resuscitating a lizard. And the clearest way to walk readers through a series of instructions is to arrange them in logical, numerical form:

A step-by-step guide.

If you've ever assembled Christmas toys or wrestled with tax returns, you know how confusing bad instructions can be. That's why step-by-step guides must be as clear, precise and user-friendly as possible. Whenever possible, add drawings or photos to illustrate key steps; as the examples on this page make evident, it's better to *show* than just *tell*.

HOW TO MAKE A HOLIDAY WREATH

What you'll need:
◆ fresh greens (you can cut home-grown evergreens or purchase them from a nursery. It takes about 7 pounds of branches to make a 12-inch wreath).
◆ wire frame (these come in a variety of sizes; a 12-inch frame costs about $1.50).
◆ preservative (this will keep greens fresh for about a month).
◆ pruning shears.
◆ wire clippers.
◆ paddle wire.

What to do:
☐ Clip the greens into hand-sized pieces. Save the fluffy ones; discard woody branches.
☐ Layer 3-4 pieces of greens into a bundle.
☐ Attach each bundle to the wire frame. Pull the wire away from the wreath's center to tighten it.
☐ Continue to attach bundles, overlapping stems with greens, until the frame is completely covered with evergreens. Alternate bundles of cedar (or other greens) with bundles of fir.
☐ Add pine cones. Loop wire around the bottom of the cone, then attach the wire to the wreath.
☐ For special trim, place dried or silk flowers amid the greens.
☐ Attach pearl or other garlands with wire.
☐ Finally, add the bow. Make your own or buy one ready-made.

Left: *This step-by-step guide displays a photo of a finished wreath but uses only text to explain the assembly process. That'll work when time and space are tight — but imagine how much more effective this guide would be if every step were illustrated.*

Right: *This full-color poster page analyzes the mechanics of hitting a baseball — the stance, the stride, the swing — with expert advice from batting coach Ken Griffey Sr. Note the freeze-frame batting sequence running along the bottom of the page.*

DIAGRAMS

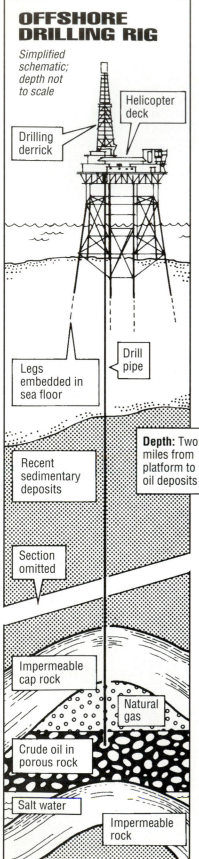

OFFSHORE DRILLING RIG

Simplified schematic; depth not to scale

- Helicopter deck
- Drilling derrick
- Drill pipe
- Legs embedded in sea floor
- **Depth:** Two miles from platform to oil deposits
- Recent sedimentary deposits
- Section omitted
- Impermeable cap rock
- Natural gas
- Crude oil in porous rock
- Salt water
- Impermeable rock

Maps focus on the *where* of a story; diagrams focus on the *what* and *how*. They freeze an image so we can examine it in closer detail, using cutaway views, step-by-step analyses, or itemized descriptions of key components.

Whatever your topic, diagrams will work best if you:

◆ **Focus tightly.** Pinpoint precisely what you need to explain before you begin. What's most essential? Most interesting? Should the diagram be active (showing how the object moves) or passive? (Notice how the passive diagrams on this page simply point to each component.) Whatever the approach — whatever the topic — keep your diagram as clean and simple as you can.

◆ **Design logically.** Let your central image determine the diagram's shape (for instance, that oil rig is a deep vertical). If you're running a sequence of images, find a perspective that lets you show the steps in the most logical order.

◆ **Label clearly.** Avoid clutter by using a consistent treatment for all callouts (sometimes called *factoids*), whether with pointer boxes, shadows, lines or arrows:

Callout   Callout   Callout   Callout   Callout

◆ **Research carefully.** You're becoming an instant expert; readers will rely on your accuracy. Do your homework. Cross-check references. Read the story. Study photos. Talk to outside experts.

In short: Become a graphics reporter.

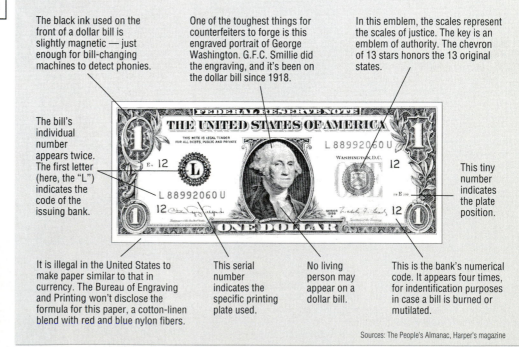

The black ink used on the front of a dollar bill is slightly magnetic — just enough for bill-changing machines to detect phonies.

One of the toughest things for counterfeiters to forge is this engraved portrait of George Washington. G.F.C. Smillie did the engraving, and it's been on the dollar bill since 1918.

In this emblem, the scales represent the scales of justice. The key is an emblem of authority. The chevron of 13 stars honors the 13 original states.

The bill's individual number appears twice. The first letter (here, the "L") indicates the code of the issuing bank.

This tiny number indicates the plate position.

It is illegal in the United States to make paper similar to that in currency. The Bureau of Engraving and Printing won't disclose the formula for this paper, a cotton-linen blend with red and blue nylon fibers.

This serial number indicates the specific printing plate used.

No living person may appear on a dollar bill.

This is the bank's numerical code. It appears four times, for indentification purposes in case a bill is burned or mutilated.

Sources: The People's Almanac, Harper's magazine

Want to explore the different components of a dollar bill? The diagram above combines history and trivia to give readers a quick visual tour — something difficult to achieve in text alone. At left, a more traditional diagram uses a cutaway view of the earth's crust to make the offshore drilling process more understandable.

DIAGRAMS

With the right topic, a diagram becomes more than just a supplementary graphic; it becomes lead art that's informational *and* entertaining. For example, these two full-page diagrams combine callouts and color images to create dynamic feature packages (notice how the turkey page uses no traditional "story" at all). Diagram packages can work with photos, too — like our "How to Build A Mechanical" on page 186 — to illustrate a step-by-step procedure. All you need is a strong image and some solid reporting to achieve professional results.

Above, a Thanksgiving feature page from the Rochester Times-Union offers facts about a turkey's voice, brain, beak and "snood." At right, a detailed look at the pope's fashions (in advance of his Denver visit).

When John Paul II steps out

When the pope arrives in Denver, he will be wearing his everyday clothes. These, like all the garb worn by Roman Catholic clergy, have their origins in the ordinary dress of early Christians and can show rank.

Everyday dress

▶ **ZUCCHETTO:** Skull cap worn by all bishops, but only the pope wears white

Pope is senior bishop
Bishops are high-ranking officials in the Roman Catholic Church. The rank includes archbishops, cardinals, some abbots and the pope, the bishop of highest rank.

▶ **RING:** Gold bishop's ring contains his choice of stone; originally, the papal ring was used like a king's, for sealing documents; pope seals with his fisherman's ring, which is not worn and is broken when he dies

▶ **CINCTURE:** Silk sash; only the pope wears white

▶ **CASSOCK:** Basic clerical garb; only the pope wears white

▶ **MANTELLO:** Long red wool cloak worn in cold weather

▶ **PECTORAL CROSS:** Contains the relic of a saint or a piece of the Holy Cross; all bishops have two: a simple one for everyday and a more elaborate ceremonial one on a silk cord; evolved from simpler crosses worn by early Christians

▶ **COAT OF ARMS:** Embroidered on the cincture; John Paul's is blue, with the letter "M" for Mary, Jesus' mother

▶ **SHOES:** Red velvet with embroidered cross; white satin during Easter

Choir dress

Worn at Mass and diplomatic functions

▶ **MOZZETTA:** Bishop's cape; like a medieval shoulder warmer; pope's is red satin in summer, red velvet in winter, white damask for Easter

▶ **STOLE:** Silk band indicating authority; only the pope wears it outside the mozzetta

▶ **ROCHET:** White linen and lace tunic

▶ **CASSOCK**

Liturgical dress

Worn when celebrating Mass

▶ **BISHOP'S MITRE WITH INFULAE (bands):** Originally a cap for Roman dignitaries; removed during most solemn parts of Mass

▶ **PALLIUM:** White wool band with six crosses; shows rank of bishop

▶ **CROZIER:** Staff; pope's differs from bishops', which is hooked like a shepherd's

▶ **CHAUSABLE:** Outer vestment; originally a large cloak

▶ **ALB:** Basic liturgical vestment; similar to Roman tunics

SOURCES: Catholic University of America, Catholic Encyclopedia for School and Home, 1993 Catholic Almanac, The Dictionary of Liturgy and Worship; research by PAT CARR

Knight-Ridder Tribune/RON CODDINGTON

MAPS

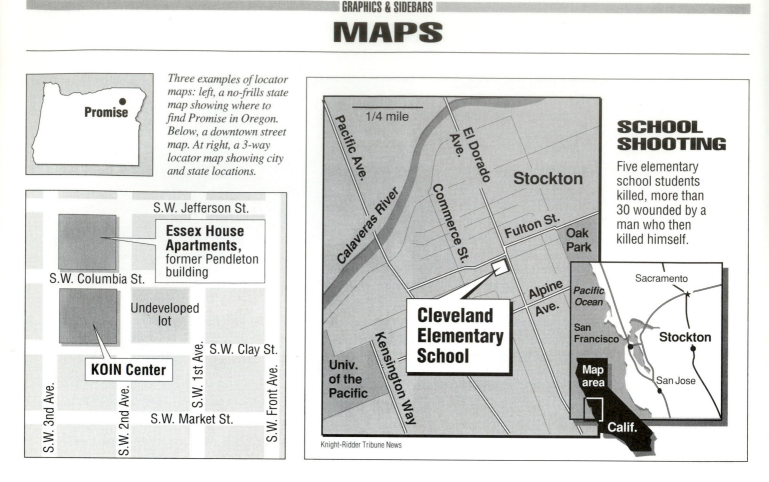

Three examples of locator maps: left, a no-frills state map showing where to find Promise in Oregon. Below, a downtown street map. At right, a 3-way locator map showing city and state locations.

Promise

S.W. Jefferson St.

Essex House Apartments, former Pendleton building

S.W. Columbia St.

Undeveloped lot

KOIN Center

S.W. Clay St.

S.W. 3rd Ave.

S.W. 2nd Ave.

S.W. 1st Ave.

S.W. Front Ave.

S.W. Market St.

1/4 mile

Pacific Ave.

El Dorado Ave.

Calaveras River

Commerce St.

Stockton

Fulton St.

Oak Park

Alpine Ave.

Cleveland Elementary School

Univ. of the Pacific

Kensington Way

Knight-Ridder Tribune News

SCHOOL SHOOTING

Five elementary school students killed, more than 30 wounded by a man who then killed himself.

Sacramento

Pacific Ocean

San Francisco

Stockton

Map area

San Jose

Calif.

Most Americans are poor geographers. They have a tough time remembering even the easy stuff, like where New York City is. (Hint: it's on the East Coast — that's the *right edge* of a U.S. map.) So how can we expect them to visualize volcanoes in Fiji? Riots in Lesotho? Train wrecks in Altoona?

With maps. Maps can enhance almost any news story, if you're ambitious enough, but they're especially important for:

❏ any story where a knowledge of geography is essential to the story's meaning (an oil spill, a border dispute, a plane crash), or

❏ any local story where readers may participate (a parade, a new gym).

Maps come in all sizes and styles — world maps, street maps, relief maps, weather maps, etc. But the maps most often produced in newsrooms are:

◆ **Locator maps:** These show, as simply as possible, the location of a key place ("X" marks the spot), or tell the reader where something occurred.

◆ **Explanatory maps:** These are used for storytelling, to show *how* an event progressed. Often using a step-by-step approach to label sequences, these maps are visually active (as opposed to passive locator maps).

◆ **Data maps:** These show the geographical distribution of data, working like a chart to convey statistical information: population distributions, political trends, weather, etc. (See our examples of each map type above).

How are maps created? They're copied. Though you can't cut a map out of a road atlas and stick it in the paper (that's a copyright violation), you *can* trace a map's highlights, then fill in your own details as necessary.

Every paper should compile a library of maps in a variety of scales, from global to local. Buy a world atlas; collect state highway maps, city and county maps, even brochures from your local chamber of commerce (showing shopping areas, local parks, hiking trails, the layout of the airport).

Be prepared. You never know where news is going to break.

MAPS

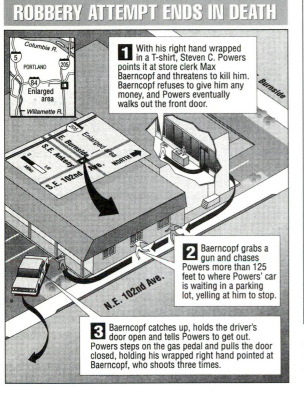

ROBBERY ATTEMPT ENDS IN DEATH

Columbia R.

5 PORTLAND 205

84 Enlarged area

Willamette R.

Burnside

Enlarged area

206

S.E. Burnside

E. Burnside Ave.

NORTH

S.E. 102nd

N.E. 102nd Ave.

1 With his right hand wrapped in a T-shirt, Steven C. Powers points it at store clerk Max Baerncopf and threatens to kill him. Baerncopf refuses to give him any money, and Powers eventually walks out the front door.

2 Baerncopf grabs a gun and chases Powers more than 125 feet to where Powers' car is waiting in a parking lot, yelling at him to stop.

3 Baerncopf catches up, holds the driver's door open and tells Powers to get out. Powers steps on the gas pedal and pulls the door closed, holding his wrapped right hand pointed at Baerncopf, who shoots three times.

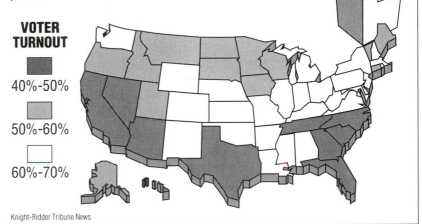

GETTING OUT THE VOTE IN THE U.S.

Low voter turnout on Election Day is a growing problem in the United States. Here is a state-by-state breakdown of the percentage of eligible voters who voted in the 1984 presidential election.

VOTER TURNOUT

40%-50%

50%-60%

60%-70%

Knight-Ridder Tribune News

At left, an explanatory map showing a step-by-step sequence of events. Note the 3-D buildings, the cutaway diagrams, the helpful arrows — all describing a complex series of events in a compact two-column box. Above, a simple data map using tint screens to illustrate state-by-state voting statistics.

GUIDELINES

◆ **Create design guidelines for all maps.** You'll save time and give your maps a consistent look if you set clear standards for abbreviations, screens, line weights, symbols — and most important:

◆ **Use type consistently.** Use designated fonts in designated sizes (sans serif will usually work best behind screens). Avoid type that's too big (over 12 point) or too small (under 8 point). Decide where you'll use all caps (countries? states?), italics (bodies of water?), boldface (key points of interest only?).

◆ **Keep maps simple.** The whole planet can fit into a one-column box, if necessary. Make your point obvious; trim away all unnecessary details. Anything that doesn't enhance the map's meaning distracts attention.

◆ **Make maps dynamic.** Don't just re-create a dull road map; add shadow boxes, screens, 3-D effects, tilted perspectives — just be careful not to distort the map's accuracy or destroy its integrity.

◆ **Keep north pointing "up."** If north isn't at the top of a map, include a "north" arrow to show where it is. Otherwise, the arrow isn't necessary.

◆ **Add mileage scales whenever possible.** They give readers perspective.

◆ **Match the map to the story.** Be sure that every significant place mentioned in the text is accounted for on the map.

◆ **Center maps carefully.** Keep them as tightly focused as possible. If pockets of "dead" space occur, you can fill them with mileage scales, callout boxes, locator-map insets or illustrations.

◆ **Assume your readers are lost.** To help them understand where they are, you may need to give your map a headline or an introductory paragraph. You may need to add a locator map to your *main* map if that makes it clearer. (For instance, if you draw a detailed street map, you should show what part of the city you're in.) Above all, include any familiar landmarks — cities, rivers, highways, shopping malls — that help readers get their bearings.

GRAPHICS PACKAGES

KRT Infographics/RON CODDINGTON

Above, one of a series of award-winning poster pages produced by The Chicago Tribune for the 1988 Winter Olympics. Each full-color page used the same basic format to analyze the techniques, equipment, rules and course layouts for top Olympic events.

The bigger the story, the more explanation it needs — and the more complex its graphics can become. That's why you'll often see dazzling graphic packages, like the ones on these two pages, combining charts, maps, sidebars and more into an encyclopedic extravaganza.

Done well, these packages present as much (or more) information as any news story. But to execute these graphics packages well, you'll need:

◆ **Time.** Some, like the Olympics page above, are part of special series that take months to assemble. Most megagraphics need at least several days to prepare and can't be rushed without dismal results.

◆ **Teamwork.** These aren't solo efforts. They demand cooperation and planning for the research, reporting, art and layout to come together smoothly.

◆ **Expertise.** Sorry to say, these packages are terribly difficult to produce. Don't tackle anything this tricky until you've honed your graphics techniques.

◆ **A firm commitment of space.** Don't let them reduce your full-page package down to 2 columns at the last minute. Get the space you need *guaranteed.*

Above all, don't overdo it. Pages like these take readers right to the edge of "information overload." Ask yourself: How much data can our readers handle?

The Middle East is frequently in the news — and because the Islamic faith plays a central role in the lives of its people, this 1993 Knight-Ridder Tribune package explains the history, beliefs, geography and architecture of Islam. Note the elegant interplay of art and text.

GRAPHICS PACKAGES

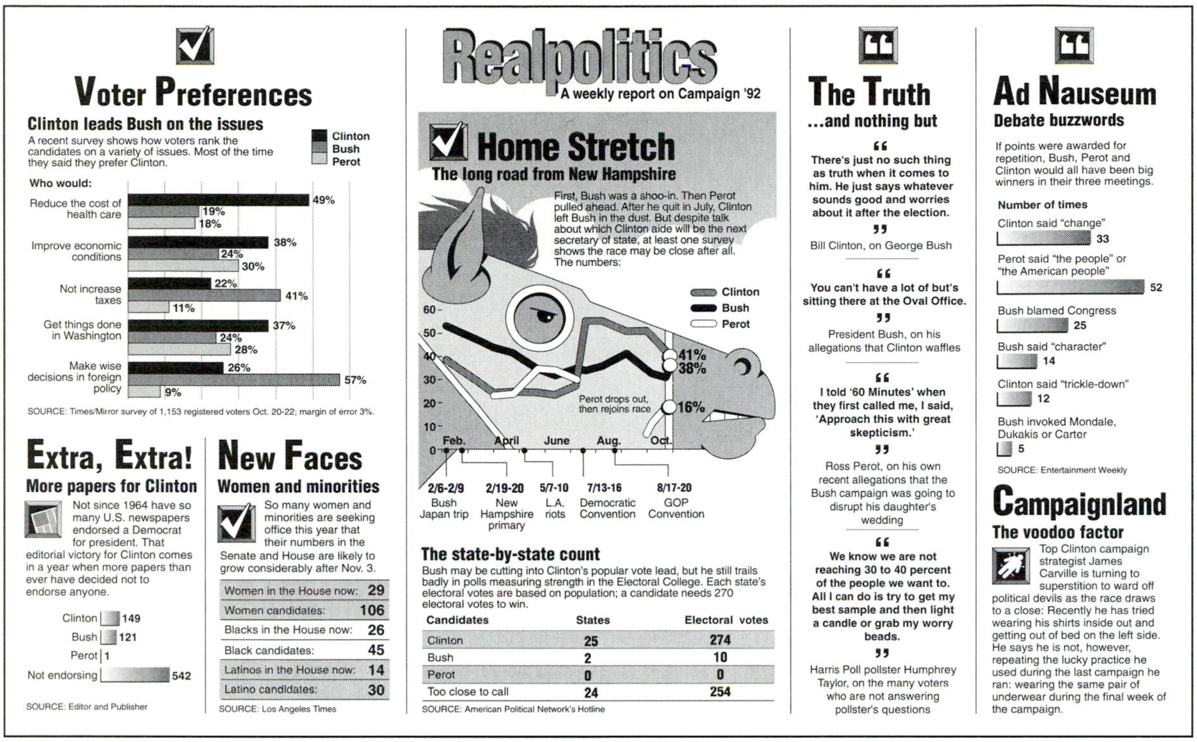

☑ Voter Preferences

Clinton leads Bush on the issues

A recent survey shows how voters rank the candidates on a variety of issues. Most of the time they said they prefer Clinton.

- ■ Clinton
- ▨ Bush
- ▨ Perot

Who would:

Reduce the cost of health care
49%
19%
18%

Improve economic conditions
38%
24%
30%

Not increase taxes
41%
22%
11%

Get things done in Washington
37%
24%
28%

Make wise decisions in foreign policy
57%
26%
9%

SOURCE: Times/Mirror survey of 1,153 registered voters Oct. 20-22; margin of error 3%.

Extra, Extra!

More papers for Clinton

Not since 1964 have so many U.S. newspapers endorsed a Democrat for president. That editorial victory for Clinton comes in a year when more papers than ever have decided not to endorse anyone.

Clinton 149
Bush 121
Perot 1
Not endorsing 542

SOURCE: Editor and Publisher

New Faces

Women and minorities

☑ So many women and minorities are seeking office this year that their numbers in the Senate and House are likely to grow considerably after Nov. 3.

Women in the House now:	29
Women candidates:	106
Blacks in the House now:	26
Black candidates:	45
Latinos in the House now:	14
Latino candidates:	30

SOURCE: Los Angeles Times

Realpolitics

A weekly report on Campaign '92

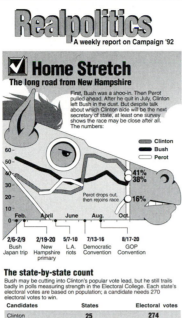

☑ Home Stretch

The long road from New Hampshire

First, Bush was a shoo-in. Then Perot pulled ahead. After he quit in July, Clinton left Bush in the dust. But despite talk about which Clinton aide will be the next secretary of state, at least one survey shows the race may be close after all. The numbers:

- ▨ Clinton
- ■ Bush
- ▨ Perot

41%
38%
16%

Perot drops out, then rejoins race

Feb. April June Aug. Oct.

2/6-2/9 Bush Japan trip
2/19-20 New Hampshire primary
5/7-10 L.A. riots
7/13-16 Democratic Convention
8/17-20 GOP Convention

The state-by-state count

Bush may be cutting into Clinton's popular vote lead, but he still trails badly in polls measuring strength in the Electoral College. Each state's electoral votes are based on population; a candidate needs 270 electoral votes to win.

Candidates	States	Electoral votes
Clinton	25	274
Bush	2	10
Perot	0	0
Too close to call	24	254

SOURCE: American Political Network's Hotline

❝ The Truth

...and nothing but

❝ There's just no such thing as truth when it comes to him. He just says whatever sounds good and worries about it after the election. ❞

Bill Clinton, on George Bush

❝ You can't have a lot of but's sitting there at the Oval Office. ❞

President Bush, on his allegations that Clinton waffles

❝ I told '60 Minutes' when they first called me, I said, 'Approach this with great skepticism.' ❞

Ross Perot, on his own recent allegations that the Bush campaign was going to disrupt his daughter's wedding

❝ We know we are not reaching 30 to 40 percent of the people we want to. All I can do is try to get my best sample and then light a candle or grab my worry beads. ❞

Harris Poll pollster Humphrey Taylor, on the many voters who are not answering pollster's questions

❝ Ad Nauseum

Debate buzzwords

If points were awarded for repetition, Bush, Perot and Clinton would all have been big winners in their three meetings.

Number of times

Clinton said "change"
33

Perot said "the people" or "the American people"
52

Bush blamed Congress
25

Bush said "character"
14

Clinton said "trickle-down"
12

Bush invoked Mondale, Dukakis or Carter
5

SOURCE: Entertainment Weekly

Campaignland

The voodoo factor

Top Clinton campaign strategist James Carville is turning to superstition to ward off political devils as the race draws to a close: Recently he has tried wearing his shirts inside out and getting out of bed on the left side. He says he is not, however, repeating the lucky practice he ran: wearing the same pair of underwear during the final week of the campaign.

The Knight-Ridder Tribune graphics service produces some of the most progressive and clever packages in the business — as these weekly Campaign '92 packages proved. Each week, these reports blended statistics, fast facts, quotes and polls to create a fascinating montage of election information.

OREGON'S WINE RUSH

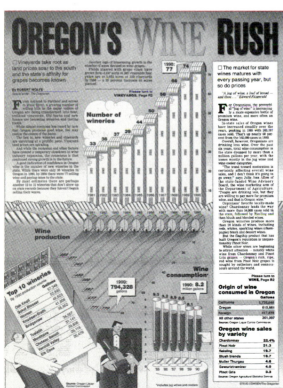

☐ Vineyards take root as land prices soar to the south and the state's affinity for grapes becomes known

By ROBERT WOLFE

For Oregonians, the proverbial "jug of wine" is increasingly a more expensive bottle of premium wine, and more often an Oregon wine.

In-state sales of Oregon wines have increased steadily over the years, peaking in 1990 with 263,397 cases sold. That's up nearly 60 percent from 166,000 cases in 1980.

Overall, however, Oregonians are drinking less wine. Over the past six years, total wine consumption in the state dropped by more than a million gallons per year, with the losses mostly in the jug wine and wine cooler categories.

"The trend toward moderation is certainly affecting overall wine sales, and I don't think it's going to go away," says Julia Ann Allen of the state-funded Wine Advisory Board, the wine marketing arm of the Department of Agriculture. "People are drinking less, but they are willing to pay more for premium wine, and that is Oregon wine."

Oregonians' favorite locally-made wine? Chardonnay leads the way with more than 34,000 cases sold in the state, followed by Riesling and then blush and blended wines.

Oregon wineries produce more than 30 kinds of wines, including reds, whites, sparkling wines (champagnes) blush and dessert wines.

But the flagship product that has built Oregon's reputation is unquestionably Pinot Noir.

While other wines are beginning to attract attention among more than 36 kinds of wines, wine from Chardonnay and Pinot Gris grapes — Oregon's rich, ripe, red wine from Pinot Noir grapes is sought by collectors and connoisseurs around the world.

Please turn to WINE, Page R2

☐ The market for state wines matures with every passing year, but so do prices

"A jug of wine, a loaf of bread — and thou..." Edward Fitzgerald

Another sign of blossoming growth is the number of acres devoted to wine grapes. Florida growers with grape vines have grown from 4,497 acres in 360 vineyards four years ago to 5,481 acres at 330 vineyards in 1990 — a 20 percent increase in wine planting.

Number of wineries

77 74 61 57 44 37 39 33

Wine production

Top 10 wineries

Wine consumption

1990: 8.2 million gallons

Origin of wine consumed in Oregon

	Gallons
California	1,725,646
Oregon	615,561
Foreign	417,479
All other states	361,097

Source: Oregon Liquor Control Commission

Oregon wine sales by variety

Chardonnay	22.4%
Pinot Noir	21.3
Riesling	19.7
Blush blends	18.7
Muller Thurgau	4.6
Gewurztraminer	4.0
Pinot Gris	3.3

Source: Oregon Winegrowers Association

Above, simple charts and tables combine to create a complex graphic analysis of Oregon's booming wine industry. Six different charts are incorporated into this colorful package, most of them drawn in an appealing cartoon style that decorates the page without detracting from the data. Note how the wine glasses, the vineyard rooftops and the wine spilling from barrels all serve as bar charts.

A Look Back

PORTLAND'S CITY HALL

The 98-year-old building is one of Portland's few remaining links between the horse-and-buggy era and the Information Age.

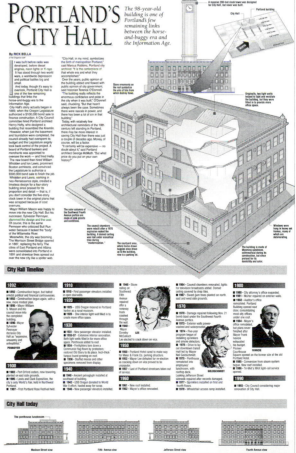

By RICK BELLA

I was built before radio was developed, before diesel engines, neon lights or X-rays. It has stood through two world wars, a worldwide depression and political battles big and small.

And today, though it's easy to overlook, Portland City Hall is one of the few remaining buildings that links the horse-and-buggy era to the Information Age.

City Hall's story actually began in 1889, when the Oregon Legislature authorized a $100,000 bond sale to finance construction. A City Council committee hired Portland architect Henry Hefty, who designed a building that resembled the Kremlin. However, when just the basement and foundation were completed, the council already had overspent its budget and the Legislature angrily took back control of the project. A board of Portland bankers and merchants was appointed to oversee the work — and fired Hefty. The new board then hired William Whidden and Ion Lewis, prominent Boston architects, and convinced the Legislature to authorize a $500,000 bond sale to finish the job. Whidden and Lewis, working in neo-Renaissance style, created a timeless design for a four-story building since praised for its proportion and detail — that is, if you don't consider the five-story clock tower in the original plans that was scrapped because of cost overruns.

Mayor William Mason was happy to move into the new City Hall. But his successor, Sylvester Pennoyer, skimmed the design and the cost. Of course, this is the same Pennoyer who criticized Bull Run water because it lacked the "body" of the Willamette River.

Meanwhile, the city was booming. The Morrison Street Bridge opened in 1887, replacing the ferry. The cities of East Portland and Albina were consolidated into Portland in 1891 and streetcar lines spread out over the new city like a spider web.

"City Hall, in my mind, symbolizes the birth of metropolitan Portland," said Marcus Robbins, Portland city archivist. "It is the centerpiece of that whole era and what they accomplished."

Over the years, public opinion of the building ebbed and flowed with public opinion of city government, said historian Terence O'Donnell. "The building really reflects the enormous confidence and pride in the city when it was built," O'Donnell said, chuckling. "But that hasn't always been the case. Sometimes there were rascals in power, and there has been a lot of sin in that building."

Today, with relatively few architectural reminders of the 19th century left standing in Portland, there may be more interest in saving City Hall than there was just a couple of decades ago. Money, of course, will be a factor.

"It certainly will be expensive — no doubt about it," said Portland architect George McMath. "But what price do you put on your own history?"

City Hall Timeline

1892
- **1892** - Construction begun, but halted amidst political and financial controversies.
- **1893** - Construction begun again, with a new, more modest plan.
- **1895** - Mayor William S. Mason and his council move into the completed building.
- **1896** - Mayor Sylvester Pennoyer cuts City Hall as "expensive, unseemly and unhealthful."

PENNOYER

1900
- **1902** - Part Orford cedars, now towering, planted as east-side grounds.
- **1905** - Lewis and Clark Exposition, the city is voted World's Fair, held in Northwest Portland.
- **1907** - First National First Rose festival held.

1910
- **1910** - First passenger elevators installed in open stairwells.

1920
- **1925** - USS Oregon moored in Portland harbor as a naval museum.
- **1928** - One stone light well filled in to create more office space.

1930
- **1931** - New passenger elevator installed.
- **1933-37** - Extensive interior renovation. Both light wells filled in for more office space. Penthouse added to roof.
- **1934** - Firefighters tore down a Communual flag flown by protesters; restored Old Glory to its place. Inch-thick fungus found growing on roof.
- **1936** - Stuffed moose and other specimens removed from display.

1940
- **1940** - Ancient petroglyph installed at southeast of building.
- **1942** - USS Oregon donated to World War II effort, hauled away for scrap.
- **1946** - New passenger elevators installed.

1948 - Stone railing on Southwest Fifth Avenue removed after a runaway truck crashed through the wall.

LEE

Mayor Dorothy McCulloch Lee elected to crack down on vice.

1950
- **1950** - Portland Hotel razed to make way for Meier & Frank Co. parking structure.
- **1952** - Mayor Lee defeated for re-election as cracking down on vice proved to be unpopular.
- **1957** - Last of Portland streetcars taken out of service.

1960
- **1961** - Mayor installs annex.
- **1962** - Mayor's office renovated.

1964 - Council chambers renovated, lights for television broadcasts added. Domed ceiling covered by drop tiles.
- **1967** - Sweet gum trees planted on north, east and west side grounds.

1970
- **1976** - Damage repaired following Nov. 21 bomb blast under the Southwest Fourth Avenue portico.
- **1973** - Exterior walls prewashed and waterproofed.
- **1974** - Four-year program begun of installing sprinklers and smoke detectors.
- **1975** - Drive to buy out downtown transit mall led by Mayor Neil Goldschmidt.
- **1976** - Penthouse remodeled into employees' lunchroom, with rooftop deck. Looking Jefferson Street sidewalk repaired after roofing damaged, roots.
- **1978** - Wheelchair access ramp installed.

GOLDSCHMIDT

1980
- **1980** - City attorney's office expanded.
- **1981** - Mortar replaced on exterior walls.
- **1982** - Auditor's office remodeled. Portland Building opened next door, consolidating most city offices under one roof.
- **1984** - Mayor's office remodeled, but plans never materialized after Mayor Frank Ivancie left office.

IVANCIE

- **1985** - Conversion from steam system begun. New roof installed.
- **1988** - Tri-Met's MAX light-rail service installed.

1990
- **1993** - City Council considering major renovation of City Hall.

City Hall today

The penthouse lunchroom

Madison Street view *Fifth Avenue view* *Jefferson Street view* *Fourth Street view*

At left, a closeup look at the architecture and history of Portland's City Hall. Notice the variety of graphic elements that comprise this package: a locator map, a cutaway diagram, a timeline, four architectural profiles — and, of course, 15 inches of text.

GRAPHICS GUIDELINES

"Graphical excellence is that which gives to the viewer the greatest number of ideas in the shortest time with the least ink in the smallest space."

Edward R. Tufte

BEFORE YOU BEGIN, ASK YOURSELF:

◆ **What's missing from this story?** What will complete the picture for those who read it — or attract readers who might otherwise turn the page?

◆ **What's bogging down the text?** A series of numbers? Details? Dates? Definitions? Comparisons? Can information be pulled out and played up?

◆ **What data needs clarification?** Statistics? Geographical details? History? Does the story overestimate the readers' knowledge?

◆ **How much time and space do we have?** Can we squeeze in a quick list? A small map? Or should we create a huge clip 'n' save poster page?

◆ **What's the point of this sidebar or graphic?** Is there one clear concept we're trying to emphasize — or are we just compiling a stack of statistics?

COMPILING & EDITING GRAPHIC DATA

◆ **Collect data carefully.** Use reliable sources, as current as possible. Beware of missing data, estimates or projections; if information is uncertain or unverifiable, you must flag it for your readers. In the line chart below, for instance, the artist has labeled two gaps in the data to avoid misleading readers. Does it work?

◆ **Edit carefully.** Every graphic and sidebar *must* be edited. Check all the numbers: totals, percentages, years. Check all spelling and grammar. Check that all details in the sidebar match all details in the text. Finally, check that all wording presents the data fairly and objectively.

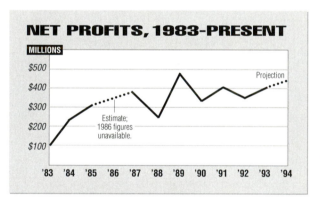

NET PROFITS, 1983-PRESENT

MILLIONS

$500
$400
$300
$200
$100

Estimate; 1986 figures unavailable.

Projection

'83 '84 '85 '86 '87 '88 '89 '90 '91 '92 '93 '94

In this line chart, we used a dotted line to indicate an estimate (for 1986) and a projection (for 1994). Does it succeed? Or does it paint a false picture for readers?

◆ **Convert to understandable values.** Avoid kilometers, knots per hour, temperatures in Celsius. Convert foreign currency to U.S. dollars. Avoid any obscure terms, jargon or abbreviations that will confuse or mislead readers.

◆ **Simplify, simplify.** What's your point? Make it absolutely, instantly clear. Depict one concrete, relevant idea — a concept readers can relate to, not something abstract, insignificant or obscure. Avoid clutter by eliminating all nonessential words and information and by focusing *tightly* on key points.

Above all, don't ever assume the reader plans to read the story's text; your graphics and sidebars must stand on their own.

PACIFIC OCEAN RECORD DEPTHS

NAME	DEPTH IN METERS	DEPTH IN FATHOMS
Mariana Trench	10,924	5,973
Tonga Trench	10,800	5,906
Philippine Trench	10,057	5,499
Kermadec Trench	10,047	5,494
Bonin Trench	9,994	5,464
Kuril Trench	9,750	5,331

In this table, we've measured the deepest depths of the ocean — in meters and fathoms. Can't fathom what it means? We need to convert those depths to FEET for the data to make more sense.

GRAPHICS GUIDELINES

CONSTRUCTING GOOD GRAPHICS

◆ **Keep it simple.** Make sidebars and graphics look easy to understand or you'll frighten readers away. Pie charts, for instance, are the bottom feeders in the great Graphics Food Chain. Many readers *hate* pie charts. So don't make matters worse; don't slice pies into a dozen pieces (with an unreadable key full of stripes and polka dots) if a few broad categories convey the same idea.

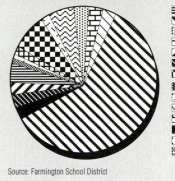

1994-95 SCHOOL BUDGET

Student services 3.5%
Instruction 64.0%
Inst. staff supp 3.4%
Utility services 1.7%
School admin. 4.4%
School support 4.3%
Transfer 0.3%
Debt service 0.0%
Contingency 1.3%
General admin. 0.7%
Business service 7.6%
Maint. serve. 1.6%
Custodial service 4.5%
Central serve. 2.7%

Source: Farmington School District

What makes this pie chart so confusing? Is it the excessive number of slices? (Exactly how many categories ARE there, anyway?) Is it the way all those stripes and dots are impossible to tell apart? Is it the use of a separate key to show percentages, rather than labeling or pointing to the pie slices themselves?

Don't cram years and years onto a line chart if only recent trends matter.

Bottom line: Don't overwork a chart. If you want to make several different points, you'll find that several charts are usually better than one.

How to lie with statistics: *Bar charts help us to visualize numbers by depicting them as bars. Tall bars are big numbers, short bars are small ones; in fact, a bar that's twice as tall as its neighbor should be worth two times as much — right? Right. Now study the chart at right. It looks like school spending in 1994-95 was about HALF of what it was in '93-94. Is that true? Or is the chart misleading?*

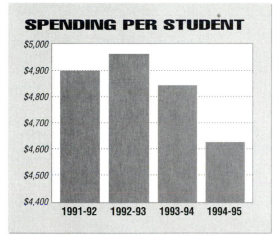

SPENDING PER STUDENT

$5,000			
$4,900			
$4,800			
$4,700			
$4,600			
$4,500			
$4,400			
1991-92	1992-93	1993-94	1994-95

◆ **Keep it accurate.** As we mentioned before, use trustworthy sources (and print their names in a source line at the bottom of the chart). Double-check their math — then have someone check *your* math when you're done.

When drawing charts, be sure all proportions are true. Slices in a pie chart should be mathematically precise; time units in a line chart should be evenly spaced; bars in bar charts should be accurately proportioned (unlike the bars above, which are disproportionate because they're not stacked on a baseline of *zero*). Some computer programs can help you plot figures with accuracy.

◆ **Label it clearly.** Make sure each significant element — every line, number, circle and bar — is instantly understandable. Add a legend, if necessary. Or write an introductory blurb at the top of the chart to tell readers what they're seeing.

◆ **Dress it up.** Add screens, 3-D effects, photos, illustrations, color — but use them to organize and label the data, not just for decoration. Sure, it's fine to use illustrations to tweak readers' attention (as if to say, *This chart is about shipping — see the little boat? Get it?*), but at too many newspapers it's become common to junk up graphics with cartoon clutter. Used poorly, these effects distort your information and distract your readers. Used with wit and flair, they can make dry statistics fresh and appealing (as in the example at right). Proceed with caution.

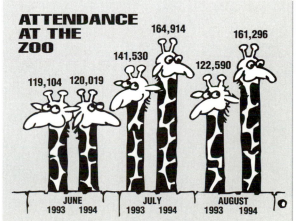

ATTENDANCE AT THE ZOO

119,104 120,019 141,530 164,914 122,590 161,296

JUNE 1993 1994   JULY 1993 1994   AUGUST 1993 1994

GRAPHICS GUIDELINES

TYPOGRAPHY FOR GRAPHICS

◆ **Develop graphics style guidelines.** You'll save time, avoid confusion and maintain a consistent look if you adopt strict standards for all type sizes, screen densities, source and credit lines, dingbats, etc. Once you determine the look you like, print up annotated samples for every writer and artist to consult.

◆ **Give every sidebar or graphic a headline.** Don't force readers to guess what a map or list means. Even a short title ("What They Earn") clarifies your intent. But as mentioned above, use consistent sizes, fonts and treatments.

◆ **Make it readable.** Avoid type smaller than 8 point (except for source or credit lines). Use boldface to highlight key words. Keep all type horizontal (except for rivers or roads on maps). Use rules and careful spacing to keep elements from crowding each other and creating confusion.

MORE ON ▶

◆ **Stylebooks:** *How to codify your paper's guidelines for text and graphics* 194
◆ **Grids:** *How some papers experiment with alternative page formats* 66

PLACEMENT & PAGE DESIGN

This 5-column story design uses two graphic elements: a dominant vertical photo and a smaller horizontal tucked into the text.

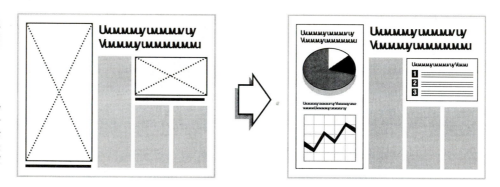

Here's that same design using a vertical graphic package as lead art, with a sidebar list boxed and dummied atop those legs of text.

◆ **Dummy graphics as you would a photo.** Graphics and sidebars are generally dummied like any other art elements. Some papers, like those below, use special page grids to accommodate graphics more easily — thus encouraging editors and designers to add them to stories more often.

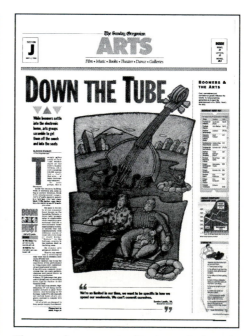

The page above runs graphics in a strip down the right side. At The Little Hawk (left), a 7-column grid creates narrow "rails" where designers place graphic extras: lists, bio boxes, quotes, etc.

There was a time, not too long ago, when all newspaper pages looked serious. Respectable. Gray. Paper was white, ink was black, and everything was locked into rigid gray rows.

Today, that's all changed. Newspapers are more reader-friendly than ever. Headlines are blue, backgrounds are violet, and photos run in eye-poppingly true colors. Feature pages look flashy. News pages look flashy. Even *business* pages look flashy. Go figure.

The best designers now carry big bags of graphic tricks. That's partly to make stories more informative, partly to make pages more lively, but mostly to keep up with a world in which *everything* competes for our attention.

Thanks to innovations in computer graphics, design standards keep rising for all informational media. Just watch the news on TV or read some "serious" newsmagazines like Time, Newsweek, US News & World Report. Their presentation is lively; their graphics are zoomy. So if your newspaper insists on being serious, respectable and gray — locking everything into rigid gray rows — you may be falling behind the times. You may be falling *asleep* (along with your readers).

In this chapter, we'll explore graphic techniques that give pages extra energy. These techniques are optional — but as time goes by, special effects like these will find their way onto every page in the paper.

CHAPTER CONTENTS

bending the rules

AS YOU HAVE SEEN, EVERY PAPER NEEDS CLEAR AND CONSISTENT RULES FOR ITS DESIGN, BUT EVERY SO OFTEN, BY BENDING THOSE RULES, YOU CAN PRODUCE SOME COOL PAGES LIKE THESE.

Just how far, though, are you willing to bend the rules? Take a closer look at this page you're reading now, for instance. We've stretched and compressed the headline. We've tilted the art. We've flipped the text sideways. Skewed it. And radically re-styled it. Just how far can we deviate from our standard design format before we look like some freakish accident? And how far can you push readers before they get tired of watching you jump up and down in your clown suit? It's hard to say. You make the call. Usually it's just a question of taste.

THE FREEP

VALERI MONTSENY · STEPHANIE CORKER · DAMON WALKER · GERALD ELLISON · BENJAMIN RANSIER · STEPHANIE NAVARRE · KRYSTAL BASS · CRYSTAL THOMPSON · MOYO...

GOOD GUIDE INSIDE

3 28 92

Ann Landers advises: "Mind your own business" and "It's not OK."
Page 2F

16-year-old Yooper has sax appeal.
Page 3F

BABY, BABY, SO COOL

by donielle self

by donielle self / freep

Aren't you supposed to abandon pacifiers by the time you're... Supposed to, yes, but one of the coolest things going... we're not talking about pacifiers for babies.

Today, some of you are wearing pacifiers just like you wear the latest jeans and hairstyles.

And to think that only a few years ago, it was your beloved mee-mo, mu-me, bo-bo, boopie, whatever.

Wearing a pacifier is not only gaining popularity on the east and west sides of Detroit, but there also have been sightings in California, Pennsylvania and New York. Recording artists Nirvana, TLC and Public Enemy member Flavor Flav have been spotted wearing pacifiers. Flavor Flav was even seen with a baby bottle once.

Like all bona fide trends, this irks older folks immensely. In fact, one Pennsylvania principal has banned pacifiers. At his school, they are popular among couples. "They share it," he explained. "They each have one, then they exchange them at the beginning of the day."

Why pacifiers, you ask?

One pacifier wearer from Detroit, Brandy Edwards says she picked up the idea from John Singleton's 1991 movie, "Boyz N the Hood." Dooky, a friend of the central character, wore a pacifier on a string and occasionally put it in his mouth.

Brandy says she also believes "it's a phase; everybody's doing it."

So the 11-year-old is not upset at comments she hears, such as, "What is that big girl doing with a pacifier in her mouth?"

Brandy wears hers on an eyeglass cord around her neck... the first to we... through her ne...

Pacifier w... no special s... old from D... saw other... being in... her frie... Fa... and... one... do...

Demetrius Woods of Detroit, above, has adopted the...

EVERYONE DESERVES TO BE HEARD

BY YOLANDA LIPPERT

A lot of older people seem to t... freedom of speech is an idea th... not apply to us. It didn't in m...

Once, an essay of mine w... by school officials; no mat... law says about my rights... censoring someone's w...

The First Amendment... Constitution of the Uni... guarantees freedom of... citizens, but several co... that doesn't apply to stu...

For an essay contest,... opposition to the racist comp... by some students at my scho... school disagreed with what I... change the essay.

I didn't care that the fac... I didn't think that they had... my essay, especially beca... totally agreed with my...

The changes were... better. My essay said... didn't take pride in... believe the essay d... competition as it... original state.

Once work... the writer any... there, to... I hope th... freedom of... everyone t... at Dear... We...

WHO SAYS? I SAY! ¡I SAY! WHO SAYS?

Brighten up the summer night with flash and flame

Shish-Kabobs!

NAME: Carolyn Hermann, 14, of Dearborn Heights, a freshman at Divine Child High in Dearborn.

ACTIVITIES: Plays on softball, basketball and volleyball teams, plays clarinet in the marching band, and writes poetry.

ACCOMPLISHMENT: "I wrote a poem for my grandmother Anna Mae Hermann's 75th birthday the summer of 1991, read it out loud, and she cried."

CLOTHES I LIKE: "Stuff that's loose-fitting, with a lot of color and designs on them. I love Levi's."

ON DATING: "I'm doing it, but it's more of, like, a friend thing. We go shopping at the mall or to movies in groups of boys and girls."

MOST FUN THIS SUMMER: "When I went to Chicago, saw the Hard Rock Cafe and then went shopping."

DREAM JOB: "To be a fire fighter. When I see the TV news about people who have been burned, I want to save them."

I LIKE TO PIG OUT ON: "Doritos."

WHEN I'M ALONE I: "Write my poems and think about stuff that happens, like if one of my friends is in a fight. I also think about what I'll do when I grow up."

IDOLS: "All fire fighters and Dustin Hoffman; he's a really good actor."

10 YEARS FROM NOW I'LL: "Be done with college and training to be a fire fighter."

NOMINATED BY: Best friend Ann Leem, 14, who attends Divine Child and lives in Dearborn Heights.

By Carol Teegardin

Get a T-shirt from The Freep for you and a friend when we feature your nominee. Write to Gotta Friend? The Freep, PO Box 152, Detroit 48231. Include your and your friend's names, ages, addresses and phone numbers. Send a photo of the nominee, but nothing you want sent back.

GOTTA FRIEND

JOHN LUKE/Detroit Free Press

---

w r i t e r

go to school?

e pacifier, and no,

pacifier because "it turns a lot of heads," and he loves attention. The 13-year-old from Detroit doesn't feel embarrassed on says he's even been told on occasion that he looks "cute with it" in his mouth.

Of course, being this hip has its down side.

Once when Farrah was driving on the freeway, she was startled when another car kept honking at her and making gestures. When it pulled up alongside, the occupants yelled, "What are you doing with a pacifier in your mouth?"

And then there's Brandy's problem. She's on her second pacifier now, and it may not be her last.

Her mom, Antoenette Foster, threw the first one away and vows to do it again.

John Luke/Detroit Free Press

It's Wednesday. It's nightti
time. You want to shake your
latest B-52's track or slam to
jam.

Only problem is that you'
bars will let you in. Well, there
at-night blues.

Naked Fun!

The Naked Fun Club
Naked Fun is an all-ag
located in the nascent
rock scene: Royal Oak.
held at the Knights of C

All it costs is $5 each
your closet and dearest
party in a dark, smoke-
It's all you could a

This summer, Roy
Productions, someon
rang

NAKED FUN
FOR ALL AGES

HOT BOX

Girlie Talk

Madonn
materia
exactly
but the
self-e
at its
sedu

NEW YORK —
Us magazine says she's through. The pope wishes she were. Many others gripe that she has gone "too far." But the old blond mare, better known Madonna, showed me what she used to be Thursday night at Madison Square Garden as she tack-led the U.S. leg of The

MICHAEL McWILLIAMS

"At this point in her career, Madonna is beyond classifications about love, sex or anything else."

her concert tour, seductively titled *The Girlie Show*.

Her performance reminded me of the newspaper that once sent a telegram to Cary Grant asking: "HOW OLD CARY GRANT?" and Grant wired back: "OLD CARY GRANT FINE. HOW YOU?" Madonna is fine, too, thank you — even if she decides to retire to a stud farm tomorrow. She's at the peak of her form, not as the cold shrew so many perceive, but as the humor-ous humanist to whom she is so loved.

Like many divas before her, she is said to be "slipping" when she's doing some of her best work, like *Erotica*, with

mime, striptease
poses, vaudevilli
maneuvers, Mar
Venus (that wi
Morocco (that

Coiffed in
Breathless and
dancers and h
donna even re
standards, ga
cally rework
ground up,
The MTV d
ningly cheer
lusetle drag

This is
as *The Ki
The Pro
upper-cr
*My Fair
Janis Jo
Mansfie
is coyle
("Like
twist; and *What*

ligned and misundersp
prising "Rain," the m
has done in years, is s
trio, accented by Ma
Imaginations." In T
died of AIDS in an
"Deeper and Deeper
twist; and *What*

THE COSBY VARIATIONS

Newspaper design is part art, part science. And that's especially true on feature pages, where you begin with the basic rules of page layout, then nudge and stretch them as far as your time, creativity, and sense of taste will allow.

For instance, here's a design exercise that demonstrates the range of options designers can choose from. Suppose you're a designer for this daily Living page. Today's cover will be entirely devoted to just one big feature story, which means you have this hole to fill:

©1985, National Broadcasting Co., Inc.

CAST YOUR VOTE ▶

On the next five pages you'll see 16 Cosby variations. Which do you prefer? To help you analyze each option, we've added checklists like this one:

YOUR OPINION

Headline .... B

Photo treatment .... C+

Impact & energy .... A–

Overall design .... B

Examine each of the variations. Then write the grades that seem appropriate.

Today's lead story — the one that will fill the entire page — is a profile of comedian Bill Cosby. It's a long piece, so you can jump as much text as you like. And as it turns out, there's only one photo available (left).

So how will you crop this photo? Arrange the text? Write and display the headline? Take a few minutes to create a solution on your own — then, over the next five pages, we'll take a close look at 16 Cosby variations.

THE COSBY VARIATIONS

1

This is a no-nonsense news approach which parks the photo in the top two legs of a 3-column layout. It works — but it's dull. The page is overrun with gray text. And the headline is too lifeless — fine for a news story, but too bland for a feature. The good news: this design could be done in a real hurry. The bad news: the page isn't much fun. There's nothing here to grab the reader.

YOUR OPINION

Headline ....

Photo treatment ....

Impact & energy ....

Overall design ....

The Bugle Beacon
Friday, April 14, 1994

LIVING

INSIDE:
Get ready
with Eddie!
C2

Cosby shares success secrets

America's favorite TV dad
wants more than laughs —
he's building a better world

By PATRICK MINIHEAD
Bugle Beacon staff writer

The Bugle Beacon
Friday, April 14, 1994

LIVING

INSIDE:
Get ready
with Eddie!
C2

Inside the world of 'Cos'

America's favorite TV
dad wants more than
laughs — he's trying
to build a better world

By PATRICK MINIHEAD
Bugle Beacon staff writer

*"All I do has to do
with some form
of education,
some form of
giving a message
to people."*

■ Please see COSBY, Page 2

2

Here, we've made the photo more vertical — a more dynamic shape — and anchored it in the middle two legs. But does it bother you that we're lopping off Cosby's hand? We've made the headline bigger and bolder, too, with a friendly reference to "Cos." Near the bottom, the text wraps around a liftout quote. Overall, though, the design is still fairly conservative.

YOUR OPINION

Headline ....

Photo treatment ....

Impact & energy ....

Overall design ....

3

Here, we've taken that catchy word "COS" and turned it into a bold display headline. Note the use of rules, the indents (at the top and right edge), the flush-right read-in. We've added Cosby's hand back, too, poking it out of the photo and dodging the text around it. Is that acceptable? (Some photographers might object.) All in all, it's a bolder design than the previous two.

YOUR OPINION

Headline ....

Photo treatment ....

Impact & energy ....

Overall design ....

The Bugle Beacon
Friday, April 14, 1994

LIVING

INSIDE:
Get ready
with Eddie!
C2

INSIDE THE COMIC MIND OF COS

America's favorite TV dad wants more
than laughs — he wants a better world

By PATRICK MINIHEAD
Bugle Beacon staff writer

*"All I do has to do
with some form
of education,
some form of
giving a
message to
people."*

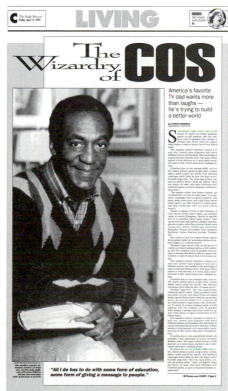

The Bugle Beacon
Friday, April 14, 1994

LIVING

INSIDE:
Get ready
with Eddie!
C2

The Wizardry of COS

America's favorite
TV dad wants more
than laughs —
he's trying to build
a better world

By PATRICK MINIHEAD
Bugle Beacon staff writer

*"All I do has to do with some form of education,
some form of giving a message to people."*

■ Please see COSBY, Page 2

4

This option is fancier still, using boxes inside boxes: The photo's in one box, the text is in another, and both overlap a third screened box. Are all those boxes distracting — or do they help organize the design elements? The headline is more decorative, too, mixing sizes, weights, typefaces and treatments. Is it all too fussy and fancy — or slick and smooth? Again, it's largely a matter of taste.

YOUR OPINION

Headline ....

Photo treatment ....

Impact & energy ....

Overall design ....

THE COSBY VARIATIONS

5

Let's move the photo back to the middle of the page to test a few variations. Note how symmetrical all four designs on this page are. Like symmetry? In this first example, the headline is centered; the two liftout quotes balance each other on both sides of the photo. Note, too, the white space in the top corners of the page. Is that space wasted, or does it help the design to "breathe"?

YOUR OPINION

Headline ....

Photo treatment ....

Impact & energy ....

Overall design ....

6

If we move the deck directly below the headline, we open up even more white space in the top corners. Is that too much now? Note how the quote fills the space below the photo. Readers reaching the end of the left leg must jump clear across the photo to continue reading. Are readers smart enough to make that leap — or will they take that opportunity to quit reading?

YOUR OPINION

Headline ....

Photo treatment ....

Impact & energy ....

Overall design ....

7

Here, we've moved the headline down, boxing it into the "dead space" in Cosby's stomach. Or IS there such a thing as "dead space" in a photo? (Many photographers would argue there isn't.) Does the headline seem to crowded? Too low on the page? One other innovation: Cosby's head now pokes up into the section header. Does that add more spunk to the photo?

YOUR OPINION

Headline ....

Photo treatment ....

Impact & energy ....

Overall design ....

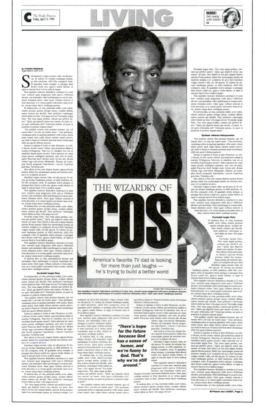

8

Here, the headline is even lower — sitting nearly at the bottom of the story. Positioning headlines that low would never work on Page One — but is it OK here? Will it be clear to readers that they should begin reading at the top of the left-hand leg? Note the decorative bars at the top and bottom of the page. And a final question: Is it better to poke Cosby's hand out of the photo, or leave it cropped off?

YOUR OPINION

Headline ....

Photo treatment ....

Impact & energy ....

Overall design ....

THE COSBY VARIATIONS

9

Since we've started cutting Cosby silhouettes, why don't we try cutting him out completely? Here, we've reverted to an earlier variation, where the text wraps along Cosby's out-stretched hand. Is that skewed text hard to read — or does it add visual variety to the page? Is the Cosby photo too huge? Finally, note how the liftout quote is now used to fill the white space beside Cosby's head.

 YOUR OPINION

Headline ....

Photo treatment ....

Impact & energy ....

Overall design ....

10

It's not often you get a chance to park your dominant image at the bottom of a design. Usually, it doesn't work (it'll either look like an ad or intrude into other stories). But here it anchors the page pretty well. Cosby's head pokes neatly into that middle column, as his fingers dangle below the bottom edge of the box. The liftout quote, too, gets a special boxed and screened treatment.

 YOUR OPINION

Headline ....

Photo treatment ....

Impact & energy ....

Overall design ....

11

Instead of cutting away the photo's background, in this variation we've cut a hole IN the photo — and around Cosby — and inserted the text block. There's enough room for a liftout quote and one leg of text. Does this technique work? Two drawbacks: There's a lot of empty space floating around near the top of the page — and there's not a lot of text. (Note, too, the slammer headline.)

YOUR OPINION

Headline ....

Photo treatment ....

Impact & energy ....

Overall design ....

12

Is this treatment clever — or tacky? We quit trying to work with the back-ground of the photo and instead created a background of our own. Some would argue it's a violation of the photograph's integrity. Or does it evoke a feeling of watching TV? Note how the photo has been electronically widened to simulate TV-tube distortion. Note, too, the screened deck and the scattered quotes.

YOUR OPINION

Headline ....

Photo treatment ....

Impact & energy ....

Overall design ....

THE COSBY VARIATIONS

MANIPULATING ART TO ADD ATTITUDE

We've just seen 12 variations that shifted photos, headlines and text around the page — but not one of those variations really used design as an extension of the *storytelling*. Yes, there were some lively shapes, some clever type treatments. But you could argue that those designs were more passive than active. Or to put it another way: Those Cosby pages could have been about *anybody*.

Remember, designers can manipulate images and headlines to enhance a story angle or create a mood — as evidenced in the two pages below. These designs have more *attitude*. Because they're more aggressive, they pack more punch. But they're riskier. And much more complicated to produce.

13 Suppose the story had a harder edge to it: analyzing Cosby's fading popularity after his hit show went off the air. That angle is captured in these graphics, which create the illusion of a disappearing Cos. The headline works with the art to create an integrated design with a clear theme.

14 How much nuttiness can you take? Remember, Cosby is a comedian — so if you're ever going to bend the rules, this may be the time. But is the head-and-headline treatment too much? The zigzag text? The deck in the bottom corner? It's a risky design — but it's got lots of attitude.

YOUR OPINION

Headline ....

Photo treatment ....

Impact & energy ....

Overall design ....

YOUR OPINION

Headline ....

Photo treatment ....

Impact & energy ....

Overall design ....

THE COSBY VARIATIONS

MAKING STORIES MORE USER-FRIENDLY

Photos, cutlines, headlines, text. Those four basic elements are fine for basic news pages. But as we learned in Chapter 6, readers prefer pages that are more active. More *interactive*. More user-friendly.

Our previous pages put all their efforts into manipulating shapes and headlines. They were exercises in decoration. But the two pages below focus on *information,* not decoration. We've changed the structure of the story to add multiple points of entry: timelines, fast facts, consumer guides.

These Cosby pages are arguably more contemporary than the rest. They're more than just page designs. They're *packages.*

Notice — both here and in the page at right — how much more traffic now flows through the page. Above, we've added a Cosby timeline (highlights of his life and career) and a guide to books, records and videos. Lots of choices for readers here — but is it worth that extra effort to produce?

15

YOUR OPINION

Headline ....

Photo treatment ....

Impact & energy ....

Overall design ....

Count the number of choices we offer the reader here — the headline, deck, photo, quote, text, consumer's guide, the facts-at-a-glance about Cosby — and you see it's a much more varied menu than those earlier pages. Content-wise, these two variations are quite similar. Which do you prefer?

16

YOUR OPINION

Headline ....

Photo treatment ....

Impact & energy ....

Overall design ....

WRAPAROUNDS & SKEWS

As we've previously seen — both in the Cosby variations and in the swipeable feature formats used in Chapter 3 — text isn't always locked into rigid gray rows. It can, instead, dodge around liftout quotes, flow around photos, and indent around logos and bugs. When a column of text does that, it's called a *wraparound*. (Some papers call it a *runaround*. And when it snakes along a jagged piece of art, it's often called a *skew*.)

Wraparounds can be used with a variety of graphic elements:

MORE ON ▶

◆ **Liftout quotes:**
Using them with wraparounds....... 126

◆ **Photo cutouts:**
Using them with wraps and skews.. 178

| Mugs | Liftout quotes | Headlines | Art or photos |

Until a few years ago, wraparounds were common in books and magazines, but not in newspapers. That's because they required a lot of time, patience and tricky typesetting codes. But with the advent of personal computers and page-layout software, type wraps have become a graphic gimmick that's much easier to play with.

Wraparounds add flair and flexibility to story designs in three ways:

◆ They let you place graphic elements in the middle of a layout without disrupting the flow of the text.

◆ They let a story's artwork interact more closely with its words.

◆ Best of all, they allow you to run graphic elements at their optimum sizes, rather than wedging everything into rigid column widths.

As you can see below, wraparounds help you save space by letting you crop photos more economically:

In the layout at left, we've cropped to the edge of the photo frame. But unless we crop into the model's skirt, we're forced to create a layout that's mostly empty white space. The layout at right, however, fits two legs of type where only one fit before. How? By cropping more tightly, poking both corners of the skirt into the text.

WRAPAROUNDS & SKEWS

GUIDELINES FOR WRAPS & SKEWS

◆ **Don't overdo it.** Any graphic gimmick will annoy readers if they see it too often, and wraparounds are *very* gimmicky. That's why they're best reserved for features — not hard news.

Remember: The text of a story is a road the reader travels; a wraparound is like a pothole in the road. Steering around one pothole is fun, but who wants to drive a road that's *loaded* with potholes?

◆ **Anchor the text block** as solidly as you can. Then start poking art into it at carefully spaced intervals. As soon as the art starts overwhelming the text, back off. (Take a look at this page. It uses several wraps — but they're shrewdly positioned along this solid column of text.)

In other words, don't let wraps create chaos. Align the text legs solidly on the page grid *first*, then add skews as enhancement.

◆ **Keep text readable.** Severe indents and sloppy spacing undermine your design (see box at right for details).

◆ **Maintain contrast** between the main text block and the object that's poking into it. As you can see here, the sidebar box at right is screened and set off with a drop shadow — and note how the sidebar's photo acts as a buffer between the sidebar text and this main text block.

◆ **Don't cut out photos** simply because you want to skew around them. That makes photographers quite angry. (For more on photo cutouts, turn the page.)

◆ **Smooth out your skews** as much as you can. Abrupt shifts in the width of the text are awkward-looking — and can be awkward to read, too.

◆ **Choose sides carefully.** Believe it or not, skews on the *right* side are preferable to skews on the *left*. Judge for yourself:

☐ When you indent an illustration or photo into a column of text, try to run at least three lines of text *above* and *below* the indented art (as we do here).

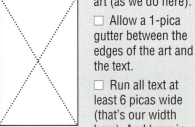

☐ Allow a 1-pica gutter between the edges of the art and the text.

☐ Run all text at least 6 picas wide (that's our width here). And keep in mind how tiring it is to read a deep, skinny totem pole of text. Try to limit all thin, indented legs to a few inches of depth, max.

Here's a block of text with a skew along its *left* edge. It looks appealing, but notice the way your eyes keep bouncing back and forth as you finish one line, then search for the beginning of the next one. That gets annoying pretty quickly, and it turns readers off.

But when text skews along the *right* edge, it's not nearly as difficult to read. Even though each line ends in a different place, your eye always knows exactly where to go to begin the next line. It's like an exaggerated ragged right. So if you have a choice, skew on the right.

◆ And finally — as we've said many times before — don't ever force readers to jump back and forth across any simple or ingenious your layout will get confused, lost or annoyed.

Take this example, for instance. the designer, that you're supthen jump across this image of — but most readers will try to get frustrated, then give up You still trying to decipher Either that, or you've got too

graphic element. No matter how may seem to you, your readers Is it worth the risk?

It may seem obvious to me, posed to start reading each line, Zippy the Pinhead to finish it read each column separately, without ever getting this far. this? You're very dedicated. much free time. . . .

© Bill Griffith

PHOTO CUTOUTS

We said earlier that photos come in three basic shapes: horizontal, vertical and square. And that's *usually* true. But occasionally, feature photos break out of the confines of the rectangle:

This fashion photo is run with background intact, cropped into a conventional vertical rectangle.

This is a partial cutout, in which the model's head and part of his arm poke out of the frame.

This is a complete cutout, with the entire gray background cut away from the model.

Many photographers and editors hate this kind of treatment. They think it's abusive — that it destroys the integrity of the photographic image. They call it "cookie-cutter art."

Artists and designers, on the other hand, consider it a handy, sophisticated technique. They call these photos *cutouts* or *silhouettes*.

Why create cutouts? It's usually done for dramatic effect. A photo that's boxed and framed seems flat and two-dimensional. A cutout, by contrast, seems almost 3-D. It pops off the page and creates an element of surprise.

It's also a good way to eliminate an unwanted, distracting background from a photograph. And it can help tighten up a story design by letting the text hug a photo's central image instead of parking several inches away.

When creating cutouts, remember:

◆ **Respect the photograph** (and the photographer). A bad crop or a silly silhouette can ruin a good photo. So when you can, work *with* the photographer. Discuss cutout treatments in advance. When in doubt, leave it alone.

◆ **Use cutouts on features** — not hard news. If you distort or violate an image, you damage its credibility. That may be OK for celebrity photos or fashion shots, but you're never allowed to change the meaning of news photos.

◆ **Use only images with crisp, dark edges.** Light skin and white clothes will fade like ghosts into the background, so be careful. And be especially careful trimming faces, fingers and frizzy hair. Crude cutouts look amateurish.

◆ **Don't cut up actual photographs.** Instead, either trim away the background from a halftone or scan, or see your printer for advice on cutting overlays.

◆ **Play them strong.** They work better the bigger they are, so don't let them drown in a sea of white space. Do it with gusto — or don't do it.

MORTISES & INDENTS

Note: *I've included this page despite nearly hysterical protests from some of my colleagues, who believe mortises are downright **evil**. One of them even wrote me a letter that went like this:*

**The preside ntboard
said boffiacijashaleet to
the newcrtteaxt taxes**

to show how you'd never stack one leg of text atop another — so why do it with photos?

To which I reply: Hey, lighten up. If you don't like it, don't do it. Nyaah!

When one text block or photo overlaps another, it's called a *mortise* or *inset*. And on this page, you can see three types of mortises: photo on photo, photo on text, and text on photo.

When creating a mortise:

◆ Inset small elements onto bigger ones.

◆ Overlap *only* into dead space, or to cover up something questionable or distracting in a photo. Avoid crowding or covering any informational part of a photo (hands, feet, background details, etc.)

◆ Mortise only photos of different scale. Never mortise any object that might mistakenly be perceived as belonging in the main photo.

◆ Maintain contrast between overlapping elements: dark onto light, light onto dark. If photos have similar values, add a gutter or shadow around the inset photo.

The three photos on this page are from a photo-essay on a monastic order. Note how the inset into the top photo uses a white gutter to keep the dark areas of both photos from blurring into each other; the text box at left adds a 4-point shadow to keep the white areas separate. In each case, the inset is relatively unobtrusive and doesn't violate either photo's center of interest (though the photographer would prefer running both photos without insets).

SCREENS & REVERSES

Ink is black. Newsprint is white. So how do we create shades of *gray?*

We do it by fooling the reader's eye. Instead of using gray inks, we create the illusion of gray by printing row upon row of tiny black dots in a *dot screen.* And the bigger those dots are, the darker the gray is. We've seen how this works in halftones (page 104), but here's how dot screens create gray tints:

0% **10%** 10% **20%** 20% **40%** 40% **60%** 60% **80%** 80% **100%**

As these examples show, screen densities are measured by percentages. A 50% screen will be half-filled with black dots, while a 100% screen is solid ink. (That ink doesn't have to be just black, either. You can create screens with any color ink, or with any combination of colors — for instance, if you look closely at a color newspaper photo through a magnifying glass, you'll see it's actually a mass of red, yellow, black and blue dots.)

Screens can be used for printing gray type: Or they can create gray rules, bars and boxes: 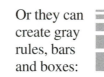 Or they can provide background tints behind type:

When screens are used to create background tints, they impair the legibility of type. It's not too difficult to read black type on a light (10%) screen, but on medium screens, it gets harder. And it's nearly impossible to read type on dark screens unless the type is *reversed* — that is, printed white instead of black.

> This is 10-point type on a white background. It's easy to read, no matter how long the story is.

> This is 10-point type on a 10% black screen. It's fairly easy to read, but works best in small doses.

> This is 10-point type **reversed** on solid (100%) black. It's easy to read, but only in small doses.

Screens and reverses dramatically expand the range of contrast on black-and-white pages. Because they're so conspicuous, they call attention to themselves and are best used to accentuate headers, logos, headlines and sidebars — especially on feature pages. They can also be integrated with photos and illustrations to create a tighter, more striking package, as in this example:

In this feature layout, the photo illustration sits above the text and its sidesaddle headline. But there's empty space in the photograph that could be put to use. . .

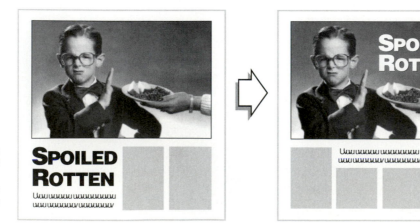

. . . and here, the headline is reversed into that photo. This connects the headline to the photo image and frees up extra space in the columns below.

SCREENS & REVERSES

GUIDELINES FOR USING SCREENS

◆ **Don't overdo it.** Don't splatter screens and reverses at random, or your paper will look like a cheap circus poster. Use special effects *only* to highlight items that are special or different: a feature headline, a column logo, an infographic. Readers regard these effects as cosmetic options, so use them only on optional items; think twice before screening hard news stories.

◆ **Don't diminish the readability of text.** *Any* screen or reverse slows readers down (and should thus be used only in small doses), but some combinations of fonts and screens create obstacles that are impossible to overcome:

MORE ON ▶

◆ **Halftones:** *How dot screens are used to reproduce photos* 104

◆ **Display headlines:** *Examples of different screens at work....* **182**

◆ **Color:** *When to use color tints and screens* **188**

Not legible:

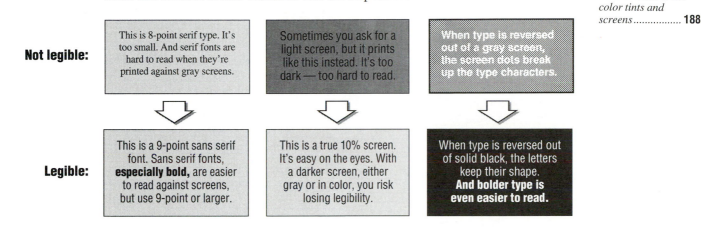

This is 8-point serif type. It's too small. And serif fonts are hard to read when they're printed against gray screens.

Sometimes you ask for a light screen, but it prints like this instead. It's too dark — too hard to read.

When type is reversed out of a gray screen, the screen dots break up the type characters.

Legible:

This is a 9-point sans serif font. Sans serif fonts, **especially bold,** are easier to read against screens, but use 9-point or larger.

This is a true 10% screen. It's easy on the eyes. With a darker screen, either gray or in color, you risk losing legibility.

When type is reversed out of solid black, the letters keep their shape. **And bolder type is even easier to read.**

◆ **Don't screen text type,** unless you want it to break apart. Gray headlines are OK, but be sure the font is big and bold, since the dot screen may give it a slightly ragged edge.

◆ **Give photos breathing room.** Avoid violating a good photo composition with a crowded reversed headline or cutline. Any added type should complement the central image — not compete with it.

This reversed headline fits poorly. By jamming so tightly against the edge of Bush's face, it disrupts the photo's composition and throws the design off-balance.

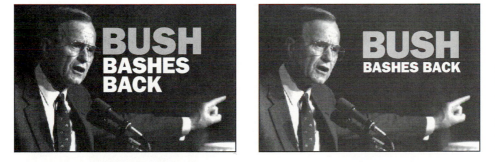

Here, the words in the headline have been restacked and repositioned, giving Bush more breathing room. The elements are now better balanced.

◆ **Don't print type against distracting backgrounds.** Look at the mottled, inconsistent background in the photo below. In such cases, a *drop shadow* behind the type may improve legibility — but proceed with caution. As a rule, type is legible *only* when it's dark against light or light against dark.

You can see how a distracting background affects (1) black type, (2) reversed type and (3) reversed type with a black shadow. Always maintain at least a 50% difference in screen value between type and its background.

1. CAN YOU READ THIS?
2. CAN YOU READ THIS?
3. CAN YOU READ THIS?

Drop shadows are made by sandwiching layers of type, one behind the other, like this:

See page 186 for more detailed instructions.

DISPLAY HEADLINES

Ordinary news stories use ordinary headlines. And then there are features.

Feature stories let you stretch beyond the confines of those routine *Council-mulls-landfill-zoning* headlines. Using type as a tool, you can make a cultural statement. Forge a new visual identity. Or craft a miniature work of art.

Some newspapers allow designers total freedom to create loud, lively headlines like those on this page. Other papers insist that feature headlines follow the same rules — and use the same typefaces — as the rest of the paper (that's to keep feature stories from looking *too* different from regular news).

So before you plunge too far off the deep end, be sure you know the limits of your editors' tastes — and the limits of your own typographic skills.

BILLY IDOL
SERIOUSLY
WIRED

THE SUNDAY OREGONIAN, JUNE 13, 1993
NORTHWEST LIVING
SECTION II
L13
Leapin' lizards! It's
DINOMANIA
The blitz of 'Jurassic Park' merchandise blends a little paleontology with a lot of hype
By MAUREEN JENKINS

TEENS IN TOUCH
REACH OUT
& BEEP
SOMEONE

RED
HOT
DEVILS
HOW
GOOD
ARE THEY?
Lemaire is ready to face Canadiens
New Jersey really hasn't been tested
The problem

NEW YORK, NEW YORK
Take a Walk on the
WILD
SIDE
Walking tours take visitors where they might fear to go alone
By TOM HALLMAN JR.
NEW YORK CITY

NBA PREVIEW
Can
Don
Chaney
pump
up
the
Pistons?
By Jerry Green
INSIDE
A look ahead?

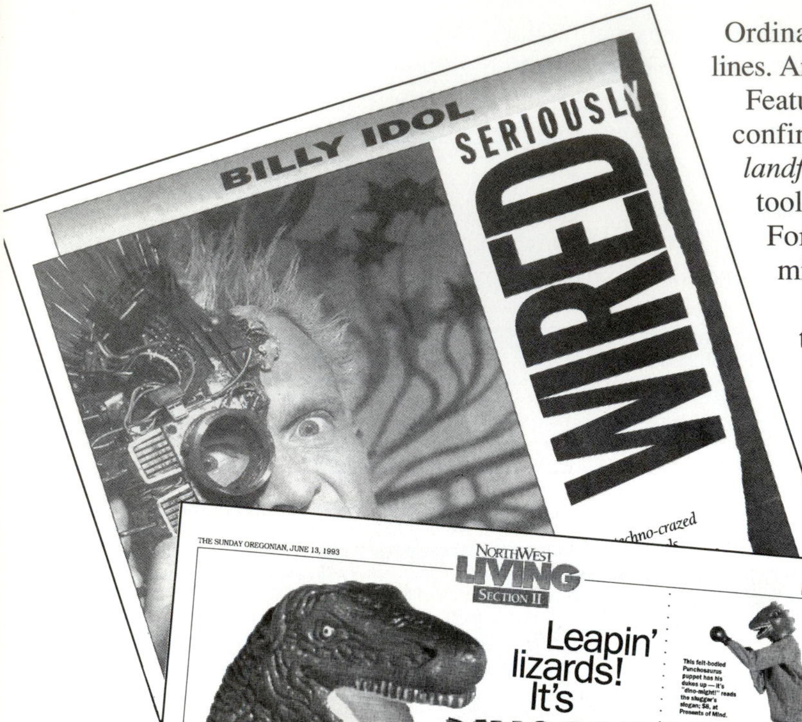

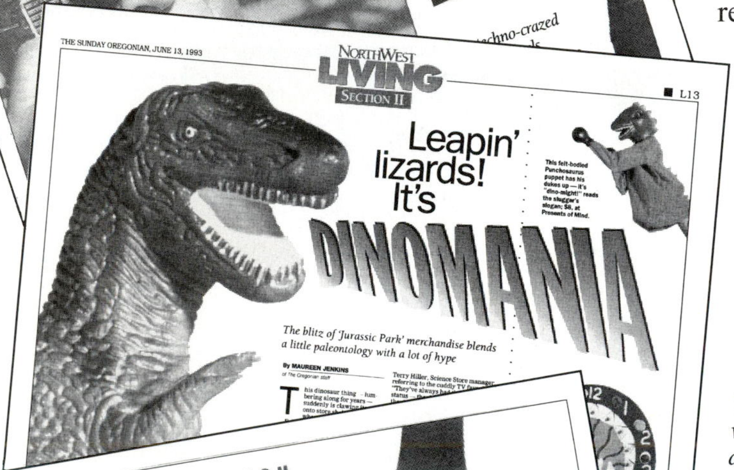

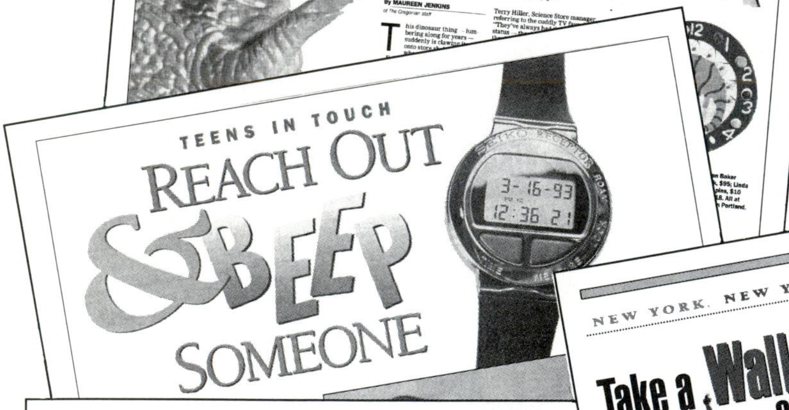

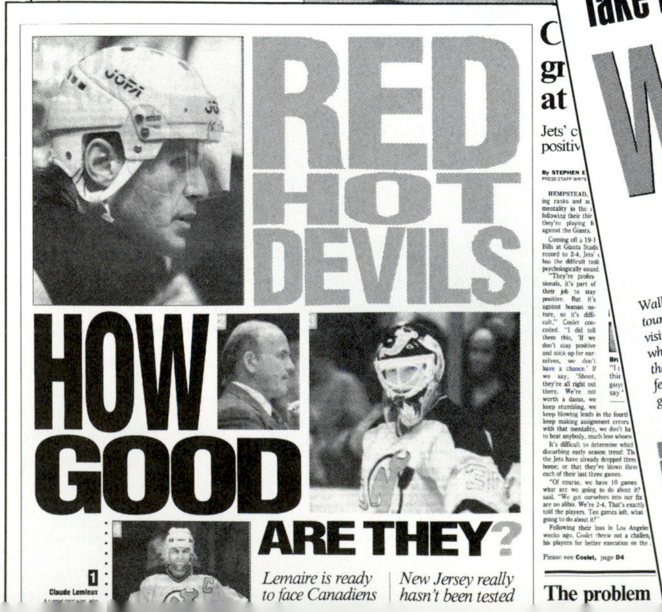

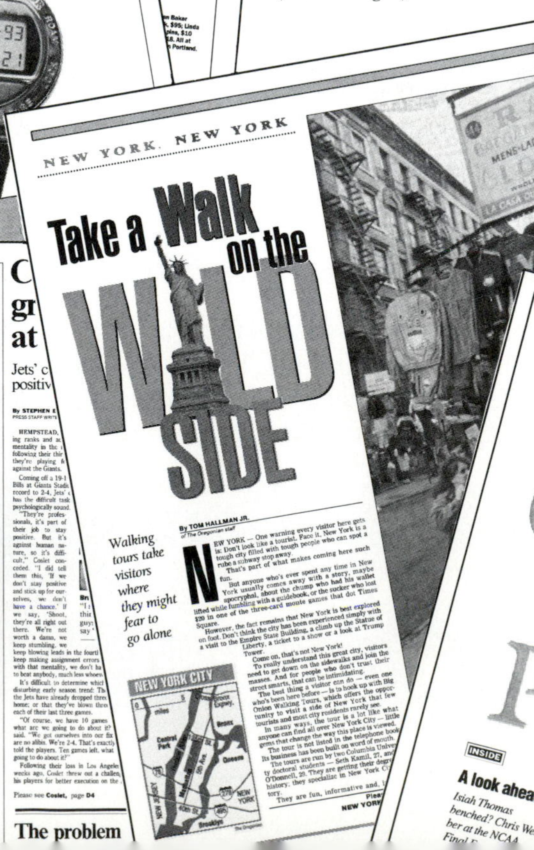

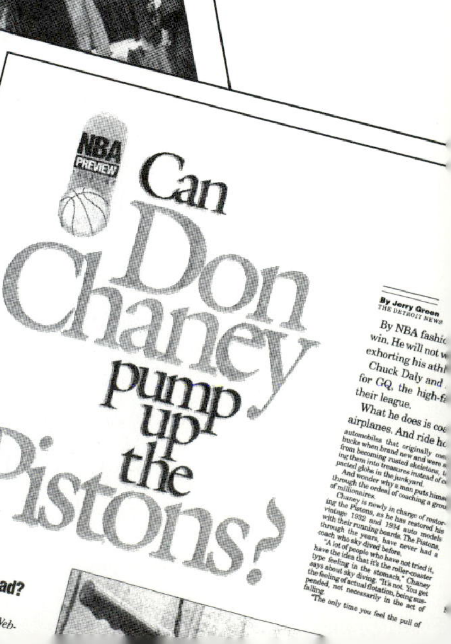

These wild & crazy display headlines were concocted at The Oregonian (left and below), The Asbury Park Press (bottom left) and The Detroit News (bottom right).

DISPLAY HEADLINES

DUMMYING & BUILDING DISPLAY HEADLINES

It can take hours — *days* — to write the perfect headline for a special story. But while you're waiting for inspiration to strike, you may need to go ahead and dummy that story, leaving a hole for the headline to fill later.

In the dummy at right, the designer left a horizontal space for a headline — which later turned out to be "Beauty and the Beast." With enough time and energy (and a big bag of fonts to choose from), you could fill that hole with a headline like this:

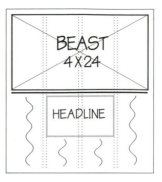

This typeface (Coronet Script) is 20% black with a 40% black shadow. The "B" is 86 pt.; the lower-case letters are 116 pt.

A 36-pt. Berkeley italic ampersand, 50% black.

This novelty font (Neuland) is reversed out of black. "THE" is 17 pt., 50% black; "BEAST" is 48 pt.

Like many designers, you may have access to dozens of typefaces and to computer programs that can crunch, curve and contort type. Fine — but go easy. Even if you're restricted to just *one* type family, you can use screens, rules and boxes to add style and variety. The headlines below, for instance, use just the Futura family. Let's take a closer look at how their components were crafted:*

Solid black type

Widely tracked type, centered over a .5-pt. rule

Solid black type

10% black box with a .5-pt. border and a 20% shadow

Type reversed out of a solid black 6-pt. bar

30% black type

Type centered over a 12-pt. bar; screen fades from 0 to 50% to 0

Solid black type

20% black type (uses two .5-pt. shadows: one white, one 50% black)

Box uses a graduated screen (from 50% top to 5% bottom). Shadow blends screens from 80% to 5%

20% black type with a 50% shadow

Type centered between .5-pt. rules spaced 2 pts. apart

Solid black type with a 20% shadow

Type reversed out of a black box with a .5-pt. reversed inline

60% black type

Type reversed out of black, with .5-pt. rules spaced 2 pts. apart

* Because screens vary from one printer to another, the densities used here may need adjustment at your paper.

DISPLAY HEADLINE GUIDELINES

◆ **Don't overdo it.** Sure, playing with type is oodles of fun. But don't turn your pages into circus posters. Use restraint. Save display headlines for special occasions: big feature stories, special news packages or photo spreads.

Too much: *Sure, it's a matter of personal taste. But if you park display headlines in every corner of the page, it'll look like rebel bands of typographers seized control of your newsroom. When you put too much emphasis on decoration, you distract your readers.*

About right: *Here, we've saved the flashy type for where we need it most: in the lead story and in that small feature in the bottom corner. Because the other stories are standard news items, they get standard headlines. This typography subliminally helps readers sort the news.*

◆ **Match the tone of the story.** Be sensitive to your topic. Use bold, expressive type when it's appropriate (below, left) — but don't impose it on topics that require more understated, dignified type (below, right).

◆ **Keep it short and punchy.** To give a display headline maximum impact, build it around one or two key words or a clever, catchy phrase. Think of popular movie titles (*Jaws, Star Wars, Ghostbusters, Home Alone*) and keep your story titles equally tight. Long, wordy headlines may be fine for hard news stories —

BABY BUNNIES SPREAD EASTER JOY

— but phrases like that seem too loud and threatening on feature pages.

So play with the story topic to draw out a short, punchy title. Then play with the phrasing to decide where the graphic emphasis should go.

DISPLAY HEADLINE GUIDELINES

◆ **Grid it off.** That's design jargon for aligning your type neatly into the story design. Wild, ragged words that float in a free-form, artsy way just add clutter and noise. And noise annoys readers.

Instead, enlarge, reduce, stretch or stack words so they're solidly organized.

This headline floats too much. It's not anchored. The leading looks awkward and uneven — and worse, none of the words align. It wastes space and calls too much attention to itself. On a busy page, this headline would just add to the confusion.

Each of these headlines is neatly stacked. The top one aligns flush right; the bottom one lines up (on a slight angle) along both sides. Notice how some words have been resized to ensure a clean fit. Note, too, how in each headline the second line manages to avoid the descender of the "g".

As you manipulate the words, watch for natural breaks in phrasing. Will key words play better wide? Narrow? Centered? Stacked vertically, a headline may work best ALL CAPS. And you may want to run a word or line in a different weight or font (be careful) for emphasis or variety.

This headline is all lower case. And as you can see, many lowercase characters don't stack well vertically; the contours of the ascenders and descenders leave uneven gaps which are difficult to fill smoothly.

The words in that middle headline flow around the uneven ascenders and descenders. Notice how the "f" and the "y" flow together; notice how the dot of the "i" has been replaced by the word "of." At right, the key words now use all caps to provide more solid, even contours.

◆ **Go easy on gimmicks.** We've all seen amazing typography on movie posters, beer bottles and record labels. But those are designed by highly paid professionals. *Your* daring headlines may look clumsy — or illegible — if you choose goofy fonts, run headlines sideways, create artsy hand-lettering. So beware, beware of gimmicky type. Do you really want readers to think you're a flake?

Novelty type: *Sorry, but some typographic cliches are hopelessly corny. Silly or gimmicky type can instantly make you look like an amateur.*

Special effects: *Twisting, tilting, stretching, shading— a little of that goes a long way. Most of the time, it just adds noise and distraction.*

Sharing letters: *Enlarged caps can add a decorative touch. But trying to share jumbo letters can be confusing. (SUNDAY CHOOL? CHOOLY?)*

Rules and bars: *The stacks in this headline go on and on and on. Too many rules, bars and words make headlines dense, dark and slow.*

BUILDING A MECHANICAL

How do you create logos like the one at right? You can build them on a computer — or you can combine type, rules and screens in a series of overlays called a *mechanical*, which your printer re-shoots on a copy camera to produce the final print. Here's how the process works:

1 *Typeset METROWEST and SOUND OFF. Make sure all the type is the size you need. Make two copies of SOUND OFF exactly the same size — in the finished logo, one will become white (reversed), while the other will be used to make the black shadow.*

2 *On a grid sheet, paste up all the elements that will print solid black. Lay down a 1-point border. Cut a black bar to hold the word METROWEST and place that at the top. Finally, position the type that will become SOUND OFF's black shadow.*

3 *Tape a clear plastic overlay to the grid sheet. On it, paste up the reverse elements (those that'll print white). Lay down a 4-point inline. Place the word METROWEST over that black bar. Place SOUND OFF so it's slightly offset from the black SOUND OFF below.*

This is the reverse overlay. The type and rules will knock out all the black or gray images from the layers below, becoming white in the final print. On this overlay, you'd write instructions like these to the printer:
REVERSE OUT OF EVERYTHING.

This overlay produces the gray screen. It will overprint gray on the layer below, but the white elements above will be dropped out of it. To get a 20% gray tint, you'd write:
20% BLACK.

The elements pasted on the grid sheet will print black. When finished, the background will be overprinted in gray and the reverse overlay (top layer) will knock out white rules and type. On this sheet, you'd write:
SOLID BLACK.

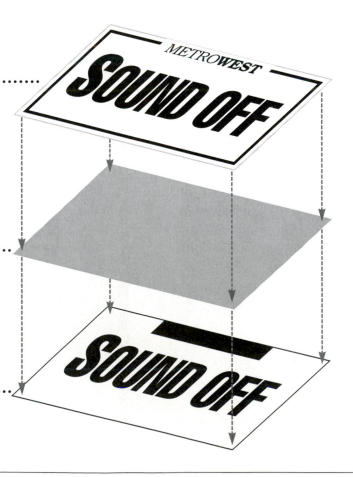

4 *Now tape down a second overlay for the background screen. Trim amberlith, rubylith (these are special red/orange overlays printers use) or black paper into the exact shape of the box. When re-shot in camera, this overlay will produce a gray dot screen.*

5 *Finally, register all three overlays (this will ensure that the elements align exactly when they're sandwiched together in the copy camera). To do that, stick two register marks in opposite corners of the grid sheet. Then place two more on each overlay, making sure they match the register marks below.*

COLOR

For years — for *decades* — newspaper editors viewed color with suspicion. Color, they stubbornly insisted, was fine for the Sunday funnies, but *news* pages should be black and white and read all over.

Time passed. TV became full color. Magazines became full color. And in the '80s, after USA Today caught on, newspapers finally realized that color isn't just decoration; it attracts readers as it performs a variety of design functions:

Advertising & promotion

There are no ads on this page, since most papers keep Page One off-limits to advertisers. But there's a color teaser, prominently located, that's designed to catch the reader's eye. And there's surely an ad on the back page of this section, since sharing color printing positions with advertisers helps defray the high cost of newsroom color production.

Standing elements

Many papers create an identity by applying color in a consistent way to various standing elements: the flag, headers, screens, reverse bars. Some papers use a specific hue to label each section of the paper (the sports header is red, the Money header is green, etc.). Others use colors to label each edition (in this example, the morning paper uses blue reverse bars; the evening paper uses red).

Quality control

Printing sharp, consistent color isn't easy. If inks aren't properly balanced, faces turn pink; the sky turns purple. That's why many papers print color control bars like this one, which mixes tints of three different inks (10% blue, 10% yellow and 10% magenta). When the press is properly inked, this bar prints a neutral gray.

Illustrations

Colorizing art is one of the easiest ways to add appeal to a page. It's just like taking crayons to a coloring book: An artist can layer one, two or a dozen colors over any black line drawing. Color drawings can be used as standing elements (like this weather icon), as logos, as supporting art in graphics, or to illustrate features. And, of course, there's always the Sunday funnies. . . .

Infographics

Charts, graphs and maps rely on screens and rules to separate elements and enhance readability. And adding color makes them even more effective. In maps, for example, readers see at a glance that blue means water, tan means land. And large-scale infographics like this one can become the centerpiece of a page — particularly when no photos are available.

Photographs

Prior to 1980, photojournalism — in both magazines and newspapers — was primarily a black-and-white craft. But at most modern papers, color photos on section fronts have now become mandatory. High-quality reproduction is still difficult and expensive, but that cost is offset by the appeal color photos have — and the added information they convey.

TYPES OF COLOR

SPOT COLOR

Ordinarily, printers use just one color of ink: black. But for a little extra money, they'll add a second ink to the press — a *spot color* — to let you print pages in a new hue.

(For even more money, you can add several spot colors to your paper. But unless you can coax an advertiser into sharing the color and footing the bill, you could blow your whole printing budget on a few flashy pages.)

Any single color — green, orange, turquoise, mauve, you name it — can print as a spot color. But because readers are so accustomed to basic black and white, any added color has instant impact. So proceed with caution. Some "hot" colors (pink, orange) are more cartoony than "cool" ones (blue, violet) — so choose hues that suit your news.

At left is a duotone, a photo reproduced using both black and a spot color. As you can see in the enlargement below, the duotone combines different-sized black and blue screened dots to create the blue-gray effect.

Like basic black, spot colors can print as either solid tones or tints. Here, for instance, are some screen percentages for a spot blue:

You add richness and variety to spot colors by mixing in black:

Pastels work best for background screens, while solid tones are best for borders and type

PROCESS OR FULL COLOR

But what if you want to print *all* the colors — the whole rainbow? You could add hundreds of separate spot colors, but that would cost a fortune (and you'd need a printing press a mile long). Instead, you can create the effect of full color by mixing and matching these four *process colors:*

By layering these four colors in different densities, a printing press can create almost any hue.

Running process color is expensive— not only for the extra ink, but for all the production work needed to prepare pages for printing. To reproduce a color photo, for instance, special software or scanners must separate the image into the four process colors — and afterwards, those negatives must be carefully registered into place. (For more on color separation, see next page.)

At left is a full color photograph which has been reproduced using all four of the process colors. As you can see in the enlargement below, the image combines different-sized cyan (blue), magenta (red), yellow and black screened dots to create the effect of full color.

Process colors can print as either solid tones or screens. Here, for instance, are the four process colors reproduced as 20% screens:

Combining different values of process colors creates new hues:

Pastels work best for background screens, while solid tones are best for borders and type

CREATING COLOR ART

How do you print full-color art using just four inks? The technology is mind-bogglingly complex, but the process is easy to understand. Here's how it works for a typical color illustration:

MORE ON ▶

◆ **Building a mechanical:** *How to add spot color to a page by cutting overlays* 186

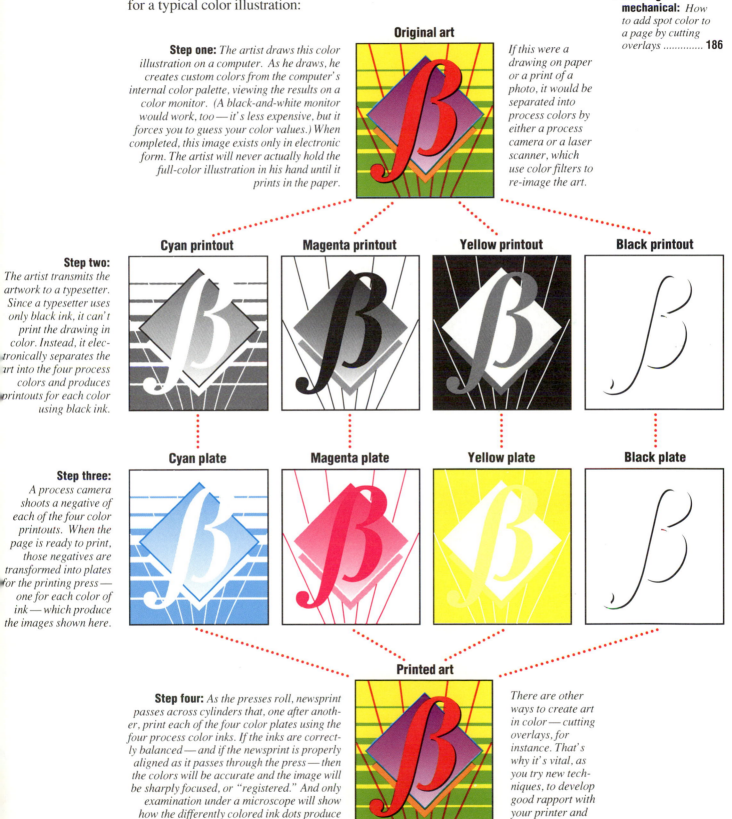

Original art

Step one: *The artist draws this color illustration on a computer. As he draws, he creates custom colors from the computer's internal color palette, viewing the results on a color monitor. (A black-and-white monitor would work, too — it's less expensive, but it forces you to guess your color values.) When completed, this image exists only in electronic form. The artist will never actually hold the full-color illustration in his hand until it prints in the paper.*

If this were a drawing on paper or a print of a photo, it would be separated into process colors by either a process camera or a laser scanner, which use color filters to re-image the art.

Cyan printout   **Magenta printout**   **Yellow printout**   **Black printout**

Step two: *The artist transmits the artwork to a typesetter. Since a typesetter uses only black ink, it can't print the drawing in color. Instead, it electronically separates the art into the four process colors and produces printouts for each color using black ink.*

Cyan plate   **Magenta plate**   **Yellow plate**   **Black plate**

Step three: *A process camera shoots a negative of each of the four color printouts. When the page is ready to print, those negatives are transformed into plates for the printing press — one for each color of ink — which produce the images shown here.*

Printed art

Step four: *As the presses roll, newsprint passes across cylinders that, one after another, print each of the four color plates using the four process color inks. If the inks are correctly balanced — and if the newsprint is properly aligned as it passes through the press — then the colors will be accurate and the image will be sharply focused, or "registered." And only examination under a microscope will show how the differently colored ink dots produce the illusion of full color.*

There are other ways to create art in color — cutting overlays, for instance. That's why it's vital, as you try new techniques, to develop good rapport with your printer and production crew.

ADDING COLOR TO A PAGE

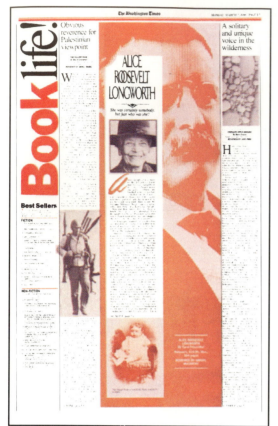

This feature page from The Washington Times demonstrates that color doesn't need to be excessive to be effective. The designer, working with a limited color palette, has carefully balanced the color elements on this page.

"We've got spot purple on this page if we want it." Ohhhh, what a dangerous temptation that is. What a quick way to turn a nice newspaper into junk mail.

Yes, color can be a blessing — or a curse. It can delight your readers or destroy your design. Using color successfully requires tight deadlines. Quality control. Extra money. Extra planning.

So plan for color. Don't treat it like a surprise gift. And above all:

◆ **Go easy.** Resist your initial urge to go overboard. Don't splash color around the page just to get your money's worth. Remember, black and white are colors, too — and newspapers have managed to look handsome for centuries without adding extra inks.

◆ **Don't use color for color's sake.** Remember, this is a *news* paper. Not the Sunday funnies. If you're deciding whether to run a color photo of circus balloons or a black-and-white photo of a bank holdup, choose the image that's meaningful — not just pretty.

◆ **Beware of colorizing false relationships.** Color creates connections, even where none actually exist. Put a *red* headline, a *red* chart and a *red* ad on the same page, and that tint will unite them all in the reader's mind. That can be dangerous.

Colors speak to each other. So if you don't want to connect elements, don't brand them with the same hue.

◆ **Be consistent.** Don't run a purple flag one day, a green flag the next; blue subheads here, red ones there. Give your pages a consistent graphic identity by using standardized colors wherever they're appropriate. Use this chart to plan ahead:

*Note the screen used in the background of this box. It's called a **graduated** screen or **blend** because it gently fades from one tint to another. Graduated screens offer a bit more texture than standard color screens, but work best when their colors remain subtle.*

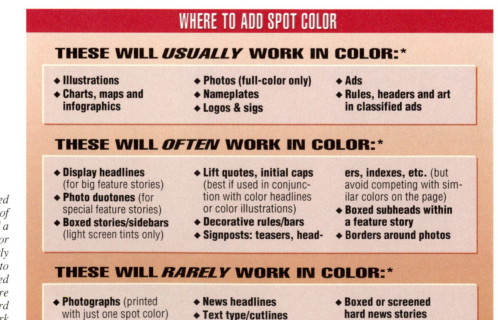

WHERE TO ADD SPOT COLOR

THESE WILL *USUALLY* WORK IN COLOR:*

- ◆ Illustrations
- ◆ Charts, maps and infographics
- ◆ Photos (full-color only)
- ◆ Nameplates
- ◆ Logos & sigs
- ◆ Ads
- ◆ Rules, headers and art in classified ads

THESE WILL *OFTEN* WORK IN COLOR:*

- ◆ Display headlines (for big feature stories)
- ◆ Photo duotones (for special feature stories)
- ◆ Boxed stories/sidebars (light screen tints only)
- ◆ Lift quotes, initial caps (best if used in conjunction with color headlines or color illustrations)
- ◆ Decorative rules/bars
- ◆ Signposts: teasers, head-
- ers, indexes, etc. (but avoid competing with similar colors on the page)
- ◆ Boxed subheads within a feature story
- ◆ Borders around photos

THESE WILL *RARELY* WORK IN COLOR:*

- ◆ Photographs (printed with just one spot color)
- ◆ News headlines
- ◆ Text type/cutlines
- ◆ Boxed or screened hard news stories

* Depending upon: (1) Your choice of tint, and (2) Whether the color creates misleading relationships between unrelated elements on the page.

ADDING COLOR TO A PAGE

Adding color to a black-and-white page is a tricky thing. Where should it go? How much is too much?

For best results, remember that *a little goes a long way.* It would be unrealistic to dictate where color can or cannot be used — but as these examples show, some choices succeed more than others:

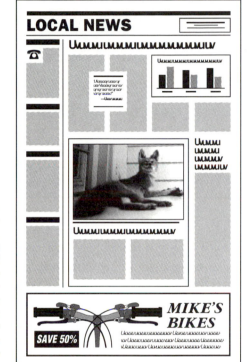

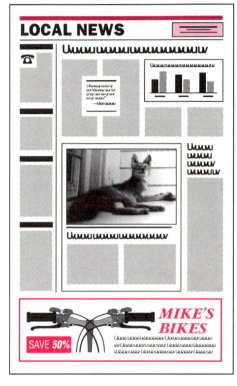

Here's a typical page in basic black. It may be gray, but it's not dull: By combining a variety of rules, bars and graphic elements, it presents an attractive mix of contrasts. It doesn't need extra decoration; any color we add should probably be functional, not decorative.

In the race to add color to this page, the advertiser got there first. And since that red ad is so distinctive and loud, any red we add to the news design may seem related to that ad. That's a problem. To maintain a distinction between news and advertising, you can choose to use a minimum of editorial color. Here, we've applied red only to the header — and we've added 20% black to it, to give it a hue that's different from that ad.

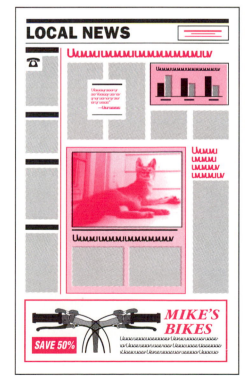

Without color in that ad, we're free to colorize our editorial layout. Still, we've used restraint — and we've applied spot color for organization, not just decoration. Adding red to the bars in the header and news briefs helps anchor the layout; adding color to the bars in the bar graph gives them sharper identity. The drawing in the news briefs has been colorized for fun, not just function — but that's OK.

*We've made some poor choices here — and now the page looks silly. Pink screens taint the credibility of the news. Red headlines and liftout quotes lose integrity. Red rules and boxes distract readers, calling attention to unimportant design elements. And that red photo? It might work for fancy feature layouts, but this is **news.** The page is weak — and worse, those colorized news elements all seem related, somehow, to Mike's Bikes.*

COLOR GUIDELINES

This Fourth of July trivia page was done on the run: The designer had no art, no budget and no time to play. But this clever solution uses only type and spot color to turn a functional layout into a patriotic pattern. The red, white and blue colors instantly communicate the theme of the story.

This page suffers from poor color choices. Green and purple — no a very popular color combo — are run as solid tones, and the lack of contrast makes the headline tough to read. The color green was probably meant to suggest money (see the dollar bill sign in the headline?) but the overall effect is dismal.

◆ **Use appropriate colors.** Colorize a page the way you'd decorate your living room. And unless you live in a circus tent, that means playing up comfortable hues (blue and tan, for instance) and playing down harsh ones (pinks and greens). The integrity of a news story will be damaged if wacky colors surround it, and the impact of a page will be negative if readers are turned off by your color choices.

Colors convey moods. "Hot" colors (red, yellow) are aggressive. "Cool" colors (blue, gray) are more relaxing. So make sure your colors produce the effect you want. And remember, too, that certain color combinations have unshakeable associations. For example:

❏ *Red* = blood, Valentine's Day.

❏ *Green* = money, St. Patrick's Day.

❏ *Red + green* = Christmas, Mexico.

❏ *Brown* = Uh, let's just say a nasty brown can *flush away* a good page design.

Like it or not, these color clichés are lodged in your readers' brains. So make these colors work *for* you — not against you.

◆ **Keep background screens as pastel as possible.** When we examined background tints back on page 180, we saw how difficult it is to read text that's buried beneath a dark screen. Well, it's a problem whether the background is black, blue, brown, or any dark color. Whenever you run text in a sidebar, chart or map, keep all underlying screens as light as you can. (These will usually be below 20%, but actual numbers vary from press to press. Check with your printer to see what the lightest printable percentages are.)

If you must add type to a dark screen, reverse it in a font that's big or bold enough to remain readable even if the printing registration is poor.

This is 10-point type over a 100% cyan screen. Because the background tint is so intense, the type is hard to read.	This is 10-point type over a 10% cyan screen. Because the background tint is pale, the type is easy to read.	This is 10-point type over a 10% magenta/ 15% yellow screen. Because the color is pastel, the type is easy to read.	This is 10-point type over a 50% cyan/100% magenta screen. Because the type is reversed and bold, it's easy to read.

COLOR GUIDELINES

◆ **Don't overreach your technology.** Color production is difficult to do well. It's costly. It's time-consuming. And in the hands of a sloppy printer, it's extremely disappointing. So it pays to learn your limits.

Drawings that look gorgeous on a computer screen often look like mud on newsprint. Color photos look worse than black-and-whites when the inking is poor or the registration is off (i.e., the color plates print out of alignment):

his color photo printed orrectly. The color inks are properly balanced, so the colors are rich nd true. The four color plates are properly ligned, so the image is crisp and well-focused.

This photo reveals the dangers of poor color production. The inks look washed out and badly balanced. And because the four plates are so far out of alignment, the image looks fuzzy — barely legible. If your color printing looks like this, you're better off using black and white.

So use color conservatively until you're certain of the results you'll get. And beware of small, detailed graphics or headlines that demand perfect color registration to succeed — or you'll face legibility problems like this:

THIS HEADLINE REGISTERS   **THIS HEADLINE DOESN'T**

◆ **Watch the volume level of your colors.** Want your page to look like a Hawaiian shirt? That's what you'll get if you use a) too many solid tones, or b) too many different colors. So go easy. Use bold, vivid colors for *accent* only, in key locations (drawings, feature headlines, reverse bars). Elsewhere, for contrast, use lighter screens or pastel blends. And if you're designing with full color, try color schemes that accent one or two hues — not the whole rainbow.

Decorative colors are like decorative typefaces. In small doses, they attract; in large doses, they distract.

◆ **Consult a color chart before you create new colors.** Some papers are afraid to mix colors, so they end up running all their color effects in basic blue, red and yellow. As a result, they look like a comics section: loud and unsophisticated.

But suppose you want to beef up your blue by adding a little black to it. How much black should you add? 10%? 50%? Or suppose you want to mix magenta and yellow to make orange. Should you simply guess at the right recipe — say, 20% magenta + 50% yellow?

Don't guess. Don't trust what you see on a computer monitor, either — a lot can change between your computer and the pressroom. Instead, ask your printer to give you a color chart (right), which shows how every color combination looks when printed. You can even create your own chart — but be sure it's printed on the same paper your newspaper uses, so all your hues are true.

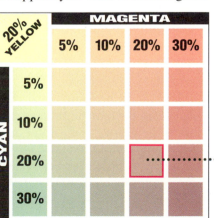

*A **color chart** shows how process inks look when they're combined. This portion of a chart, for instance, shows the tints you get when you add magenta and cyan to 20% yellow. The box highlighted at left shows the tint that results from mixing 20% yellow, 20% magenta and 20% cyan.*

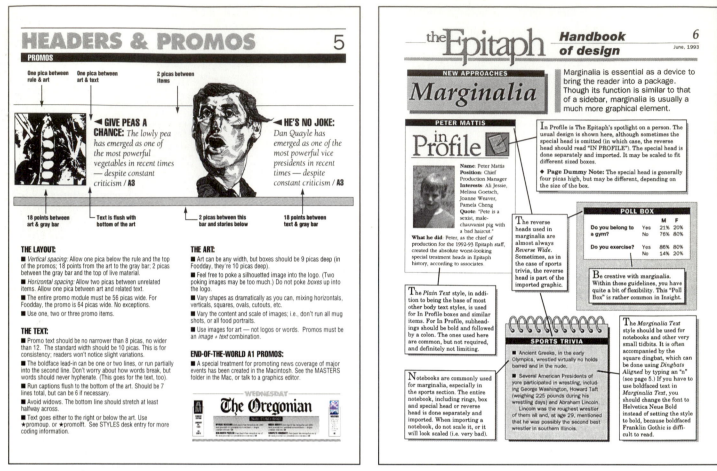

This sample page from The Oregonian design stylebook explains how to produce the daily promos on Page One. Note the detailed guidelines for sizing the art, positioning the text, spacing each element. Fine-tuning these details in advance can help goof-proof any newspaper.

During the 1992-93 school year, The Epitaph unveiled one of the most innovative designs of any high school newspaper. Their 11-page stylebook codified all major components of the design, from decks and dingbats to the marginalia on the Sports page explained here.

Imagine you've just redesigned your newspaper. And it's perfect. Gorgeous. A newspaper *the very angels in heaven read unto one another.*

It could happen.

The problem is, designing a newspaper (as we've spent the last 193 pages finding out) is a complicated affair. And once your paper is perfectly planned, how do you codify all those messy details — those logos, bylines, liftout quotes and pie charts — so that, should you get hit by a bus, other staffers can make pages look as gorgeous as *you* would?

Answer: Create a design stylebook.

If you're a reporter or editor, you're probably familiar with writers' stylebooks, those journalistic bibles that prescribe when to capitalize words like *president* or abbreviate words like *avenue.* Newspapers need design stylebooks, too, to itemize the do's and don'ts of their designs, to catalog all the tools in their typographic toolbox.

Stylebooks aren't intended to stifle creativity. They're meant to save time, so that staffers on deadline don't waste energy wondering, "How dark is that screen in our logos?" or "Are we allowed to write COMIC BOOK headlines?"

The best stylebooks are detailed and complete, like those shown above. For a checklist of design elements to include in your stylebook, see page 211.

MORE ON ▶

◆ **Redesigning your paper:** *How style-books play a key role in the process ......* **21**

APPENDIX

QUESTIONS ▶ 37

Why ask why?

1 **Typeface:** Helvetica.
Weight: Bold — though technically, this is an extra-bold weight called *Helvetica Black*.
Size: 36 points.

2 ◆ We've italicized the type.
◆ We've tightened the tracking (or kerning) so the letters are now overlapping.
◆ We've expanded the set width (or scaling) of the type — to 150% of its regular width.

3 The following characteristics apply to the type in this box:
◆ Sans serif   ◆ Light weight
◆ 12 point   ◆ Condensed
◆ Tight tracking   ◆ Flush left
◆ 14 points of leading
◆ Phrase is written downstyle (normal upper and lower case).

> Here is another
> typographic brain-teaser

Extra credit: The type in this example is Futura Condensed Light.

4 ◆ The type is now all caps.
◆ The type is now centered.
◆ The type is now reversed.
◆ The tracking has been increased.

> **HERE IS ANOTHER
> TYPOGRAPHIC BRAIN-TEASER**

5 The box is 13 picas wide; 3 picas and 6 points — or 3p6 — deep.
(Remember, the horizontal measure is always given first.)

6 The box has
a 1-point border.

Best picture: "Schindler's List"
Best actor: Tom Hanks in
  "Philadelphia"
Best actress: Holly Hunter in
  "The Piano"

● **Best picture:** "Schindler's List"
● **Best actor:** Tom Hanks in
  "Philadelphia"
● **Best actress:** Holly Hunter in
  "The Piano"

7 The text in the column on the right:
◆ Uses bullets (dingbats) to highlight each new category.
◆ Uses boldface type for each new category.
◆ Adds a few points (3) of extra leading between categories.
◆ Uses a hanging indent.

7 Drawing a page dummy, as we've explained, isn't an exact science. But if you measured those components carefully, you'd probably draw a dummy like this:

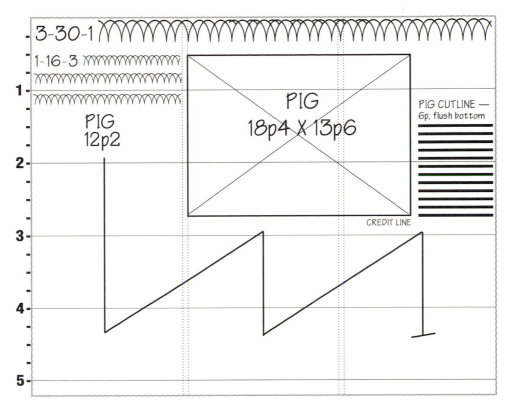

As you can see, the headline is three columns wide; the deck below the headline is one column wide; the text is divided into three legs, each one column wide. But the photo and cutline don't line up evenly with the other columns: the photo is a column-and-a-half wide and the cutline is a half-column wide. Those are called *bastard* measures. Yes, they're odd — but as you'll see later, they add variety to story designs.

8 Type specifications can vary, depending upon the software you use (this headline was created on a Macintosh running Quark Xpress), but here are the key typographic components:

Larry *is flush left, 51-point lowercase Times. The spacing on both sides of the "a" has been tightly kerned.*

The ampersand *is flush left, 57-point Times. The set width (scaling) is expanded to 220%. It rests on the same baseline as the word "Curly," but it has been moved behind the "M."*

MOE *uses 76-point Helvetica Black. The set width (scaling) is expanded to 130%. The tracking is -23. The letters are screened 30% black.*

Curly *is flush right, 57-point Times Bold. The set width (scaling) is 100%. The tracking is -13.*

QUESTIONS ▶ 63

1 A 5-inch story should be dummied either in one leg 5 inches long or in two legs 2.5 inches long. You should avoid dummying legs shorter than 2 inches, which rules out a 3-column layout for this story.

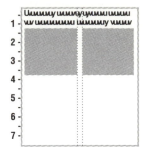

Though styles vary from paper to paper, this story might use a 1-30-3 headline on Page One, and a 1-18-2 (or3) or 1-24-2 (or 3) at the bottom of an inside page.

On Page One, this 2-column layout might use a 2-30-2 or 2-24-2 headline. At the bottom of an inside page, it would become a 1-line headline: 2-18-1 or 2-24-1.

2 Your three best options are a 1-column format, a 2-column format and a 4-column format (in the 4-column format, the mug could be dummied at either the right or left side).

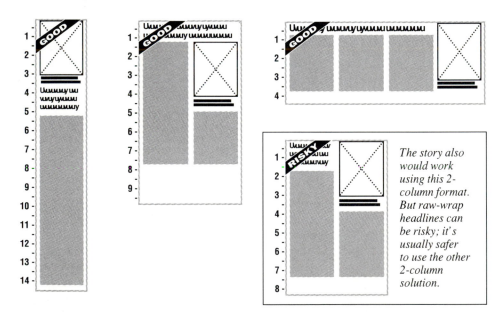

The story also would work using this 2-column format. But raw-wrap headlines can be risky; it's usually safer to use the other 2-column solution.

In a 3-column layout, the headline would need to run above the photo, with roughly a half-inch of text below the photo. That's not enough; you *must* dummy at least 1 inch of text in every leg. For this layout to work, you need either more text or a smaller mug indented into any of the three legs.

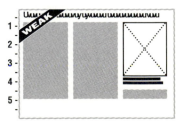

EXERCISE ANSWERS: STORY DESIGN

3 **1.** Avoid dummying photos between the headline and the start of the text. As a result, this story seems to begin in the second column.

2. The headline wraps clumsily around that left-hand mug. Ordinarily, all lines in a news headline should align evenly with each other (here, both lines should be 4 columns wide).

3. Mug shots shouldn't be scattered through the story, but grouped as evenly as possible. The two middle legs might work best in this layout.

4. Mug shots should run at the top of each leg of text, not at the bottom.

---

4 Because this is the day's top story — and because that photo grows more dramatic the bigger it runs— you should run the photo *at least* 3 columns wide. (A 2-column treatment of that photo would weaken its impact and make the story seem relatively insignificant.)

But because it's a busy news day, you can't afford to devote *too much* real estate to this story — which is what would happen if you ran the photo 5 or 6 columns wide.

So the best approach is one that uses the photo either 3 or 4 columns wide. Here are the most common, dependable design options:

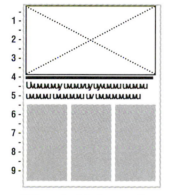

This vertical design uses the photo 3 columns wide, which means it's 23 picas deep — or just under 4 inches. This is a good, clean, reliable solution.

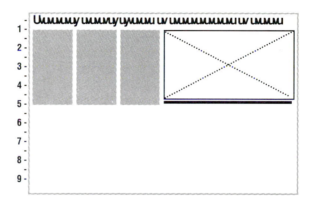

This horizontal design also uses the photo 3 columns wide. The text fits snugly alongside the photo, and everything squares off cleanly. But there's a problem with the banner headline: Half of it covers just the photo, not the text. That treatment (called an "armpit") looks thin and ungraceful.

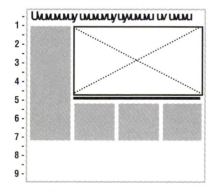

Another good solution using the photo 3 columns wide, with an L-shaped text block. (With a shorter story, the legs under the photo might be too shallow.)

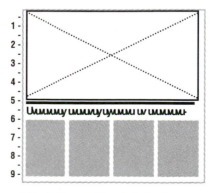

This design runs the photo 4 columns wide. From the photographer's point of view, it's the best solution, since the big photo gives the story drama and impact.

EXERCISE ANSWERS: STORY DESIGN

5 Most designers would choose the tighter, vertical shot of Springsteen as the lead photo. The horizontal photo is interesting, but less dynamic; Springsteen's face is obscured, and there's too much empty black space between Springsteen and the woman giving him that salute.

Your design options for this story are limited. Since the vertical photo is so strongly directional to the left, it must be dummied somewhere along the right side of the layout. With that in mind, these become the two most common solutions using a strong dominant photo:

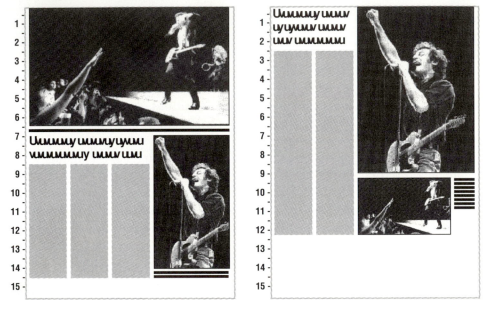

Using the horizontal photo as lead, you'd need to play it 4 or 5 columns wide to give it impact. If you played it 4 columns wide, it might not be as strong, the layout might not be as clean, and the second photo might be too similar in size. This is the better solution — though the story would need to lose an inch, and the second photo is cropped a bit tight.

Using the vertical pho as lead, you'd need to play it 3 columns wide give it impact (playing 4 columns wide woul make it way too huge) The only remaining question, then, is when to put the second pho Here, we sized it a bit larger than 2 columns wide, so both photos could share a cutline. It's less blocky than r ning both photos the same width — and it f

6 **A.** There's no need to use a raw-wrap headline in this layout. That last leg of text might collide with text from another story. Instead, the headline should be one line, 4 columns wide across the top of the story.

B. The photo is poorly placed. It should never be dummied between the headline and the start of the text. Instead, it should scoot over one or two columns to the right.

C. This story design is not rectangular. Assuming the photo belongs to that top story, the text should square off along the bottom edge of the photo. To do that, either the text must be deeper or the photo must be shallower.

However: If both stories related to that photo, you could argue that the two stories and one photo together form one package, shaped rectangularly. And that would be acceptable.

D. Both photos are sized too similarly. One needs to be clearly dominant for this design to work best.

E. The reader is forced to jump blindly across the photo in the middle two legs. That's occasionally permissible for some feature pages, but it's awkward and risky for news layouts.

F. Headlines should generally cover only the text; this head is too wide. And photos should not be sized identically like this — one should dominate. *But* if this were a before/after sequence that needed to create visual impact, this treatment might be effective.

EXERCISE ANSWERS: PAGE DESIGN

1 The box below is 40 picas wide. Using 1-pica margins and gutters, here are the text widths for 2-, 3- and 4-column layouts:

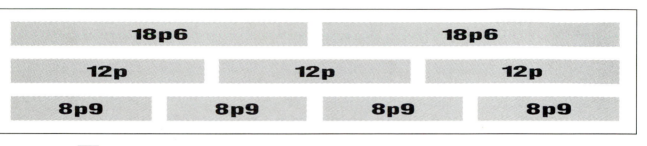

2 Here are three acceptable layouts — and one that just won't work:

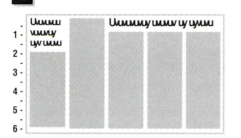

This layout lets you run both stories at their full lengths. The smaller story uses a raw-wrap headline; its second leg of text keeps the headlines from butting. This layout works best when used, as it is here, at the top of an inside page.

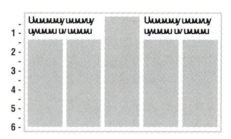

This layout uses a raw-wrap headline for the longer story; that third leg of text keeps both headlines from butting. The smaller story has been cut an inch to fit. This layout may look odd, but it satisfies the page's requirements.

This layout forces you to trim the smaller story by an inch while boxing it beside the first story. This treatment works best if the smaller story is a special feature; otherwise, avoid boxing stories just to keep headlines from butting.

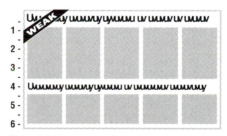

Note: *This common solution may have been your first response — but it won't work here. Those long horizontal headlines take up too much space and force you to cut the stories more than an inch apiece. They won't fit.*

3 **A.** The page has no dominant element; all three stories have the same weight and impact, and all the headlines are the same size. In addition, everything is horizontal and static. The page needs more art, and that photo should not be dummied at the bottom of the page.

B. The photo is ambiguous — which story does it go with? Are all those stories at the top of the page related? You can't be sure. The boxed story on the left butts awkwardly against that banner headline (this is sometimes called an "armpit"). The lead story is not a rectangular shape. And the right-hand leg of text seems to come up an inch short.

C. The page is off-balance; all the art is on the left side, forcing four stories to stack up along the right edge. The page seems divided into two sections (for this reason, you should avoid deep gutters running the full depth of the page). And there's not enough text under the mug shot.

EXERCISE ANSWERS: PAGE DESIGN

4 The best solution is **B**; it's well-balanced and correctly organized. What's wrong with the others? In example **A**, the entire midsection of the page is gray and type-heavy, while the top of the page uses two small, weak headlines that could mistakenly be related to that big photo. In example **C**, the photo is ambiguous (it could belong either to the story alongside or below) and headlines nearly collide. In example **D**, the lead photo is ambiguous again, and both photos are bunched together.

5 Many page designers park promo boxes and indexes in the bottom right corner of the page, as "page-turners" that send you off into the paper. Using that philosophy, our first solution (below left) would be preferable. But if you choose to use the promo box as a graphic element to break up those gray stories, you could slide it toward the middle instead (below right). In either case, it works best at the very bottom of the page.

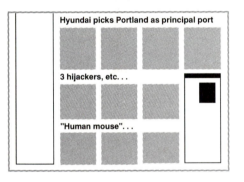

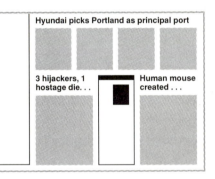

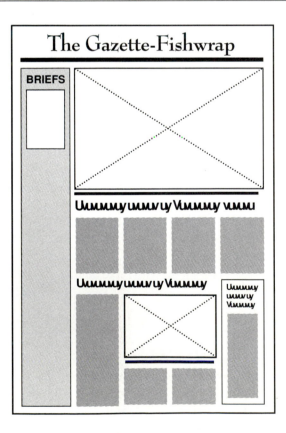

6 If the lead photo is strong, you should play it as big as possible — and in this case, there's room to run it 4 columns wide at the top of the page. Once that photo and its story have been anchored, your options are limited for those other two stories. This solution balances the art, mixing horizontal and vertical shapes. The small story is boxed to keep the headlines from butting — but that's OK, since it's a "bright" feature that deserves special treatment.

EXERCISE ANSWERS: PAGE DESIGN

The solution at right is clearly the better of the two. It avoids any nasty collisions between stories (though those two headlines in the middle of the page do butt a bit — if you prefer, you can box the short feature on the right). That story with the mug shot is the only one that needed to be trimmed to fit; it lost an inch and a half.

Though those two left-hand legs run a bit deep, it's acceptable. To lessen the problem, you could either add a deck or park a liftout quote halfway down (either in the right-hand leg or, better still, *between* the two columns, with the text wrapping around). Either way, you'd need to trim an inch or so from the text.

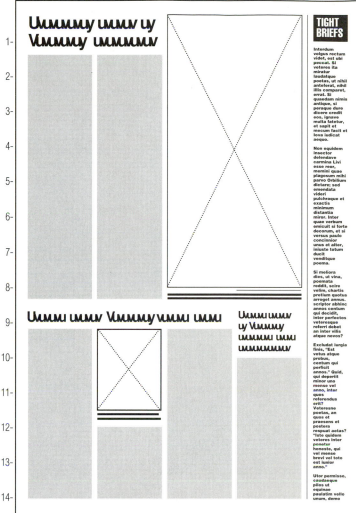

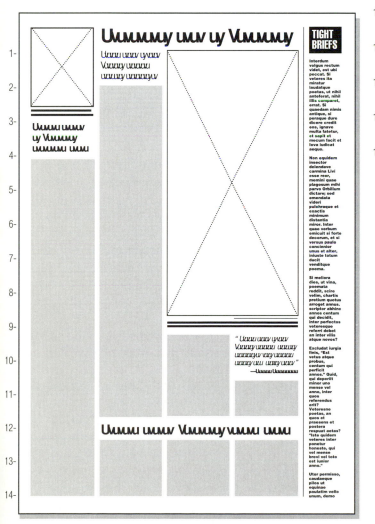

You could argue whether the layout at left succeeds or not — but since some designers will try it, we might as well discuss it.

The problem, of course, is in the upper-left corner: the juxtaposition of that mug shot and the lead story's headline. Is it confusing? Yes. Would it work better if we ran a column rule between those two butting stories or boxed the lead story? Maybe. But readers might still think that mug shot is connected to the headline beside it — which it isn't.

To make the text fit, we had to trim 3 inches from that left-hand leg. And, as you can see, we padded the lead story a little by adding a liftout quote and a deck.

EXERCISE ANSWERS: PHOTOS & ART

1 The two strongest images — the ones that say "woman jockey" in the most arresting way — are the race photo and the tight portrait. The other two should be supporting photos; they're informational, but not really interesting enough to dominate the page.

Here are three likely layouts using the race photo as the lead. If you've created a radically different page, congratulations — but check the guidelines on page 110 to be sure you haven't made some mistakes.

In this design, the race photo is used as the lead shot and runs across the top of the page, sharing a cutline with the photo below. (That's a photo credit floating below the cutline in the right margin.) The other two photos are stacked across the bottom of the page.

Note how the page is divided into three horizontal layers. In the second layer, the photo and text could have swapped positions, with that photo at the left side of the page — but then we'd have two similarly sized photos parked one atop the other. To avoid that, we could transpose the two bottom photos — but then the mug shot would be looking off the page. This layout, then, balances its elements well and avoids violating the directionality of the mug.

This layout isn't very different from the one at left. The race photo runs big across the top; together, the four photos form a "C" shape with the story tucked in the middle. (The page at left forms a backwards "C.") The sidesaddle headline treatment provides an alternative to the more standard approach used at left. The headline and deck form one wide column; the text sits beside it. (That leg is pretty wide; it could be indented or run as two legs instead.)

One final note: All three of these layouts close with the shot of the jockey washing her horse. Does that seem like an appropriate "closer"? Or would we make a stronger exit by closing with the shot of the jockey walking off the track, splattered with mud?

This design, like the one at left, uses the small portrait to set up the headline; pairing those two elements shows instantly *who* is on the fast track. The cutline beside the mug also describes the action in the lead photo below. The other two photos stack along the bottom of the page, with the photo credit floating in the left margin.

Note how headline, text and two vertical photos are all given an extra indent.

If there's a drawback to this layout, it's that it uses a big headline, a big deck, big photos — and a small amount of text. At some papers, editors may prefer to downsize those photos and increase the amount of copy.

EXERCISE ANSWERS: PHOTOS & ART

These layouts represent three common design approaches using the portrait of the jockey as the dominant photo. That portrait is strongly directional. As a result, your options are more limited, since you must position the lead photo looking *into* rather than *off of* the page.

Getting all four photos to fit properly is tricky when you're working around a directional dominant photo. In this case, the race photo is used as a scene-setter at the top of the page. The lead portrait runs below it, sharing a cutline. The other two photos fit in the space below the lead photo.

Some would say this is a very clean design, with the art aligning on one side of the page, the text running in one leg alongside. Others might find it too off-balance, with a preponderance of weight on the left side.

That leg of text is a bit too deep. We're relieving the gray by indenting a liftout quote halfway down.

Here, the lead photo runs at the top of the page, and the other photos arrange themselves in the rectangular module below. Note how the shapes and sizes of the photos vary. This helps to avoid static, blocky configurations.

If there are drawbacks to this design, they would be:

1) The excessive white space along the left edge of the page, around the cutline and photo credit. That's hard to avoid, however. It's hard to size that horse-washing photo much wider. The cutline, too, is about as big as it should be.

2) The small amount of text. Playing these photos as big as they are doesn't leave much room for the story. This is a very photo-heavy layout.

Here's a page that gets a bit crowded at the top but seems to work anyway. Three photos are grouped together in a tight unit; the race photo, however, is set apart from the rest for extra emphasis (and to give the page more of a "racing" feel).

The racing photo also could have been dummied in the right-hand three columns instead of the center three; in that case, a 2-line, 2-column deck would have been preferable. But as it is, this design produces a more symmetrical page.

EXERCISE ANSWERS: PHOTOS & ART

2 Several additional images would enhance this selection of photos. Among them:

◆ A stronger racing shot — one with clearer details and a greater sense of motion, perhaps shot from a more dramatic angle.

◆ More emotion — the thrill of victory, the agony of defeat. These four photos fail to capture any athletic dramatics.

◆ An interaction shot, showing how this woman jockey relates to her colleagues in a male-dominated sport.

◆ Detail shots — whips, boots, saddles, even trophies — especially some racing apparel or artifact that is unique to this jockey.

3 Here are some of the major problems on these pages. Remember: When it comes to page design, tastes can be very subjective. You don't have to agree with every nitpick — but you should understand the principles that underlie our design guidelines.

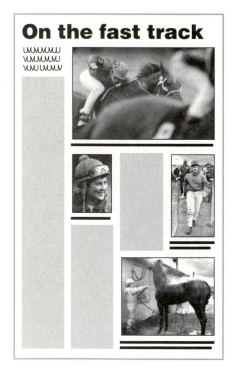

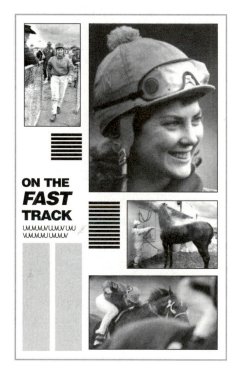

The text snakes around the photos in a clumsy, unattractive way— and that first leg of text is way too deep. There's no white space designed in to this page, which results in a layout that feels dense and crowded, more like a typical news page than a photo spread. And that feeling is reinforced by the sizes of the photos — the lead photo isn't quite dominant enough, and there's no sense of interplay among the rest of the pictures.

The lead photo faces off the page. If this page design were flopped, that problem could have been avoided. But there's still a problem with that big cutline blob in the center of the page. It's unclear which photo or photos it belongs to. (Does the bottom photo have a cutline?) There's too much trapped white space in the middle of the page. There's also too much white space above the headline. Finally, those two legs of text may be too thin — one wider leg would be better.

Overall, this page looks handsome, but there are some subtle problems. It's divided into three very separate chunks: 1) big photo, 2) gray text and 3) small photos. There's no interplay between elements; in fact, this seems like a formulaic page design that you could plug *any* photos into. In addition, there's no white space, and the shapes are too blocky and static. It's also difficult to determine which cutline describes the center photo in the bottom row.

4 **A.** The photographer's crop for this photo comes in tightly on both police officers but leaves a bit of air between them and the sides of the frame. The top crop almost reaches that officer's head; the bottom crop leaves a bit of foreground pavement below the suspect's shoes.

    B. After you properly crop the photo, it should measure roughly 16 picas wide by 12p8 deep. Using a proportion wheel, there are two ways to find the photo's depth if its width were enlarged to 45 picas:

1. Find the original cropped width (16) on the inner wheel. Line that number up with the new width you need (45) on the outer wheel.
2. Find the original cropped depth ($12^2/_3$) on the inner wheel. The number it lines up with — 36 — will be the new depth of the photo.

OR you could try it this way:

1. After proper cropping, your original photo measures 16 by 12p8. On the proportion wheel, line up 16 on one wheel, $12^2/_3$ on the other.
2. As you look around the wheel, all the figures will be paired in the ratio of $12^2/_3$:16. So if you check 45, it's lined up with 36.

NEWSPAPER DESIGN
REPORT CARD

Whether you're a weekly or a daily, a small student tabloid or a big-city broadsheet, the same design standards apply. To see how you rate, answer each question by marking the corresponding box *yes* (worth two points), *somewhat* (worth one point) or *no* (zero points). You can earn up to 10 points per category or 100 points overall. Your score will help you assess your graphic identity *and* your appeal to readers.

		no (0 pts.)	somewhat (1 pt.)	yes (2 pts.)	score/comments
headlines & type	Do news headlines intrigue, inform and invite readers in?	☐	☐	☐	
	Do feature headlines project a friendly, appealing personality?	☐	☐	☐	
	Do decks summarize and sell stories to browsers?	☐	☐	☐	
	Do headlines and text use an effective mix of styles and weights?	☐	☐	☐	
	Are all typographic details consistent and professional-looking?	☐	☐	☐	
photos	Are photos active and engaging (rather than dull and passive)?	☐	☐	☐	
	Are photos cropped, sized and positioned properly?	☐	☐	☐	
	Are photos sharp, clear and well composed?	☐	☐	☐	
	Are key photos in color — and is the color well balanced?	☐	☐	☐	
	Do enough photos appear throughout the entire paper?	☐	☐	☐	
graphics & artwork	Do maps, charts and diagrams enhance text where necessary?	☐	☐	☐	
	Is graphic data meaningful, accurate and understandable?	☐	☐	☐	
	Are sidebars and agate material typographically well-designed?	☐	☐	☐	
	Are drawings and artwork clean and well executed?	☐	☐	☐	
	Is there witty/insightful art on the opinion page?	☐	☐	☐	
special page designs	Are special pages active, attractive and well balanced?	☐	☐	☐	
	Are display elements — art and type — given bold treatment?	☐	☐	☐	
	Are headers and logos polished and eye-catching?	☐	☐	☐	
	Is color used effectively in photos, graphics, standing elements?	☐	☐	☐	
	Do themed pages get distinctive packaging (formats, grids, etc.)?	☐	☐	☐	
inside pages	Is the content organized, logical and consistent?	☐	☐	☐	
	Do layouts use modular shapes with strong dominant elements?	☐	☐	☐	
	Is there a mix of briefs and analysis throughout the paper?	☐	☐	☐	
	Is each page's contents labeled with a consistent header style?	☐	☐	☐	
	Are jumped stories well labeled and easy to find?	☐	☐	☐	

NEWSPAPER DESIGN
REPORT CARD

	no	somewhat	yes	score/comments

the basic fixtures

	no	somewhat	yes
Are liftout quotes used often and effectively?	☐	☐	☐
Are margins and spacing uniform and appropriate?	☐	☐	☐
Are column logos and sigs consistent, attractive and helpful?	☐	☐	☐
Do rules, boxes and screens effectively organize material?	☐	☐	☐
Are bylines and jump lines well designed and positioned?	☐	☐	☐

volume & variety

	no	somewhat	yes
Does the front page combine hard news with "softer" features?	☐	☐	☐
Have major stories been packaged with short, effective sidebars?	☐	☐	☐
Do key pages give readers a sense of motion and activity?	☐	☐	☐
Is there an effective blend of live news and regular departments?	☐	☐	☐
Do stories appeal to a broad range of tastes and interests?	☐	☐	☐

ads & self-promotion

	no	somewhat	yes
Do front-page promos catch the reader's eye in a lively way?	☐	☐	☐
Did you offer any contests or giveaways? Sponsor any events?	☐	☐	☐
Can readers phone in for the latest scores, weather or headlines?	☐	☐	☐
Are ads well designed? Arranged in neat, unobtrusive stacks?	☐	☐	☐
Have you given readers reasons to anticipate your next issue?	☐	☐	☐

user-friendliness

	no	somewhat	yes
Is there a complete index in a consistent, obvious spot?	☐	☐	☐
Are some stories interactive (quizzes, tips, Q&As, checklists)?	☐	☐	☐
Do you run complete calendars (for meetings, sports, events)?	☐	☐	☐
Is it clear how to reach key staffers (by phone, fax, letter, etc.)?	☐	☐	☐
Is reader input packaged on pages besides the editorial page?	☐	☐	☐

personality

	no	somewhat	yes
Does your paper's personality match that of its target audience?	☐	☐	☐
Are regular columnists given mug shots? Anchored consistently?	☐	☐	☐
Is the paper's flag sophisticated-looking and contemporary?	☐	☐	☐
Are there any surprises on Page One?	☐	☐	☐
Will anything in today's paper incite reactions from readers?	☐	☐	☐

the grading scale

90-100: Outstanding! A top-notch publication.
70-89: Good, but could still use new ideas and improvements.
50-69: Average — possibly dull. Thinking about a redesign?
below 50: Sorry, but you're old-fashioned. Your readers are probably bored. It's time to consider a major overhaul.

YOUR TOTAL SCORE ▶

REDESIGNING YOUR NEWSPAPER

THE 10 STEPS TO A SUCCESSFUL REDESIGN

1 **Assess your strengths — and your weaknesses.** Every newspaper and every staff is unique. Some excel in photography. Some crank out award-winning text. Some are loaded with graphic wizardry. How would you evaluate *your* staff? Are you low on photographers? (Better emphasize type and graphics.) Got reporters who can't write long stories? (Try pre-packaging lots of briefs and sidebars.) Scrutinize your staff so your redesign plays to your strengths.

2 **Gather examples.** Get a feel for current design trends by collecting a variety of papers from across the country: the good, the bad and the ugly. Get samples of award-winners, trend-setters and papers recently redesigned. Study them closely. Analyze headlines, bylines, flags, liftout quotes, column rules, grids — *everything* — and weigh them against your own.

3 **Make a shopping list.** Do you know what your readers (remember them?) want you to change? If not, *ask*. Send out a survey or print one in the paper. Pinpoint specific items that need replacement or repair.

Try to set some limits. Determine what's sacrosanct (your flag?), what's *got* to go (your sky boxes?), what's optional (maybe a fancy index would be nice, but not essential). Are you ready to explore new packaging innovations — or do you just want a typographic facelift?

Itemize all the changes you want to make. Then set a timetable — but keep it flexible.

4 **Build prototypes.** Explore a variety of alternatives. Try to present several options (ranging from conservative to radical) for each design component you test. Try mixing and matching these new elements as you proceed.

Tip: Always use bland art and dull stories in prototypes. If a design works with bad material, you know it'll work with strong stuff.

5 **Test it.** Don't be secretive. Share your prototypes with the newsroom — better yet, test them on readers in a focus group, if possible. Let fresh eyes discover the bugs you've overlooked.

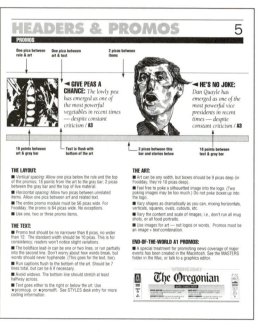

6 **Write a design stylebook** *(like the sample shown above.) Consider this your production cookbook, providing detailed recipes for every item on your design menu. Make it as comprehensive as possible. Load it with examples and diagrams. This may be your only chance to codify each change, so don't cut corners.*

7 **Train the staff.** Hold sessions for copy editors and designers. Meet with the production staff to explain changes in detail. Consider producing real-time pages to test the production process and expose oversights. If you're a big paper, train phone operators to monitor readers' complaints.

8 **Promote it.** Any time you monkey with your paper, you've got two options: a) Phase in changes quietly, or b) Launch them with fanfare. The first option gives you more control; the second is riskier, but fun. Either way, create promotional ads to show readers how you've improved their paper.

9 **Launch it.** *(Ulp! Good luck!)* Expect some hysterical overreactions from whiny readers. Stay cool. Stay objective.

10 **Follow through.** Enforce rigidly. Appoint a style cop to nail all design violations. Set up a design bulletin board to display successes and failures. Hold regular post-mortems; be prepared to make modifications. Just think: Once everything works perfectly, you can start planning your next redesign.

REDESIGNING YOUR NEWSPAPER

A REDESIGN CHECKLIST

Every newspaper needs to update its image every few years. But planning a redesign can be overwhelming. Where do you begin? Which options should you consider? Try using this checklist as a starting point.

HEADLINES & TEXT

☐ **THE FLAG** ....Must be unique and expressive, like a corporate logo. Should we try a modern, stylish typeface? Special graphics effects? Color?

☐ **HEADLINES** ....Want them bold and punchy? Or sleek and elegant? Want to try alternative forms (hammers, kickers) — or add topic labels?

☐ **DECKS** ....Should complement the main headline's typeface. Do we add them to *every* story? Want different styles for news & features?

☐ **STANDING HEADS** ....Choose one expressive, stylish type family for all page toppers, logos, sigs, etc. Want screens, reverses, other graphics effects?

☐ **TEXT** ....*Must* be comfortable to read. What's the ideal size & leading?

☐ **SPECIAL TEXT** ....Want a sans-serif alternative for graphics, sidebars, briefs? Should be a font with versatility (strong boldface, italic, etc.).

ARCHITECTURE & DESIGN

☐ **PAGE GRIDS** ....Do we want a new system of column widths and packaging formats? Will this work with ads — or just on open pages?

☐ **PAGE HEADERS** ....Where do we want them — at the top? Sideways? Indented? Can they incorporate graphic extras (factoids, calendars, etc.)?

☐ **BRIEFS** ....Should we treat them like a fundamental building block and run them throughout the paper? Can we include art? How often?

☐ **SPECIAL FEATURES** ....Polls. Quotes. Stats. Calendars. Quizzes. Contests. Letters. Cartoons. Can we build these into standing page formats?

☐ **RULES & BOXES** ....They're a key part of our overall look. Want them loud? Quiet? Decide on ideal line weights. Box styles. Screen densities.

☐ **PROMOS & INDEX** ....How prominent? How flexible? How much art can we add?

☐ **ADS** ....Can we keep ad stacks modular? Cleared from key pages?

CONTENT & ORGANIZATION

☐ **SECTIONING** ....Can we re-structure the news into innovative topics and departments? Can we create special themed pages or packages?

☐ **SEQUENCING** ....What's the most interesting, effective flow of topics through the paper? Where can we pile ugly ad stacks to do the least damage?

☐ **NON-TEXT OPTIONS** ....Can we re-package information in a variety of forms — *besides* text & headlines? Can we anchor these alternative formats?

☐ **INTERACTIVITY** ....How user-friendly are we? Are readers given the chance to speak, participate, interact? How often do we write news you can *use?*

OTHER ELEMENTS

☐ **LIFTOUT QUOTES**
☐ **COLUMN LOGOS**
☐ **REVIEW/PREVIEW BOXES**
☐ **BYLINES**
☐ **JUMP LINES**

☐ **JUMP HEADLINES**
☐ **INITIAL CAPS**
☐ **CUTLINES**
☐ **CUTLINES FOR STAND-ALONE PHOTOS**

☐ **CREDIT LINES**
☐ **EDITOR'S NOTES**
☐ **MAPS & CHARTS**
☐ **REFERS**
☐ **CORRECTIONS**

GLOSSARY

Agate. Small type (usually 5.5 point) used for sports statistics, stock tables, classified ads, etc.

Air. White space used in a story design.

All caps. Type using only capital letters.

Armpit. An awkward-looking page layout where a story's banner headline sits on top of a photo or another headline.

Ascender. The part of a letter extending above the x-height (as in *b, d, f, h, k, l, t*).

Attribution. A line identifying the source of a quote.

Banner. A wide headline extending across the entire page.

Bar. A thick rule. Often used for decoration, or to contain type for subheads or standing heads.

Bar chart. A chart comparing statistical values by depicting them as bars.

Base line. An imaginary line that type rests on.

Bastard measure. Any non-standard width for a column of text.

Blow up. To enlarge a photo or illustration for reproduction.

Body type. Type used for text (in newspapers, it usually ranges from 8 to 11 points).

Boldface. A heavier, darker weight of a typeface; used to add emphasis (the word "boldface" here is in boldface).

Border. A rule used to form a box or to edge a photograph.

Box. A ruled border around a story or art.

Broadsheet. A full-size newspaper, measuring roughly 14 by 23 inches.

Bug. Another term for a sig or logo used to label a story; often indented into the text.

Bullet. A type of dingbat, usually a big dot (●), used to highlight items listed in the text.

Bumping/butting heads. Headlines from adjacent stories that collide with each other. Should be avoided whenever possible.

Byline. The reporter's name, usually at the beginning of a story.

Callouts. Words, phrases or text blocks used to label parts of a map or diagram (also called *factoids*).

Caps. Capital or uppercase letters.

CD-ROM. Computer disks (CDs) with huge amounts of memory, used for photo archives, font libraries, interactive games, multimedia programs, etc.

Caption. A line or block of type providing descriptive information about a photo; used interchangeably with *cutline*.

Centered. Art or type that's aligned symmetrically, sharing a common midpoint.

Character. A typeset letter, numeral or punctuation mark.

Clip art. Copyright-free images you can modify and print as often as you like.

Column. A stack of text; also called a *leg*.

Column inch. A way to measure the depth of text or ads; it's an area one column wide and one inch deep.

Column logo. A graphic device that labels regularly appearing material by packaging the writer's name, the column's name, and a small mug or drawing of the writer.

Column rule. A vertical line separating stories or running between legs within a story.

Compressed/condensed type. Characters narrower than the standard set width; i.e., turning this M into M.

Continuation line. Type telling the reader that a story continues on another page.

Continuous tone. A photo or drawing using shades of gray. To be reproduced in a newspaper, the image must be converted into a *halftone*.

Copy. The text of a story.

Copy block. A small chunk of text accompanying a photo spread or introducing a special package.

Copyright. Legal protection for stories, photos or artwork, to discourage unauthorized reproduction.

Crop. To indicate where a photo should be trimmed before it runs in the paper; usually done by making crop marks in the margins of the photo.

Cutline. A line or block of type providing descriptive information about a photo.

Cutoff rule. A horizontal line running under a story, photo or cutline to separate it from another element below.

Cutout. A photo where the background has been removed, leaving only the main subject; also called a *silhouette*.

Deck. A small headline running below the main headline; also called a *drop head*.

Descender. The part of a letter extending below the baseline (as in *g, j, p, q, y*).

Disk. Used to store computer information: *hard disks* are the internal memories for computers; *floppy disks* are small, square, removable cartridges; *CDs,* also removable, store vast amounts of information.

Dingbats. Decorative type characters (such as bullets, stars, boxes, etc.) used for emphasis or effect.

Display headline. A non-standard headline (often with decorative type, rules, all caps, etc.) used to enhance the design of a feature story, photo spread or news package.

Doglegs. L-shaped columns of text that wrap around art, ads or other stories.

Dot screen. A special screen used to produce

tiny rows of dots, thus allowing newspapers to print shades of gray.

Double burn. The process by which two different elements are overlapped when printed (for instance, printing type on top of a photo); also called *overprinting.*

Double truck. Two facing pages on the same sheet of newsprint, treated as one unit.

Downstyle. A headline style that capitalizes only the first word and proper nouns.

Dpi. The number of dots per inch a printer prints. The higher the dpi, the finer the resolution of the output.

Drop head. A small headline running below the main headline; also called a *deck.*

Drop shadow. A thin shadow effect added to characters in a headline.

Dummy. A small, detailed page diagram showing where all elements go; also, the process of drawing up a layout.

Dutch wrap. Text that extends into a column alongside its headline; also called a *raw wrap.*

Duotone. A halftone that uses two colors, usually black and a spot color.

Ear. Text or graphic elements on either side of a newspaper's flag.

Em. An old printing term for a square-shaped blank space that's as wide as the type is high; in other words, a 10-point em space will be 10 points wide.

En. Half an em space; a 10-point en space will be 5 points wide.

Enlarge. To increase the size of photos or artwork.

Expanded/extended type. Characters wider than the standard set width: i.e., turning this M into **M** .

Family. All the different weights and styles (italic, boldface, condensed, etc.) of one typeface.

Feature. A non-hard-news story (a profile, preview, quiz, etc.) often given special design treatment.

Fever chart. A chart connecting points on a graph to show changing quantities over time; also called a *line chart.*

Filler. A small story or graphic element used to fill space on a page.

Flag. The name of a newspaper as it's displayed on Page One; also called a *nameplate.*

Flat color. An extra color ink added to a page; also called *spot color.*

Float. To dummy a photo or headline in an empty space so that it looks good to the designer, but looks awkward and unaligned to everyone else.

Flop. To create a backwards, mirror image of a photo or illustration by turning the negative over during printing.

Flush left. Elements aligned so they're all even along their left margin.

Flush right. Elements aligned so they're all even along their right margin.

Folio. Type at the top of an inside page giving the newspaper's name, date and page number.

Font. All the characters in one size and weight of a typeface (this font is 10-point Times).

Four-color. The printing process that combines cyan (blue), magenta (red), yellow and black to produce full-color photos and artwork.

Full frame. The entire image area of a photograph.

Graf. Newsroom slang for "paragraph."

Graph. Statistical information presented visually, using lines or bars to represent values.

Grid. The underlying pattern of lines forming the framework of a page; also, to align elements on a page.

Gutter. The space running vertically between columns.

H and J. Hyphenation and justification; the computerized spacing and aligning of text.

Hairline. The thinnest rule used in newspapers.

Halftone. A photograph or drawing that has been converted into a pattern of tiny dots. By screening images this way, printing presses can reproduce shades of gray.

Hammer head. A headline that uses a big, bold word or phrase for impact and runs a small, wide deck below.

Hanging indent. Type set with the first line flush left and all other lines in that paragraph indented (this text is set with a 10-point hanging indent).

Header. A special label for any regularly appearing section, page or story; also called a *standing head.*

Headline. Large type running above or beside a story to summarize its content; also called a *head,* for short.

House ad. An advertisement promoting the newspaper or a newspaper feature; small house ads are often used as fillers.

Hyphenation. Breaking a word with a hyphen at the end of a line (as in those previous two lines).

Indent. A part of a column set in a narrower width. The first line of a paragraph is usually indented; columns are often indented to accommodate art, logos or initial caps.

Index. An alphabetized list of contents and their page numbers.

GLOSSARY

Infographic. Newsroom slang for "informational graphic"; any map, chart or diagram used to analyze an event, object or place.

Initial cap. A large capital letter set at the beginning of a paragraph for decoration or emphasis.

Inset. Art or text set inside *other* art or text.

Italic. Type that slants to the right, *like this*.

Justification. Mechanically spacing out lines of text so they're all even along both right and left margins.

Jump. To continue a story on another page; text that's been continued on another page is called the *jump*.

Jump headline. A special headline treatment reserved for stories continued from another page.

Jump line. Type telling the reader that a story is continued from another page.

Kerning. Tightening the spacing between letters.

Kicker. A small, short, one-line headline, often underscored, placed above a larger headline.

Laser printer. An output device that prints computer-generated text and graphics, usually at a lower resolution than professional typesetters.

Layout. The placement of art and text on a page; to *lay out* a page is to design it.

Lead-in. A word or phrase in contrasting type that precedes a cutline, headline or text.

Leading. Vertical spacing between lines of type, measured in points.

Leg. A column of text.

Legibility. The ease with which type characters can be read.

Letter spacing. The amount of air between characters in a word.

Liftout quote. A graphic treatment of a quotation taken from a story, often using bold or italic type, rules or screens.

Line chart. A chart connecting points on a graph to show changing quantities over time; also called a *fever chart*.

Line shot. Reproduction of a photo or artwork resulting in only two tones: black and white (no screened shades of gray), as opposed to a *halftone*.

Logo. A word or name that's stylized in a graphic way; used to refer to standing heads in a newspaper.

Lowercase. Small characters of type (no capital letters).

Margins. The space between elements on a page.

Masthead. A block of information, including staff names and publication data, often printed on the editorial page.

Measure. The width of a headline or column of text.

Modular layout. A design system that views a page as a stack of rectangles.

Mortise. Placing one element (text, photo, artwork) so it partially overlaps another.

Mug shot. A small photo showing a person's face.

Nameplate. The name of a newspaper as it's displayed on Page One; also called a *flag*.

Offset. A printing process, used by most newspapers, where the image is transferred from a plate to a rubber blanket, then printed on paper.

Orphan. A short word or phrase that's carried over to a new column or page; also called a *widow*.

Overlay. A clear plastic sheet placed over a pasted-up page, containing elements to be screened, overprinted, or printed in another color.

Overline. A small headline that runs above a photo; usually used with stand-alone photos.

Pagination. The process of generating a page on a computer.

Paste-up. A page assembled for printing where all type, artwork and ads have been placed into position (usually with hot wax). To *paste up* a page is to place those elements on it.

Photo credit. A line that tells who shot a photograph.

Pica. A standard unit of measure in newspapers. There are 6 picas in one inch, 12 points in one pica.

Pixel. The smallest dot you can draw on a computer screen (short for "picture element").

PMT. A photographic paper used for shooting halftones. Short for photomechanical transfer; also called a *velox*.

Point. A standard unit of measure in printing. There are 12 points in one pica, 72 points in one inch.

Porkchop. A half-column mug shot.

Process color. One of the four standard colors used to produce full-color photos and artwork: cyan (blue), magenta (red), yellow or black.

Proof. A copy of a pasted-up page used to check for errors. To check a page is to *proofread* it.

Pyramid ads. Advertisements stacked up one side of a page, wide at the base but progressively smaller near the top.

Quotes. Words spoken by someone in a story. In page-design jargon, a *liftout quote* is a graphic treatment of a quotation, often using bold or italic type, rules or screens.

GLOSSARY

Ragged right. Type that is not *justified;* the left edge of all the lines is even, but the right edge is uneven.

Raw wrap. Text that extends into a column alongside its headline; also called a *Dutch wrap.*

Refer (or reefer). A line or paragraph, often given graphic treatment, referring to a related story elsewhere in the paper.

Register. To align different color plates or overlays so they're perfectly positioned when they print.

Reverse. A printing technique that creates white type on a dark background; also called a *drop out.*

Roman. Upright type, as opposed to slanted (italic) type; also called *normal* or *regular.*

Rule. A printing term for a straight line; usually produced with a roll of border tape.

Runaround. Text that wraps around a photo or artwork; also called a *wraparound* or *skew.*

Sans serif. Type without serifs: This is sans serif type.

Scale. To reduce or enlarge artwork or photographs.

Scaling. The overall spacing between characters in a block of type.

Scanner. A computer input device that transforms printed matter (photos, illustrations or text) into electronic data.

Screen. A pattern of tiny dots used to create gray areas; to *screen* a photo is to turn it into a *halftone.*

Serif. The finishing stroke at the end of a letter; type without these decorative strokes is called *sans serif.*

Sidebar. A small story accompanying a bigger story on the same topic.

Sidesaddle head. A headline placed to the left of a story, instead of above it; also called a *side head.*

Sig. A small standing head that labels a regularly appearing column or feature.

Silhouette. A photo where the background has been removed, leaving only the main subject; also called a *cutout.*

Skew. Text that wraps around a photo or artwork; also called a *wraparound* or a *runaround.*

Skyboxes, skylines. Teasers that run above the flag on Page One. If they're boxed (with art), they're called *skyboxes* or *boxcars;* if they use only a line of type, they're called *skylines.*

Solid. A color (or black) printed at 100% density.

Spot color. An extra color ink added to a page; also called *flat color.*

Spread. Another term for a large page layout; usually refers to a photo page.

Stand-alone photo. A photo that doesn't accompany a story; usually boxed or labeled to show it stands alone; also called *wild art.*

Standing head. A special label for any regularly appearing section, page or story; also called a *header.*

Style. A newspaper's standardized set of rules and guidelines. Newspapers have styles for grammar, punctuation, headline codes, design principles, etc.

Subhead. Lines of type, often bold, used to divide text into smaller sections.

Summary deck. A special form of deck, smaller and wordier than most decks, that capsulizes the main points of a story.

Table. A graphic or sidebar that stacks words or numbers in rows so readers can compare data.

Tabloid. A newspaper format that's roughly half the size of a regular broadsheet newspaper.

Teaser. An eye-catching graphic element, on Page One or section fronts, that promotes an item inside; also called a *promo.*

Tint. A light color, often used as a background tone, made from a *dot screen.*

Tombstoning. Stacking two headlines side by side so that they collide with each other; also called *bumping* or *butting heads.*

Trapped white space. An empty area, inside a story design or photo spread, that looks awkward or clumsy.

Tripod. A headline that uses a big, bold word or phrase and two smaller lines of deck squaring off alongside.

Underscore. To run a rule below a line of type.

Uppercase. Type using capital letters.

Velox. A photographic paper used for shooting halftones. Short for photomechanical transfer; also called a *PMT.*

Weight. The boldness of type, based on the thickness of its characters.

Well. Ads stacked along both edges of the page, forming a deep trough for stories in the middle.

White space. Areas of a page free of any type or artwork.

Widow. A short word or phrase that makes up the last line of text in a paragraph. (See *orphan.*)

Wraparound. Text that's indented around a photo or artwork; also called a *runaround* or *skew.*

X-height. The height of a typical lowercase letter.

INDEX

INDEX

ACKNOWLEDGMENTS

Finishing a book is like winning an Oscar — you *can't* leave the stage until you've thoroughly thanked everyone who labored behind the scenes.

The author is sincerely grateful to the following friends and colleagues:

◆ **Editing:** Patty Kellogg, without whose insight, meticulous eye and relentless enthusiasm this book would never have been finished; Mark Wigginton, for pretending to listen to me whine; Katherine Miller; John Hamlin; Dan Gustafson; Rob Melton; Jack Kennedy.

◆ **Art and photography:** David Sun; Joe Spooner; Ron Coddington; Judy Treible; Bill Griffith; Fred Ingram; Steve Gibbons; Joel Davis; Steve Dipaola; Randy Rasmussen; Michael Lloyd; Ben Brink; Tim Jewett; Ross Hamilton; Steve Nehl; Kraig Scattarella; Dana Olsen; Lois Bernstein; Pat Minniear.

◆ **Contributors of pages & images:** Harris Siegel; Kevin Rivoli; Marty Bonvechio; Jim Denk; Miguel Buckenmeyer; Warren Watson; Dale Peskin; William McGrath; Mitchell Hayes; Tom Porter; T. J. Hamilton.

◆ **The Brown & Benchmark staff:** Kassi Radomski; Stan Stoga; Deb DeBord — I truly appreciate your patience and support.

◆ **Ocean pollution and estuaries:** Krystyna Wolniakowski.

◆ And of course, most of all, once again and always: Robin.

CREDITS   The following photographers, artists and publications were not previously identified in text or cutlines:

Front cover: Fred Ingram (lead art); Steve Gibbons (Eddie Van Halen photo); Ron Coddington (David Letterman drawing), reprinted by permission, Knight-Ridder Tribune Information Services.

4 (bottom), 5 (top): From the professional library of Vergil S. Fogdall.

6: The Oregonian.

9 (left), 182: ©1993 Asbury Park Press. Used with permission.

12: Photo by Randy Wood.

13: Photo by Kraig Scattarella.

17: Photo by Pat Minniear.

18: Engravings electronically enhanced by David Sun.

20: Illustration by David Sun.

22: The Chicago Tribune.

23: Weekly World News.

28: All photos copyright Associated Press and Wide World Photo, Inc., except Oswald photo, copyright 1963 by Bob Jackson, and Truman photo, The Bettman Archive.

29: Photos by Kraig Scattarella (top); Joel Davis (left); Tim Jewett (right).

30, 34, 38: Photo by Kraig Scattarella.

33: The Orange County Register.

36: The Oregonian.

42: The White House.

46: Copyright 1985 Lois Bernstein/The Virginian-Pilot.

53: Photos by Max Gutierrez (top left); Robert E. Shotwell (bottom left and top right); Holley Gilbert (bottom right).

63: Photo by Michael Lloyd.

64: Photos by Claudia J. Howell

(left); Ross Hamilton (right).

76: The Orange County Register.

86: Both photos copyright Associated Press and Wide World Photo, Inc.

91, 100: Photo by Steve Gibbons.

92: Photos by Randy L. Rasmussen (top); Michael Lloyd (center and bottom).

101: Photo by Dana Olsen.

102: Photo by Randy Wood.

104: Photo by Tim Harrower.

105: Illustration by Joe Spooner.

106: Photo by Michael Lloyd.

108: Photos by Tim Jewett.

112: Photos by Dana Olsen (left); Doug Beghtel (center); Randy L. Rasmussen (right).

119: Photos by Randy L. Rasmussen.

120: Photo by Steve Nehl.

121: The Sun News (Myrtle Beach, S.C.)

122: The Sun News

123: The Miami Herald (left); The Oregonian (center); The Washington Times (right); The Philadelphia Inquirer (bottom).

125: Logos by Jim Denk, The Detroit Free Press (bottom).

126: (bottom left) Copyright Associated Press and Wide World Photo, Inc.

137: Page designed by Michael Mode, The Oregonian.

142: Steve Cowden, The Oregonian.

146: Ecological art by Joe Spooner; burglar art reprinted by permission, Knight-Ridder Tribune Information Services.

156: Photos by Joel Davis.

157: Lizard drawings by David Sun; photo by Dana Olsen; page from The Oregonian.

159: Graphic reprinted by permission, Knight-Ridder Tribune Information Services.

160: The Oregonian (left); school shooting map reprinted by permission, Knight-Ridder Tribune Information Services.

161: The Oregonian (left); voter turnout map reprinted by permission, Knight-Ridder Tribune Information Services.

162: Islam page reprinted by permission, Knight-Ridder Tribune Information Services.

163: The Oregonian (bottom two pages); Realpolitics page reprinted by permission, Knight-Ridder Tribune Information Services.

168-169: Times Publications (left); The Detroit Free Press (center); The Anchorage Daily News (top right); Detroit News (bottom right).

170: Photo courtesy of The National Broadcasting Company, Inc.

176: (top right) Ron Coddington, reprinted by permission, Knight-Ridder Tribune Information Services; photo by Jesse Gerstein for Oscar de la Renta, spring 1989 (bottom).

177: Zippy the Pinhead mug courtesy of Bill Griffith.

180: Photo by William Duke.

181: Photos by Randy L. Rasmussen.

182: Photo by Tim Jewett.

183: Photo by Michael Lloyd.

181: Photos by Steve Dipaola.

188: Photo by Tim Jewett (top); Michael Lloyd (bottom).

193: Photo by Paul Peterson.

Back cover photo: Robin Harrower.